Cahokia's Countryside

Engraving by Theodor de Bry (1590)

Mark W. Mehrer

Cahokia's Countryside

Household Archaeology,

Settlement Patterns,

and Social Power

NORTHERN ILLINOIS UNIVERSITY PRESS   DEKALB 1995

Published by Northern Illinois University Press,

DeKalb, Illinois 60115

Manufactured in the United States using acid-free paper

Design by Karen Gibson

Library of Congress Cataloging-in-Publication Data

Mehrer, Mark.

Cahokia's countryside : household archaeology, settlement patterns, and social power / Mark W. Mehrer.

p.   cm.

Includes bibliographical references.

ISBN 0-87580-565-5 (acid-free paper)

1. Mississippian culture—Illinois—American Bottom.
2. Cahokia Site (East Saint Louis, Ill.) 3. Land settlement
patterns, Prehistoric—Illinois—American Bottom. 4. American Bottom (Ill.)—Antiquities. 5. Illinois—Antiquities.

I. Title.

E78.I3M47   1995

977.3'8901—dc20   94-45750

CIP

To ALM and PVM

Contents

Figures

Tables

Preface

This study is the result of several years of research and personal growth. My professional curiosity about American Bottom archaeology was first piqued during 1976–1977 fieldwork at a small Mississippian site on a small stream in the dissected uplands overlooking the Mississippi River floodplain. The site, which the crew named Lab Woofie after ourselves (we were the lab crew assigned to this site at the beginning of winter while that year's field crews were busy tying off their season's digs), turned out to be an unplowed Stirling phase homestead. Our excavations at Lab Woofie were directed by John Kelly, who had recently given me the opportunity to do Illinois archaeology with the fledgling FAI-270 project. Dale McElrath and I supervised the excavations there, and our casual efforts to interpret the organization of daily life at that site began the quest that produced the study in hand. During our excavations it became clear to us that in order to understand that settlement and its place on the landscape, we had to make sense of the buildings, pits, and scatters of debris. Joyce Williams, Bob Williams, Larry Kinsella, and many others helped us dig that site. They brought plenty of experience, good common sense, and fearless speculation to help inspire our interpretations. As an errant lab crew, we explained to visitors that we were merely holding the fort and that the University of Illinois would soon send an expert to take over. Eventually, Guy Prentice, the "expert from U of I" arrived to help finish the fieldwork, analyze data, and report on the project. I am grateful to these individuals for being stalwart colleagues through the years. In some ways, this episode was the first attempt at household archaeology in the American Bottom. Looking back, I can see that we were all fortunate to be able to pursue this household perspective unselfconsciously—that is, without realizing that we were treading new theoretical and methodological ground.

The following years of fieldwork, analysis, and reporting at the Range site provided on-the-job training for me as I worked with people who would become the current experts in Cahokia region archaeology. Tom Emerson, George Milner, Dale McElrath, Andy Fortier, John Kelly, Sissel Johannessen, Paula Cross, and Cricket Kelly were all hands-on site directors and special analysts for the bulk of the work completed during the FAI-270 project. We were able to shrug off the then popular dictum that a 10% sample of any site was sufficient. We were able to dig entire sites because the project's leaders had ideas of their own. We were encouraged, indeed, directed, to go after complete site plans—community plans—with heavy equipment and to bring back all the details. We did. The results include dozens of community plans of many types from all ages.

This work was done during the decade and a half following 1975. We worked with the intellectual illumination provided by an earlier generation of Cahokia scholars who had spent the previous decade and a half exploring the American Bottom and laying the archaeological foundation on which we lived, worked, and built. A few of those long-established experts are James Anderson, Charles J. Bareis, Leonard W. Blake, Hugh C. Cutler, Melvin Fowler, Michael L. Gregg, Robert L. Hall, Alan Harn, Patrick Munson, Patricia L. O'Brien, Paul W. Parmalee, James Warren Porter, Harriet M. Smith, Joseph O. Vogel, Howard D. Winters, and Warren L. Wittry. These are the people whose articles, reports, correspondence, and conference papers we studied as though they were scriptures. Many were the times when two or more of us gathered to debate the archaeological equivalent of "how many angels will fit on the head of a pin?" basing our arguments on "the literature" as it stood then.

My years at the University of Illinois at Urbana-Champaign (UIUC) tempered my thinking with discipline and hard work. R. Barry Lewis, Charles J. Bareis, James Brown, Norman Whitten, Dmitri Shimkin, David Grove, Joseph Casagrande, Linda Klepinger, Thomas Riley, and Clark Cunningham all took an interest in my work. During this time the first analytical results were coming in from the FAI-270 project. One challenge was to place these results into context with the culture history of North America. Another was to interpret them in an anthropological manner. The notion of social power as control of energy was new to me, but it seemed to be a tool well-suited to archaeology. It was during this time that I realized household archaeology had become a recognized pursuit in other parts of the western hemisphere. Other archaeologists were apparently coming to realize that studying the family in prehistory was useful. Household archaeology brings fieldwork and analysis together to examine prehistoric families as the basic units of society. Understanding the families of prehistory is essential to understanding the majority of people who lived then. Studying temples and tombs reveals little about how most people conducted their daily lives; household archaeology is at the heart of such discovery.

Since the mid-1980s, there has been a great deal of work at the Cahokia site. This work was done after my analysis had been completed, but it can be incorporated into the conclusions here. Much of this Cahokia work was performed by William Woods and his Southern Illinois University-Edwardsville ICT-II project team, which included Jim Collins, Neal Lopinot, George Holley, and Rinita Dalan. In a separate effort, Timothy Pauketat, then of University of Michigan, courageously and successfully tackled the project of reanalyzing and interpreting the results of the 1960s excavations at Cahokia's Tract 15A, Dunham Tract, and Kunnemann Mounds.

The present study was possible because of the vast quantity of high-quality data collected, analyzed, and published by the hardworking members of the FAI-270 Archaeological Mitigation Project community since 1975. There are too many project members to list, but I thank them all for the opportunity to work with a large, coherent body of well-reported data. I wish to acknowledge the assistance of the Illinois Department of Transportation, which funded the FAI-270 project, and Chief Archaeologist John A. Walthall, who always ensured we had the resources we needed. The project was administered by Professor Charles J. Bareis of the Department of Anthropology at UIUC, where project materials are curated.

The small-site household information, which forms the bulk of the hard-data for this study, was assembled and analyzed for my dissertation research at UIUC under the direction of R. Barry Lewis. The conclusions of that study resulted in a regional settlement model. After my degree program was completed, the results of the two detailed analyses of Cahokia data became available. Fitting my model to downtown Cahokia was the "Ah Ha!" experience that inspired this book. Thanks to Jim Collins for sharing his insights and the results of his labor among Cahokia's ICT-II households. Thanks also to Tim Pauketat for sharing with me the results of his admirable analysis of Cahokia's Tract 15A, Dunham Tract, and Kunnemann Mound data.

I also wish to thank all my colleagues who kept me informed of their latest ideas. George Milner gave me updates on his refinements of the Julien and Turner-DeMange data as he continued to analyze them. Tom Emerson and Doug Jackson helped with the BBB Motor data. Sissel Johannessen advised me about the ethnobotany of the region. Paula Cross provided assistance with the faunal data. Mike Hargrave and Gerald Oetelaar gave me updated information on the Bridges site. Chuck Bentz offered data from his analysis of the 1976 Lunsford-Pulcher site excavations. Preston Staley introduced me to cluster analysis and discriminant analysis.

In addition to my association with these colleagues, through the years I have been fortunate to share many enthusiastic and enlightening discussions of American Bottom archaeology—its past, present, and future—with Fred Finney, Bill Green, Ned Hanenberger, Tom Maher, Guy Prentice, Chris Szuter, and Joyce Williams. Steve Ozuk was a peerless Ranger when we supervised the Range site digs together. Carl Merry shared his innovative ethnoarchaeological analysis of the Grand Valley Dani.

My wife, Dr. Denise Hodges, not only made this book possible but also made the process of writing it worthwhile. Without her unflagging support and encouragement, it would never have happened.

I thank all these fine colleagues and their institutions for their assistance. Thanks also to Daniel Coran, Wendy Warnken, Julia Fauci, Karen Gibson, and the rest of the NIU Press staff for their hard work in the editing and publishing process. I am, of course, solely responsible for the views and conclusions in this book.

Cahokia's Countryside

Chapter 1

Introduction

This book synthesizes Mississippian settlement and social systems in the American Bottom using an abundance of recent data and an anthropological framework of theory. In the chapters that follow, a model of regional cultural evolution will be presented that is based on a thorough quantitative analyses of a large body of hard data. Complete data for over eight hundred features from small sites in Cahokia's countryside were culled from the total available in the region as of the mid-1980s. These features were selected for their completeness and representativeness for small Mississippian sites in the American Bottom.

The present treatment of the rise and fall of Cahokia is different from previous studies in that it incorporates the latest available data in large measures. As a result, the interpretations are firmly grounded in hard evidence and current archaeological systematics. The book uses theories of cultural evolution and social power to consider the roles and the lives of the masses of people, the commoners, rather than those of the elite classes. We still know little of how Cahokia's elites lived, even though we know a bit about how they were buried. Cahokia probably had the most sophisticated society in North America—it certainly had the largest and the most mounds.

This study offers an understanding of what happened to the houses and house-life of commoners living in the countryside as town-life evolved from village-life during the panregional development of complex society. The quantity and quality of data available from the American Bottom region are well-suited to address this issue—many small sites in the region have been recently excavated to illuminate this evolution. The analysis in this book demonstrates that some common dimensions of human settlement are sensitive to regional trends of social complexity. For example, homesteads responded to changes in the way the communities of the region were integrated with one another socially, politically, and economically. The results of the analysis show how life at homesteads changed as nearby towns grew and prospered. The interpretations herein are cast in general terms in order to describe the effect of regional cultural processes on the domestic order of rural settlers—an aspect of social change common around the world.

During late prehistory (A.D. 800–1400)[1] in the Central Mississippi River Valley, social, economic, and political developments at regional ceremonial centers[2] had substantial and significant effects on nearby farm communities. These effects include the formation of well-planned towns, the construction of monumental public architecture such as mounds, plazas, and palisades, and the emergence of a variety of specialized domestic building types such as sweat lodges and storehouses. Long-term trends in the spatial organization of buildings, households, and communities were closely tied to the shift from a simple, ranked society to a more complex, stratified social organization.

Two simple distinctions can illustrate the dramatic significance of this shift. One major distinction between ranked and stratified societies is that high-status individuals in ranked societies do not have privileged access to the basic necessities of life; those in stratified systems do (Fried 1960:721–722, 1967). Another important distinction is that stratified societies have elite social classes whose members inherit their high status from their ancestors, while ranked societies do not. To understand the context of these changes, we must set the stage by laying out the region's landscape and the history of archaeological work there.

THE AMERICAN BOTTOM REGION

Our study area is the northern portion of the American Bottom, which extends about 50 km from Alton to Columbia, Illinois. It is at the hub of a potentially vast communication and transportation network of major waterways—the Mississippi, Missouri, and Illinois Rivers—that drain much of the northern and western parts of the continent (Figure 1). Approximately 250 km south of this triple confluence, the Mississippi joins the Ohio River, which drains much of the northeastern part of the continent. The American Bottom is on the northern border of the Central Mississippi Valley archaeological subarea, which is the smallest subarea in the Eastern Woodlands. The subarea adjoins the Upper Mississippi Valley, the Lower Mississippi Valley, and the Ozark, Southeast, and Ohio Valley subareas (Willey 1966:6, 248). Understandably, the region had diverse ties to distant prehistoric cultures in all directions. The sites in this study are from only the northern portion of the cartographic extent of the American Bottom, but for convenience the study area will be referred to interchangeably as the American Bottom, the American Bottom region, or the Cahokia region.

The American Bottom is unique because of the large number of late prehistoric mounds and mound complexes that are scattered over its floodplain and

Figure 1. Location of the American Bottom region at the confluence of major waterways in the midcontinent of North America.

adjacent uplands. Cahokia is the largest of five major mound centers in the region; the others are the Mitchell site, the St. Louis Group, the East St. Louis Group, and the Lunsford-Pulcher site (Figure 2). Cahokia encompasses over 15 square kilometers (Fowler 1973a:1, 1989) and contains 120 mounds, including Monks Mound, the largest man-made structure north of Teotihuacán (Figure 3). A string of mounds that connects Cahokia proper with the East St. Louis Group (Bushnell 1904, 1922:93, Fig. 99; Moorehead 1929:118, Fig. 11) emphasizes the arbitrary nature of the modern site boundaries.

Cahokia's interregional ties allowed for far-reaching if not always intense cultural interplays. In late prehistory, the American Bottom was on the periphery of a widespread Pan-Southern cultural tradition (Hall 1975b:24) characterized by ranked societies, maize agriculture, temple-towns, and distinctive

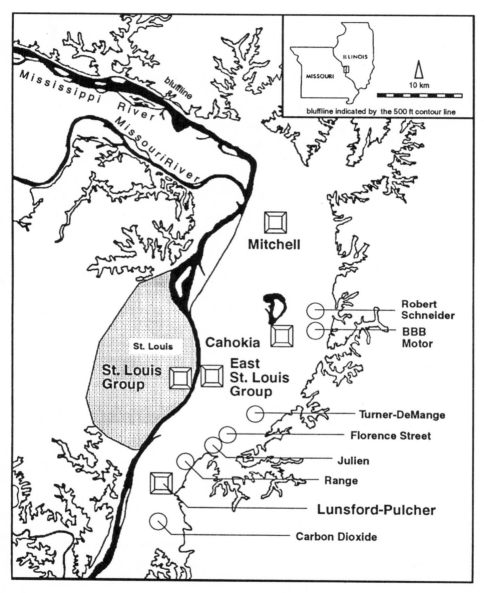

Figure 2. Locations of the seven analyzed sites and five major mound groups nearby.

Figure 3. Monks Mound. Top: aerial view looking toward the northwest (courtesy of Cahokia Mounds Museum, Illinois Historic Preservation Agency). Bottom: 1892 photograph of the mound viewed from the south (courtesy of Missouri Historical Society).

ceramics. Beyond the periphery, Cahokia also had limited yet specific cultural ties to distant regions such as Aztalan in Wisconsin (Barrett 1933; Goldstein 1991), the Red Wing area of Minnesota (Gibbon 1979; Gibbon and Dobbs 1991; Johnson 1991; Rodell 1991), the Mill Creek area of northwestern Iowa (Anderson 1987; Tiffany 1991), and the Steed-Kisker area of Kansas and Missouri (O'Brien 1978a, 1978b). Cahokia also had direct connections with the Lower Mississippi River Valley (Brain 1991; Perino 1967; Phillips et al. 1951; Phillips 1970; Williams and Brain 1983). Cahokia has often been seen as the Mississippian heartland from which colonists, immigrants, and intruders brought social revolution and/or political subjugation to these regions (Smith 1984). However, critical examination (Smith 1984) has dispelled the heartland concept and the need to invoke a center from which the various late prehistoric traditions in the Southeast and Midcontinent spread.

Recent discussions have considered systematic modes of interaction between Cahokia and its distant neighbors (Anderson 1987; Claflin 1991; Conrad 1989; Farnsworth et al. 1991; Finney 1991; Harn 1978, 1991; McConaughy 1991; Markman 1991; Stoltman 1991a, 1991b). For example, Anderson (1987:226–229) has designed a model based on cultural processes, such as economic and political influences, that explains how the rise and fall of Cahokia, as part of the broader Middle Mississippian tradition, probably influenced the development of the Mill Creek culture in extreme northwestern Iowa. In this case, the rising Mississippian chiefdom at Cahokia expanded its regional trade networks, thereby spreading ideological and subsistence innovations along with useful and novel artifacts.

The American Bottom was probably more developed sociopolitically than any other region in the Southeast, and due to its location it was probably known more widely among prehistoric groups than other large centers (Hall 1991). Because adequate data from other regions is not currently available, it is not possible to know to what extent Cahokia dominated these other regions politically or culturally. The number and size of the earthworks in the Cahokia region have led to exaggerated claims for the region's sociopolitical role in prehistory. Cahokia has been considered an urban settlement (e.g., Fowler 1975; O'Brien 1972b) as well as the center of a formal state-level society (Gibbon 1974). Nevertheless, these arguments have not gained universal acceptance (Hines 1977). Although the precise apex of sociocultural development in the American Bottom is an intriguing question, the focus of this study is on how the configuration of common households, buildings, and other features sheds light on the development and decline of the region as a whole.

The source of the American Bottom's social complexity and its impact on other regions have been the subjects of speculation. For example, Cahokia was one of the last places to be considered a point of direct and powerful Mesoamerican influence (e.g., Porter 1973:159). Several decades ago, Mesoamerica was considered the source of cultural inspiration throughout the late prehistoric Southeast (Phillips 1940), but the Mesoamerican connection is no longer viewed as an overwhelming or even definitive influence (Brown 1985).

Natural Setting

The American Bottom is at the border of east-central Missouri and west-central Illinois. Much of the Illinois land is rolling plains; much of the Missouri land is open hills (USDI 1970). The most salient geographic feature of this area is the 5 to 18 km-wide stretch of the Mississippi River floodplain. In early holocene times, the main channel of the river meandered widely between the bluffs to the east and west. Eventually it became entrenched at the western margin of the floodplain, where it has remained relatively stable for the past 4000 to 5000 years (Munson 1974; Kelly et al. 1979), leaving an undulating floodplain formed by meander scars, point bars, and natural levees. This reticulate pattern of swells and swales created sloughs, backwater lakes, and marshes that formed a complex system of permanent and intermittent waterways extending from the river on the west to the bluffs on the east (White et al. 1984). Point bars and levees, rising 1.5 to 3.0 m above the water, made up the high ground on the floodplain. Extensive waterways were undoubtedly convenient for transportation across short distances, but the river and its tributaries provided the main route between the American Bottom and distant places.

Because of rich biotic zones created by the region's topography and waterways, rich resources were virtually everywhere. Extensive archaeological floral and faunal analyses have been conducted recently (Johannessen 1984; Kelly and Cross 1984; Lopinot 1991), and so the prehistoric use of this rich natural environment is known in some detail (for studies on the physiography and biotic zones of the region, see Chmurny 1973; Gregg 1975b; White et al. 1984). For about three thousand years leading up to Mississippian times, the procurement of food in the American Bottom became increasingly localized and intensified, as people became increasingly sedentary and reliant on farm or garden crops (Johannessen 1984:205–214, 1993a, 1993b). This picture fits well with our current understanding of how people developed the production of plant food in the floodplain settings of the Midwestern central riverine area (Johannessen 1993a; Smith 1992). The production of storable surpluses of food, beyond the needs of mere subsistence, through labor-intensive innovations in agriculture is a key notion for understanding the social relations among large and small sites in the new regional model presented in this study.

History of Investigations

The American Bottom region has long been recognized as the setting for important prehistoric events. Explorers of the eighteenth and early nineteenth centuries made observations of the area, and during the 1880s the Smithsonian Institution's mound exploration project identified a number of sites in and around the American Bottom (Thomas 1894:131–134). Later, Bushnell (1904, 1907, 1908, 1922) investigated sites along the Mississippi River in Missouri, where among other discoveries he identified the remains of late prehistoric salt-making.

Programmatic archaeological investigations were started in the 1920s by the University of Illinois at Urbana-Champaign and later by the Illinois State Museum, the University of Chicago, and the University of Michigan. A small state park was formed around the central mound group of the Cahokia site in 1924 largely as the result of Moorehead's Archaeological Survey of the Cahokia Region project (Moorehead 1922, 1923, 1929) and his lobbying (Griffin 1984:xv).

During the New Deal era of the 1930s and 1940s, surveying and excavating were performed along the Mississippi River in both Illinois and Missouri (Adams 1940, 1941, 1949; Adams and Magre 1939; Adams and Walker 1942; Blake 1942; Kelley 1933; Munger and Adams 1941; Perino 1947a, 1947b; Thomas 1938; Titterington 1938, 1947; Walker and Adams 1946). As a result of these investigations, the archaeological literature for the area flourished during this time (Griffin 1941, 1949; Titterington 1935, 1943). Investigators used the Midwest Taxonomic Method (McKern 1939) in addition to other more localized schemes (e.g., Adams 1940) to define the region's various traditions (Bennett 1944; Deuel 1938; Wedel 1945; Wray and Smith 1944) and to rough out a sequence of foci and aspects. Their taxonomic findings still permeate the chronological and typological systems now used in the American Bottom.

After the Central Mississippi Valley Archaeological Survey project (Griffin 1977; Griffin and Spaulding 1951) of 1949 and 1950, there was a hiatus in large-scale projects in the Cahokia region during the 1950s, when institutional fieldwork in Illinois concentrated on the Illinois River valley and southern Illinois. Nevertheless, publication of research drawing on data from this region continued unabated (e.g., Blake 1955; Dick 1955; Grimm 1950; Parmalee 1957; Perino 1959; Smail 1951; Temple 1957; Titterington 1950; Wagner 1959; Williams and Goggin 1956). Two projects, the "Coordinated Study of the American Bottoms" (Fowler 1962, 1963, 1964) and the "Historic Sites Survey Project" (Linder et al. 1975; Porter 1971, 1972, 1973, 1974a), were performed during the 1960s and 1970s. Much of the work conducted on or near the Cahokia site by the Coordinated Study is outlined in Fowler's three unpublished annual reports (1962, 1963, 1964). Published accounts of this episode of Cahokia archaeology, edited by Fowler (1973b, 1973c) and Brown (1975), include the analytical results of some of the work completed in the 1960s. Additionally, O'Brien's (1972a) and Vogel's (1975) analyses of Cahokia ceramics and Griffith's (1962, 1981) stylistic study of Ramey Incised pottery derive from earlier fieldwork. Current treatments of past work at Cahokia continue to become available (Ahler and DePuydt 1987; Fowler 1989; Pauketat 1991, 1994; Skele 1987, 1988).

Highway salvage excavations at the Cahokia site during the 1960s reveal much about late prehistory. Regional surveys of the American Bottom show the wide distribution of settlements from as early as 4000 B.C. (Brandt 1972; Harn 1971; Munson 1971). Synthesis of data from survey and excavation produced a chronology spanning from A.D. 600 to 1500 (Fowler and Hall 1972, 1975). With this improved understanding of the region came models of social development characterizing late prehistory (Fowler 1974).

Kelly (1980:163–221) discusses several models for Cahokia's emergence originating in work completed during the 1960s and 1970s. An important unknown factor during these decades was the number and role of small moundless settlements. Shifting patterns of large and small sites across the landscape and evidence of increasing socioeconomic complexity throughout the region raised questions about whether or not people were moving to the large sites and whether or not there were any very small sites after A.D. 1000.

In the late 1970s and early 1980s planning for highway construction called for more archaeological investigations in the region. Much of this work was done by members of the FAI-270 Archaeological Mitigation Project (e.g., Bareis and Porter 1984; Kelly et al. 1979), who produced the data on small sites that is analyzed in this study.[3] An important aspect of the FAI-270 project was its emphasis on recovering entire community plans through the excavation of large contiguous areas. One of the important results of this work was that many sites were completely, or nearly completely, mapped and excavated, creating a great deal of new information about prehistoric settlement patterns throughout prehistory. It was the recovery of this information about whole communities that stimulated an interest in the archaeology of households in the American Bottom.

Another important result of work in the 1970s and early 1980s was a revised and expanded outline of the chronological periods represented in the American Bottom. This new chronology was more detailed than any previously devised. It extended from 3200 B.C. through the Historical period after European settlement. This improved chronology set a new baseline for further work in the region by revealing previously unknown details of settlement, subsistence, technology, trade, flora, fauna, and many other aspects of prehistoric life.

In the late 1980s excavations were performed in the Cahokia site to make room for a new interpretive center. The awkwardly dubbed Interpretive Center Tract II, or ICT-II, became the focus of intensive excavations from 1984 through 1986 (Collins 1990; Holley 1989; Lopinot 1991). Also during the late 1970s and throughout the 1980s the palisade at Cahokia was a focus of research (Dalan 1989; Holley et al. 1990; Holley et al. 1993; Iseminger et al. 1990). Massive soil slumping on the slopes of Monks Mound in the late 1980s spurred excavations there (Collins and Chalfant 1993). The results of these investigations are among the first from Cahokia to be analyzed and reported according to modern standards. Another product of these times is the reanalysis of Cahokia's Tract 15A and Dunham Tract by Pauketat (1991, 1994). These late-1980s findings are used in the present study to complement my small-site data in order to construct a regional model of Mississippian settlement and social power.

Regional Chronology

As previously noted, the recently revised chronology of the region provided the groundwork for further investigations (Figure 4). The information used to devise that chronology, and information from continued work in and around Cahokia, has allowed scholars to revise and to update their theories about how and why the regional social system evolved the way it did. The settlement patterns are of special importance here.

We can follow a long-term trajectory of increasing settlement complexity that began during the Late Archaic period (3200–600 B.C.). At that time, communities were characterized by low labor investment in shelter and storage facilities; that is, shelters were not elaborate or permanent and storage pits were not large or numerous. Clusters of pits represent the household as a basic unit in the organization of community layouts. The earliest known shelters in the region are from this Late Archaic period (Fortier 1993; McElrath et al. 1984:46; McElrath and Fortier 1983; Phillips et al. 1980; Phillips and Gladfelter 1983). The oldest known American Bottom domestic structure with well-defined walls, from the Early Woodland period (600–150 B.C.), was excavated at the Florence Street site (Emerson et al. 1983). Other Early Woodland components have scatters of debris that probably represent small temporary shelters since wall foundations are not evident (Emerson and Fortier 1986; Fortier 1985a; Fortier et al. 1983; Fortier et al. 1984a:66; Williams and Lacampagne 1982). The first evidence of precise and formal planning of domestic architecture occurs during the Middle Woodland period (150 B.C.–A.D. 300). At the Truck #7 site, an occupation of Hill Lake phase times had a large (10 m diameter), precisely geometrical, circular structure with a clearly defined posthole foundation (Fortier 1985a).

During the Late Woodland period (A.D. 300–800), complex, permanent settlements, characterized by substantial shelters and abundant storage pits, represent a new high level of investment of labor and material resources (Fortier et al. 1984b; Hargrave 1991; Kelly 1990a; Kelly et al. 1984a, 1987). Buildings during this period were semisubterranean pit-houses built inside hand-excavated basins, with their floors well below ground. They were strongly constructed of numerous wall-posts set into foundation holes that extended below the floors. Storage and roasting pits were plentiful. These features together mark the beginning of settled community life in the region. Buildings in these settlements were occasionally laid out with a degree of

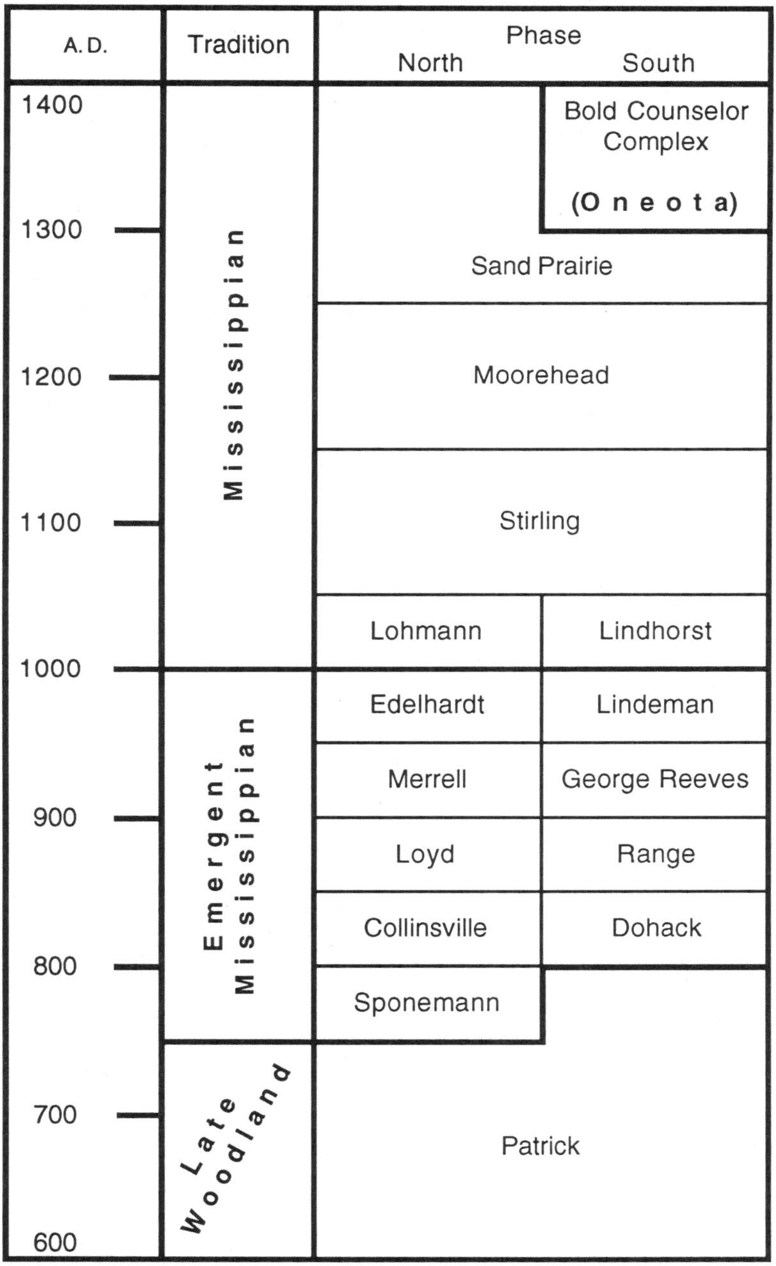

A.D.	Tradition	Phase	
		North	South
1400	Mississippian		Bold Counselor Complex (O n e o t a)
1300		Sand Prairie	
1200		Moorehead	
1100		Stirling	
1000		Lohmann	Lindhorst
	Emergent Mississippian	Edelhardt	Lindeman
900		Merrell	George Reeves
		Loyd	Range
800		Collinsville	Dohack
		Sponemann	
700	Late Woodland	Patrick	
600			

Figure 4. American Bottom chronology. The sequence of phases differs in the northern and southern portions of the study area.

formal planning, with buildings arranged around a central courtyard or plaza. Individual households can be recognized in the clustered arrangements of buildings and pits.

Emergent Mississippian (A.D. 800–1000) times show increasing development and growth of community planning (Kelly 1990a, 1990b; Kelly et al. 1984b). Hut-compounds were elaborations on the spatial themes established in Late Woodland times. Community layout became even more formalized than it had previously been, with residential buildings arranged around a courtyard that held either a large communal building or a set of four large storage pits closely surrounding a central post. In a series of successive reoccupations of the Range site, Emergent Mississippian communities became more densely populated, with more buildings concentrated in smaller village areas. Substantial buildings, representing considerable investment of resources, plus the evidence of reoccupation at the Range site, indicate that the people had a long-term commitment to that location. At this time, inhabitants of the region added maize, a hallmark of the Emergent Mississippian period, to a long-established set of cultivated plant species. Maize quickly became a major high-yield, storable commodity (Johannessen 1984:203). Increases in human population, expanded use of natural and domesticated resources, and the specialization of domestic and communal facilities seem to have stimulated the diversification of local styles of art and technology within the region. The stylistic variety of this time has been interpreted to represent two separate series of chronological phases: one for the northern portion of the American Bottom and one for the southern (Figure 4; Kelly et al. 1984b).

During the Mississippian period (A.D. 1000–1400), a hierarchy of diverse settlement types developed. At its highest level, it was characterized by temple-towns with complex, obviously formalized community plans. At its lowest level, it was characterized by relatively simple isolated homesteads laid out more casually on the landscape. At Cahokia, the highest-level site, mounds around plazas were flanked by residential districts, and an inner precinct was demarcated by a palisade. The lowest level sites include many small nonmound settlements that are the focus of this study. The basic modes of public architecture, house construction, and ceramic technology here were common throughout much of the Midwest and Southeast at that time. Settlement diversity continued within the region from the Emergent Mississippian period onward.

MODELS OF SETTLEMENT AND SOCIAL COMPLEXITY

The origin of social classes is an important question for the social sciences. What happened when life became complex enough to require elite classes and a hierarchical chain of decision making? How did this take place and why? Ethnoarchaeological studies can be useful, but ethnology lacks the time depth necessary to observe long-term developments. Ethnographic observation, itself an outside Western influence, alters the course of cultural change even under ideal circumstances.[4] For example, the considerable impact of foreign influence has been made clear in the debate over the nature of the "tribe" as a stage in the evolution of complex society. It now appears that examples of this seemingly essential stage of cultural evolution may be largely the result of foreign influences.[5]

Examples of civilizations that have undergone long-term cultural development without strong foreign pressures are available only through archaeological research. Such cases are rare, but they are essential to our understanding of the nature of cultural evolution. Indeed, an ideal way to study the development of complex society is to examine archaeological examples where there were no foreign influences to skew the patterns of cultural development in peculiar ways. However, archaeological studies often focus on temple-towns and their elite inhabitants to the exclusion of the populace who were commoners and only occasionally walked in the shadows of the monuments they built. Approaches to the identification of complex society have focused on the distribution of tools, ornaments, and monumental architecture as indicators of elite status (Brown 1971; Larson 1972; Peebles 1971, 1983; Peebles and Kus 1977). These discoveries identified the presence and extent of social ranking but did not show what it meant in the daily lives of most people. In this way, rare, large, and elite places have commanded archaeological attention, while little is known of the small, relatively simple settlements that make up most of the archaeological record. This is true even though an understanding of small sites is a powerful aid to the understanding of large sites and regional systems (Binford 1964:432; Lewis 1982:83; Smith 1978c:499-500).

The shift from simple to complex society, where it occurred, created new regional systems of decision making and resource allocation that required a new settlement system with new settlement patterns at all levels in the society. Recent studies of settlement, architecture, and proxemics reveal that a people's ideology, society, and economy are expressed in the ways that they organize their homes, work places, and communities.[6] Furthermore, the results of these studies reinforce the usefulness of reconstructing prehistoric spatial organization in cultural terms rather than simply in terms of the demands and limitations imposed by the natural environment. Thus, the distribution of facilities, tools, and even debris, as this study will show, may be examined as evidence of social, ideological, and economic forces. From the results of this investigation, I reconstruct the shifting framework of spatial organization for the social, economic, and ritual aspects of domestic and community life in the built environment of nonelite prehistoric groups in the American Bottom. Trends of change in settlement and social organization are modeled based on households as functional parts of a hierarchical system—a system in which small, medium, and large communities were joined with one another in complex networks that were controlled in part by authorities in the largest towns. This system developed without foreign coercion. The model is fitted with the latest information from the Cahokia site to form an overview of Mississippian social development throughout the American Bottom. The results include details and trends that are relevant in southeastern North America and anywhere else complex societies have emerged.

There are commonly accepted notions about the way the American Bottom developed. They derive from archaeological knowledge of this and other regions and from historical, geographical, political, and economic concepts (Emerson 1989, 1992; Emerson and Milner 1982; Fowler 1975, 1991; Fowler and Hall 1978; Hall 1991; Kelly 1980, 1991; Milner 1982, 1986, 1990, 1991; Milner and Emerson 1981; O'Brien 1972b; Pauketat 1993, 1994; Woods and Holley 1991; Yerkes 1991). The direction of cultural evolution in the American Bottom during the Emergent Mississippian and Mississippian periods is clear. An elaboration of the social system, and hence the settlement pattern, is evident in the formation of large temple-towns, smaller temple-towns, dispersed communities, and farmsteads. As population increased and exotic imports proliferated, elites were buried with exotic wealth items and art abounded with complex symbolism—all are indications of complex systems of handling the information, goods, and services that people needed. Organizational structures were devised to control the growing energy-flow associated with, but not limited to, the increasing production and consumption of subsistence resources. The swelling population, expanding resources, and ever-widening trade networks were integrated through increasingly complex sociopolitical and economic ties. This situation is comparable throughout much of southeastern North America, where a variety of similar regional expressions of the Middle Mississippian tradition characterize late prehistory.

The American Bottom has many excavated sites that document the entire range of social hierarchy (Fowler 1974, 1975; Fowler and Hall 1978; Kelly et al. 1984b; Milner et al. 1984). The small sites in this study illustrate the lowest social order. The highest order is illustrated at Cahokia. At Cahokia's Mound 72, for example, an important man was escorted into the next world by dozens of young retainers apparently selected to die with him. This example illustrates a high-status individual's power over others' lives, an extreme case of one person controlling others' access to the basic necessities of life. However, it is beyond the scope of this work to marshal all the evidence supporting the evolution of Cahokia's complex society or to detail the historical events that punctuated the rise and fall of Cahokia's dominance. The subject of the present book is the nature and extent of growing social power in the region and the resulting integration of isolated country households with crowded temple-towns.

Until now, little was known of the households that were the building blocks of Mississippian society and the roles they played in the society at large. But trends in regional social organization can be observed in Cahokia's countryside, especially in the spatial organization of buildings, features, and debris. As small hinterland settlements became more and more influenced by the increasingly organized towns, the patterned arrangements of their domestic activities changed to meet increasingly structured obligations and opportunities. These obligations and opportunities included the tribute of goods or services, participation in ceremonies, and access to commodities through extensive trade networks or redistribution events like feasting or gift-giving (Smith 1978c:490–491). For example, prominent families during Cahokia's heyday had sweatlodges or meeting houses where they apparently hosted their less affluent neighbors during local ceremonies. Likewise, private interior storage pits came in and out of fashion as the regional hierarchy of social statuses rose and fell. In the domestic sphere, activity areas were systematically allocated in this way to accommodate the new distinctions of labor and status that came with the communication and decision-making processes peculiar to the new social system. Such decisions were made to form alliances, to wage wars, and to regulate production on the basis of information flowing into the regional centers (Peebles 1983:193–194). The new distinctions of labor and status include the role of the family farm as an economic unit that participated in the self-sufficient subsistence economy and specialized to some degree in the production of agricultural surplus. Later, as complex society disintegrated near the end of the Mississippian period, a corresponding decrease in the systematic use of space by householders occurred as some social roles disappeared. New patterns of space allocation are evident in the floor plans of buildings and in household arrangements of buildings and pits.

The object of this study has been to build a model of Mississippian society emphasizing the role of households in the changing local and regional settlement system. This has been done first by identifying the standards of vernacular architecture, household organization, and small-community planning and then by interpretating the temporal trends of these standards in a regional synthesis. Findings from extensive excavations at many small sites answer questions about households as parts of the regional system. The results show how Mississippian notions of space utilization and activity organization changed with time. Social stratification at small sites is demonstrated where it was previously unrecognized (Fowler 1974:32–33). When the results of this study are considered in the context of organizing principles common to farming communities everywhere (Chisolm 1962; Fowler 1983; Netting 1989, 1993; and Reynolds 1974), a regional model is developed.

We can make three working assumptions for the purposes of this analysis. First, chronological change in the built environment will reflect the effects of an increasingly complex society on people at small settlements. Second, changes in the distribution of debris, facilities, and buildings will show the increasing importance of craft, subsistence, and civic-ceremonial, as opposed to gender-related, divisions of labor as expressions of social complexity among hinterlanders. Third, dedication of space to various craft activities will have varied among households and fluctuated through time. However, full-time craft specialization, such as pottery or stone tool manufacture, is not expected at small sites. Full-time craft specialization is a hallmark of complex society, but it seems unlikely to have been popular in a rural setting where family farmers provided for their own subsistence and produced a surplus to sustain others who did not provide for themselves.

This study presents a model of how settlements in the region developed and declined. The model is a synthesis of data from sites throughout the Cahokia region that builds on a foundation of long-standing knowledge including earlier models. Fowler (1974:27) proposed two alternate models of settlement for the Mississippian period. One model is characterized by a series of hierarchically stratified community types; the other model is characterized by population nucleation.

The community stratification model proposes a four-tiered hierarchy of settlement types. Cahokia, representing the highest order of settlement with its numerous large mounds, is the only first-tier site. Second-tier settlements are smaller multimound complexes, exemplified by the Mitchell, Lunsford-Pulcher, St. Louis, and East St. Louis Mound groups. Third-tier settlements, such as the Lohmann site, have single-mounds (Esarey and Pauketat 1992). The fourth tier is made up of "a number of small, moundless sites that have been characterized as hamlets, villages, and farmsteads . . . [which] seem to cluster around the larger communities" (Fowler 1974:32). The community stratification model assumes that sites of all types were contemporaneous.

The population nucleation model differs from the community stratification model in that only the first and second tier sites were occupied during the Stirling and Moorehead phases (Fowler 1974:32). This model was derived primarily from survey data (Harn 1971), which tend to be insensitive to shell-tempered ceramics that are diagnostic of the Stirling and Moorehead phases (shell-tempered ceramics deteriorate relatively quickly when exposed to the elements in plowed fields).

Both models were problematic because of the quality of the data on which they were based (Fowler 1974:32). The nucleation model has proved to be nonviable because small sites have been discovered for all Mississippian phases, contrary to what the model called for. The community stratification model was better than the nucleation model, but it did not explain how the four-tiered hierarchy arose from its Late Woodland antecedents, how stable it was, and how it finally collapsed.

Partly in response to these shortcomings, Milner (1990) recently added dynamic qualities to the community stratification model. In his model, Milner proposes a segmented regional polity made up of nearly identical, quasiautonomous territories, each dominated by the elite social stratum at its temple-town. According to this model, Cahokia dominated the entire polity through networks of relations among territorial elites. The social landscape of the regional polity would have shifted according to the changing fortunes of various territorial segments in relation to one another. The present study explains why such dynamic disequilibration should be expected in a sociopolitical context such as Cahokia, even though investigators still lack confirming archaeological evidence for it.

RATIONALE

During late prehistory, the development of settlement in the American Bottom was characterized by gradual rather than revolutionary change. Early in the record, nucleation of settlements during the Emergent Mississippian period is apparent in a sequence of increasingly dense and complex community plans (see Kelly 1990a, 1990b; Kelly et al. 1984b). Later, in the Mississippian period, this continuing process was accompanied by developments in public architecture such as mounds, plazas, and palisades at town-and-mound centers, which were a new settlement type. Although, as we have seen, it has been speculated that small settlements disappeared as part of the nucleation process (Fowler 1978; Fowler and Hall 1978), this did not in fact happen (e.g., Milner et al. 1984). Instead, isolated homesteads became the smallest unit of permanent settlement, probably representing the nuclear or extended family as a basic socioeconomic group.

The cultural patterns of settlement, society, economy, politics, and religion in the area make up what is referred to as the "regional system." All the intricate changes in the regional system are expressed in ways that are more or less clear in the archaeological record of the region. Social and economic changes occurred relatively early at the growing mound centers (Collins and Chalfant 1993; Fowler 1974:19–23; Holley et al. 1993), marking the rise of complex society (e.g., Adams 1975, 1988; Fried 1967:185–226). The impact of these changes on tiny settlements has until recently been unrecognized. The clues have not been simple or easy to identify. At one time, for example, the arrival of maize from Mesoamerica was thought to be the principle cause for the sudden development of complex society. Now it is known that the relative amounts of various important foods people had at these small farming sites went essentially unchanged for several centuries during the Emergent Mississippian and Mississippian periods (Johannessen 1984, 1993; Kelly and Cross 1984; Rindos and Johannessen 1991), thus eliminating any simple, subsistence-related explanation for social change. In fact, maize was an important addition to an already long-established agricultural complex of domesticated native plants. This study will suggest that although maize was an important new source of energy in the region, there was a complex mechanism of social interaction and evolution driven by a whole set of new ways of channeling information and controlling energy.

The model of Mississippian settlement presented in this book was built on the basis of answers to three important questions. First, how did major trends in the region affect small-settlement layout? We will see that changes in social and economic conditions can be inferred from the waxing and waning in popularity of special kinds of activity areas and facilities as well as from changes in the patterns of architecture, household organization, and community planning.

Second, how were changes in production, storage, and redistribution of subsistence commodities correlated with changes in the local organization of socioeconomic groups, the hierarchical organization of civic or religious authority, and the local and regional centralization of authority? These correlations are evident over time in the spatial organization of economic activity areas, storage pits, granaries, cemeteries, meeting houses, cult houses, sweatbaths, and households within and among communities.

Third, how were the gender-based division of labor, craft specialties, civic-ceremonial functions, and subsistence activities expressed in vernacular architecture? The rules or norms governing the allocation of space for these purposes were apparently expressed in the patterned distributions of activity areas, hearths, benches, prepared floors, storage pits, refuse pits, and other features within and among buildings of various sizes, shapes, and constructions. These three questions are addressed in this book using data from three decades of survey and excavation.

This research is oriented toward the micro and the semi-micro levels of settlement (e.g., Butzer 1982:232–234; Clarke 1977:11–15). The basic unit of analysis is an individual feature, such as a house basin, a storage pit, or a posthole. Taken together in archaeological context, these units are considered in hierarchical groups: an individual building is composed of a structure with its interior facilities and debris contents; a household is made up of buildings and exterior pits; a community is made up of housholds and other elements.

At a low hierarchical level of analysis, individual features are analyzed according to their temporal, spatial, morphological, and content characteristics. Relatively higher levels of analysis examine distributions of features and debris: buildings are analyzed according to their construction and floor plans; spatial configurations of households are analyzed; communities are studied for patterns in the arrangement of households with respect to one another. Important patterns are compared with data from nearby sites that were not included in the analysis.

There are a few biases in the archaeological record that derive from the way that sites in the region were formed and preserved. These biases were first examined in a series of pilot studies (Mehrer 1982a, 1982b, 1983, 1986b) that used some of the data in this study. For example, the construction of one prehistoric facility may have disturbed the remains of an older, previously abandoned one. In this way, debris from the older facility may have been inadvertently redeposited into the fill of the newer one. Sometimes pits were reused after they had temporarily fallen into disuse. Buildings were occasionally repaired or completely replaced on the spot. In this study, the occupational history of a site, the disposal of refuse, and post-abandonment disturbances—all potential biasing factors—are considered in an effort to control their effects on the interpretation of analytical results.

This inquiry does not rely on special samples or complex laboratory techniques, and for that reason the methods and interpretations are readily applicable to many other regions of the world. As stated before, wherever pre-state or emerging-state societies are studied archaeologically, questions arise about how and why society became increasingly more complex. This study has demonstrated that archaeological findings from prehistoric rural settings can shed light on this question—on how and why such societies change. The pace of cultural development can be measured by counting and weighing the castoffs of daily life and by studying the layout of domestic scenes. Culture evolves in the mundane lives of ordinary farm families just as it does for the elite classes living in large centers.

Chapter 2 offers a theoretical framework for the middle-range approach applied in this study; some controversial aspects of regional late prehistory are also addressed. Chapter 3 describes the research methods used in this study and defines special terms. Chapter 4 presents the analysis of debris, features, buildings, and households. Chapter 5 interprets the results of analysis in regional context, compares and contrasts them with other sites in and around the American Bottom, and proposes a model of rural households as functional units in the evolution of the region's complex society. Finally, Chapter 6 presents the conclusions of the study and considers their relevance to research in this and other regions.

Chapter 2

Theoretical Perspectives
on Settlement in the Cahokia Region

The use of theory in this study is pragmatic, not rhetorical. The aim of the study is to test hypotheses and apply theories to the results of those tests in order to present a coherent picture of late prehistory in the American Bottom. Several middle-range theories link the archaeological record to prehistoric behaviors so that the organizing principles of those behaviors can be understood (Binford 1987:452); a general or high-range theory of cultural evolution provides a framework within which to coordinate generalizations about those principles. Therefore, the first practical problem in this study is one of middle-range theory—to isolate archaeological patterns that reflect prehistoric behaviors organized by traditional prehistoric norms, standards, or customs. The second practical problem is to coordinate the interpretations using a high-range theory. To be useful, such a theory must be general enough to apply beyond the study region and to bear on general problems such as the rise of social complexity.

Three late prehistoric conditions in the study region influence the character of its record: the lengthy duration of occupation in the region; the relatively stable systems of sedentary settlement and horticultural livelihood; and the perishable nature of architectural building materials. These factors helped to create an archaeological record that is often a palimpsest of repaired, reused, abandoned, destroyed, and disturbed facilities.

The character of the American Bottom's archaeological record makes it appropriate to look at the region from five specific theoretical perspectives: site formation processes, activity area studies, vernacular architecture, household archaeology, and social power. These perspectives range from relatively mechanical to abstract. The mechanical matters of interpreting feature and debris distribution are considered in terms of how the archaeological record of a site is formed by natural and cultural forces (Schiffer 1976) and how different kinds of activities mark sites with various types of discarded debris and abandoned facilities (Cameron and Tomka 1993; Kent 1984). From a less mechanical perspective, sites and communities are considered in terms of their built forms—that is, in terms of their architecture, household organization, and community layout. These perspectives joined together can help illuminate the family's place on the natural and cultural landscape of ancient times.

The "conjunctive approach" was first presented by Walter Taylor in 1948 as an effort to understand, "the interrelationships which existed *within* a particular cultural entity" (Taylor 1964:5; emphasis in original). Taylor's approach incorporates the widest range of relevant data to produce a comprehensive picture of a prehistoric culture rather than a comparison of some relatively minor aspects of one culture with those of another. This study builds on many published single-site analyses of settlement, subsistence, population, chronology, technology, natural setting, flora, fauna, and bioanthropology.[1] Those analyses were conducted in the spirit of Taylor's conjunctive approach and their various results were used in concert to refine the regional chronology, among other things. By analyzing much of that data again and then interrelating the new results via several theoretical perspectives, the present study examines the region's settlement system as a composite of its social, economic, and political dynamics as they are expressed on the landscape through the inhabitants' built environment.

Any site's position in the natural and cultural environment is intertwined with the social, economic, and political aspects of the regional system. It is clear that a settlement's economic potential is directly related to its distance from natural resources and trade partners; its political position is related to its distance from authority figures and its place in the hierarchy of different types of sites; its social situation is related to its proximity to extended family, friends, and neighbors. In the same sense, the typical family's size is also a factor in society, politics, and economy. A settlement's size and configuration are factors of its population, its social position in the region, its standing in the settlement hierarchy, and its economic potential. Of course, the cultural and natural debris that make up the archaeological record are important indicators that reflect not only the family's social, political, and economic status but also the history of the site's occupancy. It is less apparant how specific elements in the archaeological record systematically express the social, political, or economic position of a given settlement within the overall cultural environment.

The constraints and provisions of the natural and cultural environment helped shape the built environment of the Cahokia region; in turn, the built forms stand as statements about the inhabitants' places in the regional system. Several recent interdisciplinary works have shown how such statements made by or through the built forms of a settlement accurately express social, political, and economic factors that are parts of the larger cultural milieu. These interdisciplinary efforts include studies of household archaeology, sociological and economic studies of family life, architectural studies of traditional architecture, and anthropological studies of intensive agricultural lifeways.[2]

Before exploring these theoretical underpinnings, it is necessary to explain a little about how archaeological sites in the study were formed and how prehistoric activities at those sites are recognized and analyzed. Because this study synthesizes the character of a group of households in the context of large-scale regional social change, its analytical goals are different from those of previous studies that sought to refine the region's chronology and to determine the cultural affiliations of its households.[3] The present analyses use the archaeological evidence of construction, repair, reuse, abandonment, destruction, discard, and disturbance—all processes of site formation—to interpret trends of regional behavior that seem to be tied to the rise and fall of Cahokia's complex society.

In this study, debris and features are analyzed as evidence for interpreting patterns of prehistoric behavior. Processes that have affected the evidence must also be understood. For example, important processes include not only how people constructed their facilities and disposed of their own refuse but also how they disturbed refuse from former occupations and inadvertently incorporated it into their own refuse deposits. Patterns of prehistoric debris disposal and the intermixing of earlier refuse are identified and controlled in this study before interpretations of historical processes or events are made from the results of analyses. Likewise, idiosyncratic behaviors, site-specific patterns, and the effects of local natural resources are taken into account.

My theoretical perspective on activity areas, as with site-formational processes, is more abstract than is customary in archaeological studies because the purpose here is ultimately to synthesize information from the sites in the region, not merely to reanalyze it. An activity area is a spatially discrete group of features, such as a building with its interior facilities or a cluster of outdoor pits. Activity areas are the smallest coherent unit of behavioral analysis in settlement studies. Late prehistoric lifeways in the American Bottom and adjacent regions were sedentary; that is, homes and communities were maintained year-round. The logistic facts of sedentary life, such as periodic cleanups and the secondary disposal of debris away from primary activity areas, have considerable impact on the archaeological record. Such conditions of sedentary life are different from those usually discussed in the literature of middle-range theory (Binford 1977, 1980, 1987; Schiffer 1976; Yellen 1977), which often deals with mobile foragers and collectors. Nevertheless, important theoretical constructs are the same in both approaches.[4] It should also be noted that primary deposits of activity-related refuse are unavailable for study here because scatters of debris on living-floors in undisturbed context are rare at the sites in this study. The debris assemblages that were found in features are commonly secondary deposits that reflect the way refuse was discarded rather than the way implements were manufactured or food was processed.

Activity areas are characterized in terms of their size, feature morphology and arrangement, and debris attributes (such as density of debris per feature volume or total number of tools and exotic artifacts). These general attributes are appropriate for characterizing the many and diverse components in this relatively large-scale study. More detailed characteristics appropriate for reconstructing events or building chronologies in a smaller-scale study would obscure most of the patterns of similarity that exist among the many and varied archaeological components.

The categories of artifactual debris in this study are gross material types such as ceramics or chert rather than more technical categories such as the ceramic's temper type or the chert's geological type. Tools have also been categorized according to raw material type rather than according to task-oriented functional categories. Stylistic and technical considerations of ceramic or tool design are especially important for interpretations of chronology and traditional affiliation, but the sites in question here already have established times and traditions.

VERNACULAR ARCHITECTURE

The buildings examined in this study were constructed of local materials by nonspecialists—the owners and users of the buildings—who applied only subtle variations in design. For these reasons the buildings are considered to be primitive by our society (Rapoport 1969:1–8). In contrast to such primitive architecture, a more complex, preindustrial vernacular order of architecture is created in societies where some individuals possess special knowledge and skills in design and construction. Examples of this architectural order include the mounds and palisades at Mississippian temple-towns that were presumably designed by people with special skills and knowledge, individuals who perhaps were full-time architectural specialists (Bareis 1975:13; Collins et al. 1986). A third order of architecture is characterized by modern or high-style buildings that are original creations designed and built by teams of full-time specialists (Rapoport 1969).

These notions of architectural order form an important theoretical scheme based on analogies from modern ethnographic architecture (e.g., Wilk 1983). Presumably, buildings in the sample were designed by nonspecialist users to meet their routine needs rather than by specialists who instead might have imposed design standards that were irrelevant to the buildings' contexts and intended uses. Likewise, the rebuilding or redesign of existing structures presumably met the actual perceived demands of daily life. For present purposes, then, the different building designs and constructions in this study can be understood as evidence for the degree and extent of cultural sharing and as an indication of variation within norms.

The perishable nature of the local building materials (wood, cane, twine, thatch, mud) is a mixed blessing to the archaeologist. On one hand, the buildings left little or no solid evidence of their superstructures; on the other hand they required periodic repair or replacement, improvements to the building that left a record. Because an edifice was designed to meet the ever-changing needs of the owner, we can be sure that as the spatial order of daily life changed, buildings were promptly redesigned or replaced appropriately.

The buildings in this study show greater technical and stylistic variation than their predecessors of the Late Woodland and Emergent Mississippian periods. Differences between the buildings are nevertheless subtle because their basic technology and raw materials are similar. Common design traits are assumed to have been traditional expressions of shared norms that were suited to perceived needs and basic technology. The lack of a highly specialized technical language and strict design rules, however, gave rise to recognizably eccentric examples.

As noted above, students of modern vernacular architecture, often termed "traditional" architecture, have come to recognize that buildings reflect their inhabitants' social, political, and economic standing. As Fuchs and Meyer-Brodnitz state, "[A]rchitecture is not the arbitrary whim of individuals but the selective outcome of a diffused, intricate, social preoccupation with construction. . . . The types and forms that best suit the purposes they serve, the meanings they carry, and the means used to carry them get accepted as norms and become the vernacular of their times" (1989:404–405).

In some studies of vernacular architecture, factors determining house forms have been identified through historical reconstruction of long-term trends. Shami states, "These include household and agricultural cycles as well as dynamics of political power and social relations in the village. Without such a holistic and contextual approach, the study of the architectural and technical characteristics of housing contributes little to the interpretation of the relationship between material and social life" (1989:452). In addition, buildings are understood in this study as a way to assign space to one or more frequently performed activities requiring some degree of privacy or shelter. Most buildings in this study were domiciles, workshops, or storerooms. Others, depending on their size, shape, location, and interior furnishings, were some combination of specialized meetinghouse, sweat lodge, and communal winter shelter.

HOUSEHOLD ARCHAEOLOGY

Vernacular architecture and household archaeology go hand in hand because the dwelling is at the heart of household archaeology (Ashmore and Wilk 1988:1; Wilk 1988:135), itself a natural outgrowth of settlement studies in archaeology (Ashmore and Wilk 1988:7). According to Bourdier and AlSayyad, "The dwelling unit is the basic architectural component of the traditional environment; the physical determinants, climatic constraints, aesthetic meanings and social practices are all important aspects of concern at this level. Settlement layouts represent a larger scale of analysis at which one can discover much about spatial organization, design symbolism and social hierarchy" (1989b:8).

Household archaeology represents an effort to understand the most basic social unit of culture, that of the family or coresidential group (Chang 1958; Flannery 1983; Flannery and Winter 1976; Hayden and Cannon 1982; Hirth 1993; Smith 1978b; South 1977a, 1977b; Wilk and Rathje 1982a, 1982b; Wilk and Ashmore 1988). The family can be considered a universal cultural trait, but defining it precisely is a problem. Because an exact definition suitable to all cultures seems unattainable (Netting, Wilk, and Arnould 1984:xix–xxvi), the term *family* will be used here simply to refer to the coresidential group of people who used the spatially discrete cluster of household facilities on a daily basis. The terms *household* and *household cluster* refer to the group of buildings and pits that served a family.

Any approach to household archaeology must be at least tangential to ethnographic and ethnoarchaeological understandings of household social and material culture. Many of the most basic inferences about archaeological remains are based on ethnohistoric and ethnographic knowledge; they take the form of inexplicit analogies that generally go unchallenged. In this manner, the analysis and interpretations of households in this study are based on the notion that the family, or coresidential group, is represented as a basic social unit by the small settlements in the study.

It is useful to take an archaeological perspective on the household in order to make inferences about the basic social units and how they were organized. The use of space within households and their spatial relationships to other similar settlements can be used to infer household and community aspects of social organization. The household, a logical aggregate of facilities and a logical subset of a dispersed rural community, has stylistic, technical, functional, social, demographic, and economic interpretive implications. For this reason, the household is a meaningful unit for archaeological comparison and contrast.

SOCIAL POWER

Because this study reveals a more complex social order in the Cahokia region than has been previously recognized, it is helpful to understand it in terms of a general theory of social power. Social power is defined as the control of energy in its various forms and flows (Adams 1975, 1977, 1981, 1988). Individuals or groups with social power have control, through word or deed, of energy production, storage, transfer, or expenditure. Social power is reflected in the ability of one individual to influence another's behavior through control of some form of energy in the society's environment (Adams 1977:388). This notion of social power is appropriate for understanding a complex, hierarchically ordered, regional settlement system that represents a ranked set of social statuses (Haas 1982:155–158). This notion also fits well with Fried's (1960,

1967) idea that high-status individuals in stratified societies have privileged access to fundamental subsistence resources. The American Bottom had such a system of social power during late prehistory.

Social power is at the heart of questions about social ranking and the transition from simple to complex societies. For Mississippian societies in general, and Cahokia in particular, the notion of social power is pertinent because most of the generally accepted scholarly ideas about the transition and its results are couched in energetic terms, especially regarding subsistence resources, tribute of commodities or labor, control over local and interregional trade, and ideological control over the annual cycle of farming activities (Barker and Pauketat 1992).

One such notion about Cahokia is that the elite commanded a great deal of other peoples' labor and skill in the execution of the large construction projects that produced the palisades and numerous large mounds at the Cahokia site. Also assumed is that the elite commanded the disposition of enormous quantities of equipment, apparatus, supplies, and energy that made these public projects important in symbolic and even thermodynamic dimensions (cf. Trigger 1990).

Another notion is that astronomical experts used the structures known as "woodhenges" at Cahokia as calendrical devices to help schedule annual planting and harvesting for farmers throughout the region as a means of centralized control of the subsistence system (e.g., Wittry 1969). The woodhenges might have been monuments in their own right, embodying complex symbolic aspects of traditional cosmology (Fowler 1991). They might also have served as land-surveying devices used to align monuments and residential districts with other parts of the townscape, as well as to plan the layout of borrow pits, ponds, refuse dumps, and other parts of the infrastructure according to an established town plan.

Yet another key notion is that Cahokia's central authorities could demand tribute of commodities, such as maize surpluses, from farmers in order to support the unpaid labor used on public works projects. Thus, in accordance with this notion, outlying farmsteads are often considered as merely extractive loci for the production of maize surpluses destined for redistribution from elite granaries.

All these notions emphasize centralized control over energetic processes. Their focus of attention is primarily on the elites of society, their roles, and how they maintained their positions and exercised their control. Most individuals in society are ignored except as they factor into these schemes as producers of surplus food and as corvée labor. The abundant source of energy that fueled such social power is generally understood to have been the maize surpluses produced by the intensive agriculturalists in the countryside who indirectly fed administrators, design specialists, and unpaid labor.

Social power is not an absolute commodity. Instead, it is widely shared, though unevenly distributed, so that almost everyone has at least some limited control over some form of energy. Even individual farmers or gardeners, for example, have a measure of direct control over subsistence production at its lowest level. Social power is categorized by two types—independent and dependent. Independent power is based directly on an individual's abilities and direct controls. Dependent power is derived from another person or group. For instance, dependent power can be granted by one individual to another, allocated by a group to an individual, or delegated by someone with power to several others (Adams 1977:388–391). Unanswered questions concern how social power was shared in and around Cahokia and how the distribution of power changed during the shift from simple to complex society. A specific issue requiring further investigation is how householders' fortunes changed as control over rapidly growing amounts of regional energy became concentrated among the new social elites accumulating power in temple-towns.

A theory of social power that is especially helpful in answering these questions is proposed by Adams (1975, 1988). According to Adams's theory, a hierarchy of social orders exists within societies—for example, bands exist within tribes, counties within states, and states within nations. Other widely held theories of social change (e.g., Fried 1960, 1967; Service 1962, 1975) are based on an evolutionary taxonomy that provides only a few mutually exclusive alternatives by which to classify the political organization of a society (e.g., band, tribe, chiefdom, or state). The major strength of Adams's theory is that it offers a way to understand small communities in the countryside without requiring all the functional details for classifying the overarching regional system. In this study, for example, we do not have to decide whether or not Cahokia was a state before we evaluate the network of households spread across the countryside. However, as we trace the trajectory of social complexity for small-scale groups, we will compare it with the social trajectory of the nearby large-scale regional centers.

Adams's theory of how individuals or groups integrate socially with one another is applicable at virtually any scale, ranging from the family to the multinational corporation. Hierarchical social ordering, or inequality of some sort, is present in all groups, even those traditionally considered egalitarian—differences in age, sex, or achievement are significant even within bands and families (Adams 1975). Adams's theory also applies to societies as they grow. The tendency within any cultural system is to grow by continually expanding the energy base and for society to become increasingly complex, through self-organization, in order to fully control that energy (Adams 1975: 137–153, 1988). Social complexity takes the familiar form of social inequality—the hierarchical ordering of statuses for individuals and groups that have different levels of control over the available resources (cf., Fried 1960:721).

According to the theory of social power, several units (individuals or groups) that recognize one another will "coordinate" when they interact with one another, granting power reciprocally among themselves on a one-on-one, relatively equal basis. Coordinating units function together as equals in some contexts but are centralized under a leader in other contexts; that is, as a group they can oscillate between these coordinated and centralized levels of integration (Adams 1975:206–217). A coordinated group will tend to centralize into a larger-scale unit as it coordinates with other similar centralized units. An example of this is the secondary state that forms when coordinated tribes or chiefdoms are confronted by a foreign state (Fried 1960:723). The processes of coordination and centralization, however, are similar at any scale.

These general notions of social power as control of energy will be useful as we consider many aspects of the settlement patterns that emerge from the settlement analyses in the following sections. To understand settlement patterns in terms of the interaction of families, communities, leaders, and followers, it is necessary to understand the functions of the various excavated facilities and the roles of the groups they represent. Facilities, by definition, are used to control energy (Wagner 1960), so it is reasonable to interpret the groups that used them in terms of their place in the regional system of energy flow that the facilities, in part, represent.

Adams (1975:203, fig. 13) uses settlement units such as neighborhood, community, town, city, and metropolitan area as "terms commonly applied to subdivisions or 'subassemblies,' operating units," of various evolutionary levels of society. Likewise, this study uses hierarchical settlement types to characterize social units and social development in terms of Adams's evolutionary theory. It is essential to understand the evolution of Cahokia's regional complex society in terms of the ways that the neighborhoods, communities, and towns interacted with one another as a larger hierarchical system even as they maintained their identity and a degree of autonomy in the process.

Chapter 3

Sites, Features, and Methodology

The way people occupied the landscape of the American Bottom changed as social, economic, and political systems waxed and waned during late prehistory. The development of complex society not only created ceremonial centers in the American Bottom but also transformed the way rural communities were organized and the way family life was conducted. In what manner and to what degree were rural households tied to the obvious developments at regional temple-towns? The aim of this chapter is to introduce the archaeogical sites and the analytical methods used to address this question.

The arrangement of buildings and pits at households and the distribution of artifacts within the households are expected to be related to the processes of cultural change experienced throughout the region. The spatial organization of rural settlements is hypothesized to have changed systematically to accommodate new activities brought about by the increasingly complex regional system of social, economic, and political relationships. This accommodation is apparent in the composition and arrangement of household facilities. It is also expected that the organization of rural settlement later responded to the regional system's decline. For example, if rural farming practices were changing and harvests were being distributed differently as a result of increasingly strong social and economic ties to regional authorities living in temple-towns, then innovations in rural domestic facilities may have accommodated those changes. Likewise, increasingly complex regional communication and decision-making processes associated with developments in leadership may have been expressed in the rural setting in the form of new local leadership roles.

To make valid interpretations, it is crucial to identify the different effects on the archaeological record of intentional and unintentional processes of site formation. An unintentional by-product of settlement activity, for example, may be the redistribution of debris from former occupations at a site. Distribution of contemporaneous debris, in contrast, may be related to intentional modes of behavior.

Patterned variety among pit features should reveal some degree of functional specialization, but evidence for primary feature use must be identified. For example, the primary use of a storage pit might have been to hold valuables; the secondary use might have been to receive the useless clutter of everyday life. Location and morphology are design elements related to a facility's initial purpose, but often a feature's content relates only to its final function as rubbish dump. In this sense, debris can convey the last, if not the first, function of a feature. To the degree that material contents pertain to features' primary functions, patterns of debris scatter will correlate with a feature typology based on location and morphology. In this way, a storage pit's contents will not ordinarily reflect its primary function, but a posthole's contents probably will.

If regional processes gradually incorporated rural dwellers, adjustments to daily routines should be visible throughout the area. Activity areas within households are hypothesized to have become more regularized as patterns of space allocation responded to the increasingly structured demands and opportunities of regional networks. Different building designs will have different patterned arrangements of interior facilities. Special households will be identifiable by their communal buildings and exotic artifacts. A greater variety of building sizes and shapes is expected to accompany increasing role specialization and social change.

As noted above, chronological trends in the distributions of debris, facilities, buildings, and settlements will show the increasing importance of the division of labor along such lines as part-time crafts, subsistence-farming, and civic-ceremonial activities, as opposed to gender-related division of labor. Craft specialties might be evident in concentrations of raw material, manufacturing tools, and by-products for the production of such items as pots, stone tools, and ornaments. Subsistence specialties might be inferred from concentrations of used agricultural implements, faunal remains, or commodity storage and processing facilities. Civic-ceremonial specialization might be apparent from community-related facilities such as sweatbaths, granaries, meetinghouses, cult houses, or other structures that lack substantial evidence of residential use. Concentrations of exotic trade items or ritual paraphernalia might also characterize civic-ceremonial facilities.

The unique occupational history of each settlement area affects the content of features—an important fact that must not be forgotten. The distribution of debris among features can be strongly biased by the presence of former occupations nearby, because debris from an earlier time can easily become mixed into later contexts. Likewise, idiosyncratic or site-specific patterns of behavior can be expected to influence the character of remains.

THE ARCHAEOLOGICAL RECORD

The major factors affecting site formation, abandonment, preservation, and disturbance in the American Bottom are the prehistoric construction of facilities, the mixing of disturbed remains among occupations, refuse disposal, the decay of organic remains, modern farming, and erosion. Late prehistoric rural settlements were composed of many types of facilities, but because the remains of buildings and pits are often found undisturbed below the plowzone, they are the most widely known.

Except for the decay of organic remains, the most obvious destructive impact has been plowing, which systematically disturbed the upper 20 to 30 cm of each site. Soil erosion and accretion has not strongly affected the topography of the sites in the sample; the ground surfaces of the American Bottom during late prehistory were essentially the same as those of today (White et al. 1984). This means surface-level refuse deposits such as shallow middens are almost always disturbed prior to archaeological recovery. Subsurface deposits in abandoned pits or house basins are also at least partially disturbed by plowing. Because of this, features and debris recovered by excavation are usually limited to those that remain undisturbed below the plowzone.

Artifacts are almost always found in feature fill or other refuse context rather than in living-floor accumulations. Remains of former occupations can be mixed into later contexts, but in these cases the distribution of culturally distinctive artifacts can often clarify the sequence of construction. Specific activities can be reflected in the debris assemblages even though portions have been lost or decayed.

The Mississippian households in this study were excavated because they were slated for imminent destruction by modern developments. Although the sample is therefore not random, the site selection criteria are independent of the prehistoric settlement criteria under study. Site locations cover a wide range of prehistorically inhabitable biotic, geomorphic, and hydrologic zones in the region. Some available sites were excluded from the whole study or only from individual analyses because of incomplete data. Nevertheless, the sample has an adequate geographical and chronological range to permit generalizations of the results to be applied to other regions. Other sites in and around the region form the basis for comparative and synthetic discussion of analytical interpretations.

Seven sites—the Carbon Dioxide (Finney 1985), Range (Mehrer 1982a), Julien (Milner 1984a), Turner-DeMange (Milner 1983), BBB Motor (Emerson and Jackson 1984), Florence Street (Emerson et al. 1983),

Table 1

Distribution of components among sites by phases.

Sites	Edelhardt Phase	Lohmann Phase	Stirling Phase	Moorehead Phase	Sand Prairie Phase	Total
Carbon Dioxide	-	x	-	-	-	1
Range	-	x	x	-	-	2
Julien	-	-	x	x	x	3
Florence Street	-	-	-	-	x	1
Turner-DeMange	-	x	x	x	-	3
BBB Motor	x	-	x	-	-	2
Robert Schneider	-	-	x	-	-	1
Total	1	3	5	2	2	13

and Robert Schneider (Fortier 1985b) sites—were selected for extensive quantitative analysis (Figure 2). Other sites will be introduced and described throughout the course of the book for regional and extraregional comparisons. Each of the seven main sites has at least one fully excavated and well-reported household-size Emergent Mississippian or Mississippian component. Each component is comprised of all the features of an archaeological phase at a site even though feature superposition within a component may indicate some time depth for it (Table 1).

The Carbon Dioxide site (11-Mo-594; Figures 5 and 6) is a small multi-component site in the southern portion of the research area. The Lohmann phase component is situated on the outer bank of the Hill Lake Meander scar 0.3 km west of the sloping bluff edge and 4.0 km from the Mississippi River. The northern limits of the site are on an alluvial fan where Hill Lake Creek emerges from the uplands. In similar American Bottom localities, Hus (1908:194) notes bottomland forest growth around backwater lakes near the bluffline. Farther from the bluff there would have been wet and dry bottom prairie, depending on elevation (Finney 1985). The Lunsford-Pulcher Mississippian mound complex (Freimuth 1974; Griffin 1977; Griffin and Spaulding 1951) is 2.2 km to the northwest.

The Range site (11-S-47; Figures 7 and 8) is a large multicomponent site situated on the point bar of the Prairie Lake Meander scar 0.4 km west of a bluff escarpment and 5.0 km from the Mississippi River. The Stirling and Lohmann phase occupations are near the point bar's crest and the prehistoric

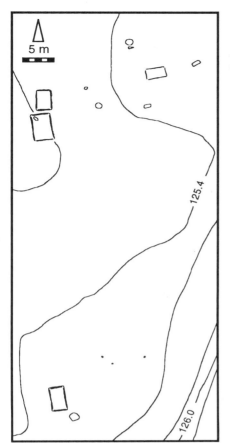

Figure 5. Plan of Mississippian features at the Carbon Dioxide site (after Finney 1985).

Figure 6. The northern feature cluster at the Carbon Dioxide site.

5 m

Figure 7.   Plan of Mississippian features at the Range site (after Mehrer 1982).

Figure 8.   An all-weather excavation shelter and the nearby bluffline at the Range site.

shores of Prairie Lake, which was seasonally flooded in late prehistory (White and Bonnell 1981:17–18). A bluff across the lake from the site rises about 70 m, exposing limestone formations containing useful cherts. The top of the loess-covered bluff forms a karst plain, and a spring emerging from the face of the bluff feeds a lake that is now canalized. Nearby are the Lunsford-Pulcher and Labras Lake sites (Phillips et al. 1980; Yerkes 1987). The Range components in this analysis are not the only Mississippian components at the site, but in the present study data for other components were not available for analysis.

The Lohmann components of both Range and Carbon Dioxide have been reassigned to the newly created Lindhorst phase by Kelly (1990a), who recognizes a distinctive limestone-tempered ceramic complex in the locality of the Range and Carbon Dioxide sites, among others, in the vicinity of the Lunsford-Pulcher mound group in the southern portion of the American Bottom. The Lindhorst phase is defined on the basis of these ceramics, which differ from contemporary Lohmann phase ceramics in the northern portion of the American Bottom. The Lindhorst ceramics are characteristically a continuation of the limestone-tempered Emergent Mississippian ceramic tradition typical of the Lunsford-Pulcher locality, whereas the Lohmann ceramics to the north are more often shell-tempered and represent a more progressive trend toward Mississippian styles than the Lindhorst ceramics. Because the present analysis was conducted before the definition of Lindhorst was published, this study will use the Lohmann phase designation for the Range and Carbon Dioxide sites to avoid confusion.

The Julien site (11-S-63; Figures 9 through 15) is a large multicomponent site occupying part of the point bar complex of the Goose Lake Meander. The site is situated on a series of ridges 2.0 km from the bluffs and 7.3 km from the Mississippi River. The excavated portion of the site is 0.8 km from the shore of prehistoric Goose Lake. The Stirling, Moorehead, and Sand Prairie phase components are included in this analysis. Nearby are the Sandy Ridge Farms (Jackson 1980a), Florence Street, Marcus (Emerson and Jackson 1987), and Bryon (Jackson 1980b) sites.

The Florence Street site (11-S-458; Figures 16 and 17) is a relatively small Sand Prairie phase site with habitation and mortuary complexes located north of the Julien site boundary. The two sites are divided only by Jerome Lane, which passes between two Moorehead phase buildings, one in each site, that were probably parts of a single late prehistoric community. Burials at the Florence Street site are not tallied in the analysis, although the mortuary complex is included as an important element in the interpretations of results.

The Turner and DeMange sites (11-S-50/447; Figures 18 through 26) are adjacent sites about 1.7 km from the bluffs and 9.5 km from the Mississippi River. They are situated on a series of ridges forming part of the Grand Marais Meander point bar. The sites are considered together here, as they were in the original analysis and description (Milner 1983), because of their proximity and contemporaneity. The Lohmann site mound complex is 2.3 km northwest of the site.

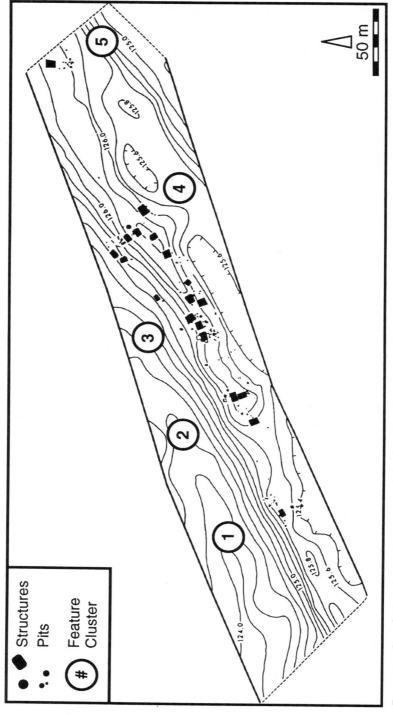

Figure 9. Plan of Mississippian features at the Julien site identifying feature clusters 1 through 5 (after Milner 1984a).

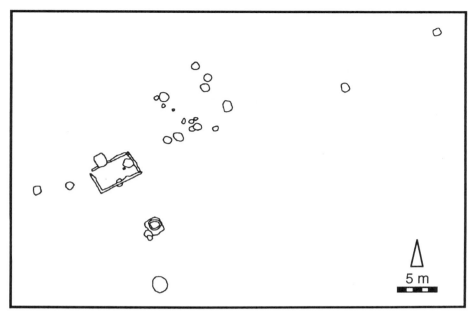

Figure 10.   Plan of cluster 1 at the Julien site (after Milner 1984a).

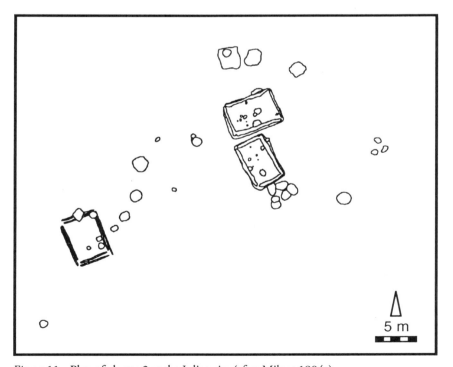

Figure 11.   Plan of cluster 2 at the Julien site (after Milner 1984a).

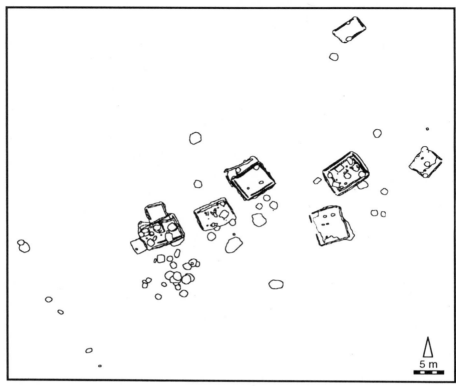

Figure 12.   Plan of cluster 3 at the Julien site (after Milner 1984a).

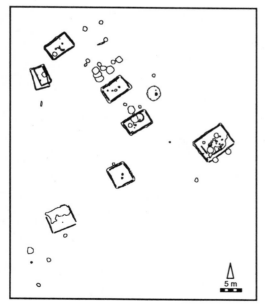

Figure 13.   Plan of cluster 4 at the Julien site (after Milner 1984a).

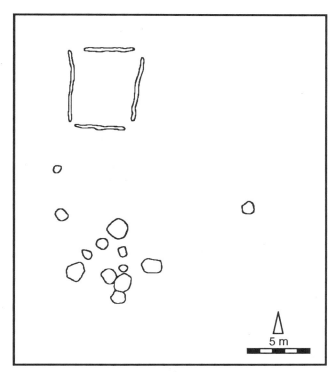

Figure 14. Plan of cluster 5 at the Julien site (after Milner 1984a).

Figure 15. Circular and rectangular structures in cluster 4 at the Julien site.

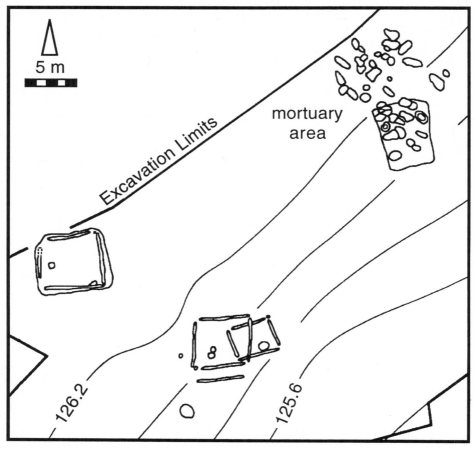

Figure 16. Plan of Mississippian features at the Florence Street site (after Emerson, Milner, and Jackson 1983).

Figure 17. Superimposed wall-trench structures at the Florence Street site.

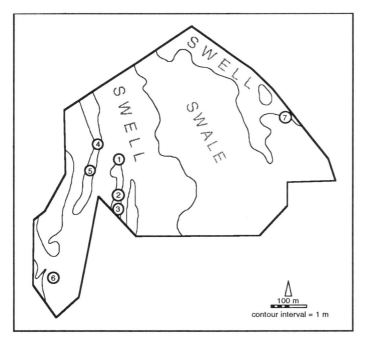

Figure 18. Plan of the locations of clusters 1 through 7 at the Turner-DeMange site (after Milner 1983).

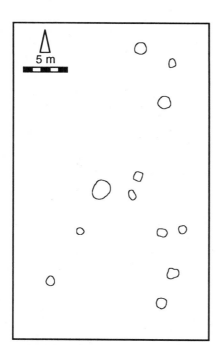

Figure 19. Plan of cluster 1 at the Turner-DeMange site (after Milner 1983).

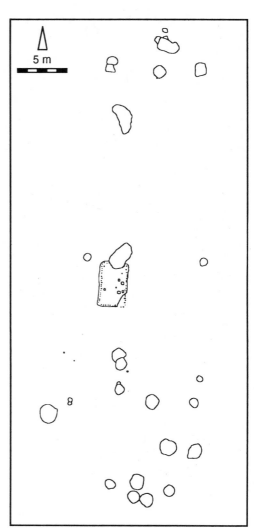

Figure 20. Plan of cluster 2 at the Turner-DeMange site (after Milner 1983).

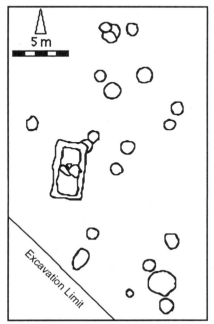

Figure 21. Plan of cluster 3 at the Turner-DeMange site (after Milner 1983).

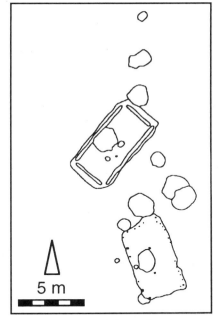

Figure 22. Plan of cluster 4 at the Turner-DeMange site (after Milner 1983).

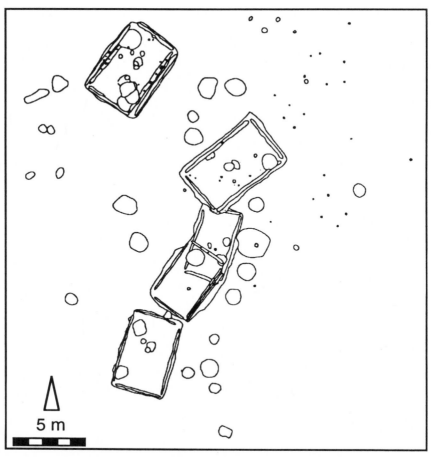

Figure 23. Plan of cluster 5 at the Turner-DeMange site (after Milner 1983).

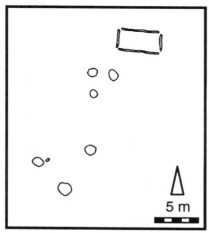

Figure 24. Plan of cluster 6 at the Turner-DeMange site (after Milner 1983).

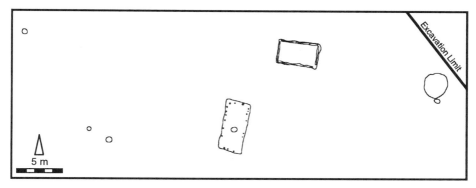

Figure 25. Plan of cluster 7 at the Turner-DeMange site (after Milner 1983).

Figure 26. Cluster 5 in progress at the Turner-DeMange site.

The BBB Motor site (11-Ms-595; Figures 27 through 30) is a multicomponent site in the northern portion of the American Bottom, 1.5 km from the bluff line and 6.5 km from the Mississippi River. It is located on what was the shore of Robinson's Lake, which was drained in the 1920s. The ridge crest is only about 40 to 60 cm above the surrounding lowland and was formerly subject to seasonal flooding. Numerous sites in the vicinity include the Cahokia, Robert Schneider, Robinson's Lake (Milner 1984b), Radic (McElrath et al. 1987), and Bishop (Kelly et al. 1979) sites.

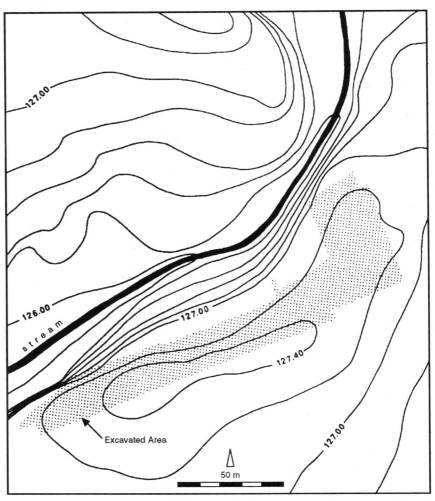

Figure 27. Plan of the BBB Motor site locality (after Emerson and Jackson 1984).

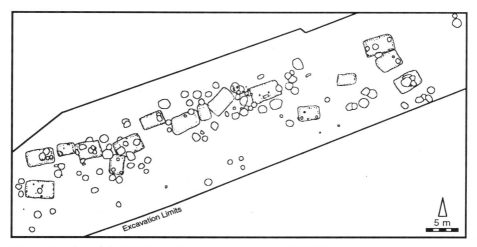

Figure 28. Plan of the Edelhardt phase component at the BBB Motor site (after Emerson and Jackson 1984).

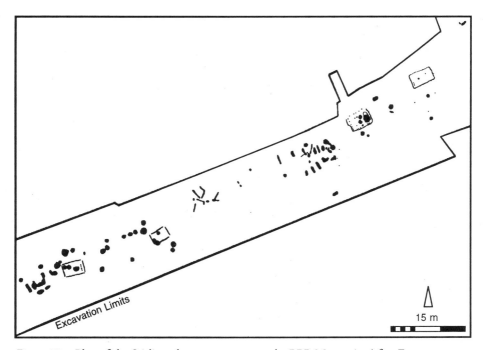

Figure 29. Plan of the Stirling phase component at the BBB Motor site (after Emerson and Jackson 1984).

Figure 30. A posthole structure of the Edelhardt phase component at the BBB Motor site.

The Robert Schneider site (11-Ms-1177; Figures 31 and 32) is a small multicomponent site 1.5 km from the bluffs and 6.5 km from the Mississippi River. The site is situated between the outer bank of the Edelhardt Lake Meander scar and the inner bank of the Robinson's Lake Meander scar, where the point bars and meander scars have been stable since Early Archaic times.

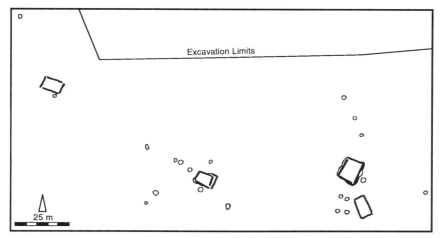

Figure 31. Plan of the Mississippian features at the Robert Schneider site (after Fortier 1985b).

Figure 32. Wall-trench structure at the Robert Schneider site.

Of the 838 features from the seven sites, there are 91 structures, 265 interior features, 443 exterior pits, and 39 other miscellaneous exterior features (Tables 2 and 3). Features are the spatial contexts for debris, and therefore locational and morphological traits of features allow interpretations of spatial organization for activity areas, buildings, households, and communities. Among basic feature categories are structures, interior pits, exterior pits, postholes, isolated wall trenches, burial pits, and hearths. A structural feature is commonly composed of a basin, a foundation, and a floor. Interior and exterior pits are classed as separate features independent of the shelters with which they were associated in the past.

Table 2

Distribution of feature types among phases.

Feature Type	Edelhardt Phase	Lohmann Phase	Stirling Phase	Moorehead Phase	Sand Prairie Phase	Unknown	Total
Structures	16	13	39	15	8	0	91
Interior Features	35	11	126	59	32	2	265
Exterior Features	97	53	227	45	10	50	482
Total	148	77	392	119	50	52	838

Debris in the analysis includes artifacts recovered from features through excavation. Materials from surface collections or unknown proveniences are not included. For the purpose of analysis, the great variety of materials found at the sites was categorized on the basis of a small set of debris types. These categories include ceramic sherds, chert debitage, chert tools, nonchert tools, unworked limestone, unworked miscellaneous stones, exotic minerals, floral remains, and faunal remains. For each feature the debris categories were quantified by count, weight, or both, depending on the data available for each site.

Ceramic counts and weights are feature totals for all sherds, including rims, bodies, appendages, and other fragments of ceramic vessels. Nonvessel ceramic items such as pipe or figurine sherds are occasionally included in the inventories, but these are so rare that ceramic counts and weights are treated operationally as vessel remains, with no loss of information.·

The chert debitage category includes mainly rejectage, cores, and hoe flakes from the manufacture, maintenance, and use of tools. Utilized flakes are counted as debris rather than tools because of inconsistencies among

Table 3

Distribution of feature types among sites by phase.

	Edelhardt Phase	Lohmann Phase	Stirling Phase	Moorehead Phase	Sand Prairie Phase	Unknown	Total
Carbon Dioxide Site							
Structures	0	4	0	0	0	0	4
Interior Features	0	1	0	0	0	0	1
Exterior Features	0	5	0	0	0	0	5
Miscellaneous	0	0	0	0	0	0	0
Total	0	10	0	0	0	0	10
Range Site							
Structures	0	7	8	0	0	0	15
Interior Features	0	5	22	0	0	0	27
Exterior Features	0	0	8	0	0	0	8
Miscellaneous	0	0	0	0	0	0	0
Total	0	12	38	0	0	0	50
Julien Site							
Structures	0	0	12	14	5	0	31
Interior Features	0	0	42	54	28	2	126
Exterior Features	0	0	44	41	7	40	132
Miscellaneous	0	0	0	3	0	2	5
Total	0	0	98	112	40	44	294
Florence Street Site							
Structures	0	0	0	0	3	0	3
Interior Features	0	0	0	0	4	0	4
Exterior Features	0	0	0	0	3	0	3
Miscellaneous	0	0	0	0	0	0	0
Total	0	0	0	0	10	0	10
Turner-DeMange Site							
Structures	0	2	11	1	0	0	14
Interior Features	0	5	30	5	0	0	40
Exterior Features	0	48	65	1	0	5	119
Miscellaneous	0	0	0	0	0	0	0
Total	0	55	106	7	0	5	173
BBB Motor Site							
Structures	16	0	4	0	0	0	20
Interior Features	35	0	16	0	0	0	51
Exterior Features	96	0	59	0	0	2	157
Miscellaneous	1	0	31	0	0	1	33
Total	148	0	110	0	0	3	261
Robert Schneider Site							
Structures	0	0	4	0	0	0	4
Interior Features	0	0	16	0	0	0	16
Exterior Features	0	0	19	0	0	0	19
Miscellaneous	0	0	1	0	0	0	1
Total	0	0	40	0	0	0	40
Grand Total	148	77	392	119	50	52	838

analysts in distinguishing utilized from unutilized flakes. Although chert debris counts do not include tools, chert debris weights do include tools. Likewise, nonchert tool weights are included in both rough rock and limestone weights. This is because of various standards of data reporting among the publications. For the Julien and Turner-DeMange sites, for example, the tool weights were published as part of the raw-material weights, and separating them was not feasible. The number and size of tools in a feature, however, are almost always so low that the significance of chert or other lithic contents is not obscured. In the rare instances when tool weights are extreme, they have been compensated for through their temporary removal from the statistical measures.

The rough rock category includes items of a variety of miscellaneous nonchert lithic raw-material types, typically glacial till or river cobbles. Sandstone, however, is classed with the rough rocks, even though there are outcrops in west-central Illinois. The limestone category includes unutilized limestone pieces, but not tools or other items made from limestone that are considered tools. Limestone is considered a separate category because it may have served such disparate technological functions as temper for pottery or as lime for maize processing and because it was a distant resource for some sites.

Chert tools include principally all unifacially or bifacially flaked tools typically categorized as points and scrapers but also include other less common tools such as hammers or grinders. Nonchert tools include igneous or metamorphic grinders and hammers as well as sandstone abraders, among other artifacts. Manufactured lithic items such as discoidals or ornaments are classed with tools since they are considered implements rather than manufacturing debris.

Exotic items are minerals such as galena, hematite, copper, limonite, red ocher, quartz crystals, and bauxite. Typically found in small quantities, they presumably were used as pigments or fetishes. Many of these materials, which occur naturally in distant regions, were traded into the American Bottom.

Faunal remains are measured by the counts and weights given in published reports. Bone tools are not analyzed separately from other faunal remains in the analysis because their presence depends to a large extent on the highly variable conditions of bone preservation.

The above debris variables are analyzed according to their distribution among the features and their associations with one another. Thus, functional interpretations of features, buildings, households, and communities are often based partly on the evidence of their associated debris.

Buildings are defined as structures plus associated interior pits or other integrated furnishings such as benches or racks that are recognizable from postmold patterns. Each building represents an integrated set of prehistoric facilities designed to shelter people, activities, and goods. Buildings of the Mississippian tradition were typically semisubterranean huts with floors well below the prehistoric ground surface. Wall foundations and interior pit facilities were dug into the subsoil below the floor. Frequently the floor, foundation, and interior features were preserved below the plowzone, and because of this the construction details, floor plan, and interior facilities are readily identifiable.

Buildings are important units of analysis in this study because built form and space utilization are basic elements of settlement patterns. Buildings are analyzed here according to their size, shape, interior facilities, and floor plan. According to these attributes, buildings are categorized into several architectural types. Functional interpretations of architectural types are based on structure size and shape, the distribution of debris, pit feature types, interior facilities, and the context of other buildings and nearby features.

Spatially discrete clusters of one or more buildings with associated exterior pits are defined as households. Households are analyzed according to the composition and arrangement of their constituent features and debris. Features are often assigned to households on the basis of proximity and chronology. Clusters of features that were defined in the published site reports were often retained in this study as households. Occasionally, however, two or more clusters were grouped together as a single household during the initial stages of this analysis. For some households, proximity and superpositioning were such that all the features could not have functioned simultaneously. Households of different phases sometimes superimposed one another, but they were usually spatially and chronologically discrete. Households are assumed to have been the settings of daily activities and special ceremonies for small coresidential groups, such as families, each of which presumably had their own domestic, political, and ceremonial functions.

ANALYTICAL UNITS: COUNTS, WEIGHTS, AND MEASURES

The basic unit of analysis is the individual feature, such as a pit, a house basin, or a posthole. These units are also considered in groups as individual buildings with their interior facilities and debris contents. Likewise, buildings and exterior pits are considered in groups as households. Finally, some groups of households are interpreted as local communities that functioned in a regional settlement system.

Feature chronology, morphology, location, and content were analyzed in this study, although all the feature variables were not available for each site (Table 4). The chronological variable is archaeological phase designation. Subphase chronology based on feature superposition is considered in discussions of analytical results.

Table 4

Data available for each site.

Variable	Carbon Dioxide	Range	Julien	Florence Street	Turner-DeMange	BBB Motor	Robert Schneider
Identification							
Household	+	+	+	+	+	+	+
Chronological							
Phase	+	+	+	+	+	+	+
Feature Metrics							
Length, Width, Depth	+	+	+	+	+	+	+
Volume	+	+	Y	-	Y	+	X
Structure Floor Metrics	+	+	+	+	+	+	+
Feature Contents							
Ceramic Count	+	+	+	-	+	-	+
Ceramic Weight	+	+	+	-	+	-	+
Chert Debris Count	+	+	+	-	+	-	+
Chert Debris Weight	+	+	+	-	+	-	+
Rough Rock Count	+	+	+	-	+	-	+
Rough Rock Weight	+	+	+	-	+	-	+
Limestone Count	+	+	+	-	+	-	+
Limestone Weight	+	+	+	-	+	-	+
Exotic Mineral Count	+	+	+	-	+	-	+
Exotic Mineral Weight	+	+	+	-	+	-	+
Chert Tool Count	+	+	+	-	+	-	+
Chert Tool Weight	+	+	-	-	-	-	+
Nonchert Tool Count	+	+	+	-	+	-	+
Nonchert Tool Weight	+	+	-	-	-	-	+
Faunal Items Data	+	+	+	+	+	+	+
Total	20	20	18	5	18	6	20

Note: + = present; - = absent; X = partially recalculated Robert Schneider site volumes; Y = calculated Julien and Turner-DeMange site volumes.

Morphological variables include both a general morphological classification of features and a set of feature metrics. The basic classification includes general categories of pits and functional categories such as hearths, smudge pits, post-holes, burials, and isolated wall trenches. General features were either interior or exterior pits whose published descriptions did not conform to functional feature types listed above. This analysis was designed to examine feature variability, especially among the general categories, so that functional aspects would become apparent.

Features were assigned to functional categories on the basis of their salient characteristics. Hearths were defined on the basis of their size, shape, and content. They were either prepared pits with evidence of burning or small, thin, ashy lenses on a floor surface. Smudge pits were also relatively small features, but they contained concentrations of charred corn cobs and twigs. The term *postmold* is used to describe the foundations of relatively small, upright poles. These were generally so small that a foundation pit was not often visible, although the outline, or "mold," of the decayed or removed post was visible. Such small poles could have been pounded into the ground without first preparing a foundation hole. For simplicity and convenience, postmolds were distinguished from postholes on the basis of an arbitrary size distinction made before excavation. Postmolds were 20 cm or smaller in diameter, and postholes were larger. Because they usually contained little or no debris, they were not classed as features and were excavated with different methods. Postmolds are not considered individually in this analysis, but posthole features are. The miscellaneous feature category includes such rare or problematic features as irregular shallow depressions, chert core caches, an *in situ* ceramic vessel, rock concentrations, exterior firestains, and unique features whose nature was unclear to the excavators. Burials were obvious because of their size, shape, human remains, and grave offerings. Isolated wall trenches were unambiguous in their definition, but their precise functions are unclear; they probably supported a variety of racks, lean-tos, or other outdoor facilities.

Measurements used in this study are based on the best available data. The metric system is used for all measurements, which are almost always taken from published data tables; map measurements were used where tables were not available. Although different authors and analysts on the FAI-270 project were responsible for the various sites, their field and laboratory methods were essentially the same.

Basin length and width of rectangular structures were measured through the center of the basin along the long and short axes at the base of the plowzone. Floor length and width measurements were made to the appropriate wall trenches or postmolds either at floor level or where necessary, at the base of the plowzone. Basin depth refers to the difference between the highest and lowest elevations reported for the basin. Rectangular basin volumes were calculated by multiplying length, width, and depth with modifications where appropriate to account for irregular feature shape or superposition. For example, basin depth as seen on a profile map may more accurately reflect the basin volume in calculations than does a simple difference in elevation, because of sloping topography or other factors. Irregular floors were measured from maps using a digitizer.

Pit length was the greatest orifice measurement, pit width was the longest measurement perpendicular to the length, and pit depth was the difference between the highest and lowest elevations. Pit volumes were calculated based on the standard mathematical formulas for the volumes of cubes, cylinders, conical sections, and spherical sections. The pit volumes published in some reports were calculated based on an erroneous formula for spherical sections, so, where appropriate, feature volumes were recalculated for this study (Macnie 1895; Thompson 1934).

A locational variable designates nonstructural features according to a typology of interior and exterior locations. This variable was designed to reveal patterns of feature placement both within buildings and around them. Interior feature locations consist of thirteen overlapping ideal possibilities distributed relative to one another and to the floor periphery (Figure 33). Exterior pit locations were determined on the basis of pit distance from the nearest house basin edge (Figure 34). My examination of these data was guided by the assumption that in prehistory a pit's placement in relation to a building was designed according to the building's size. Exterior features were designated as either near or far from a structure. The distance equal to the width of the structure basin (or floor, where necessary) was used as the measure distinguising near and far. Exterior pit locations were further differentiated by their position relative to the structure's orientation. Thus features were either near or far from a structure's long wall, short wall, or corner.

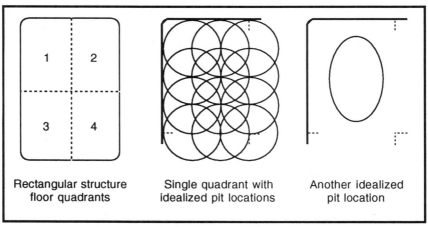

Rectangular structure floor quadrants

Single quadrant with idealized pit locations

Another idealized pit location

Figure 33. Idealized locations of interior features.

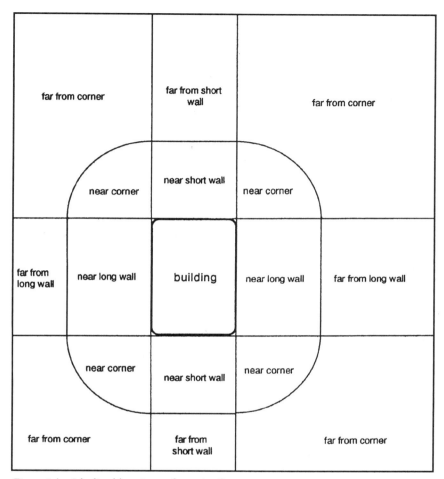

Figure 34. Idealized locations of exterior features.

Feature content variables are counts and/or weights for several debris types. These are ceramic sherd count and weight, chert debitage count and weight, chert and nonchert tool counts, limestone and miscellaneous stone debris weights, exotic item count and weight, and floral and faunal count and weight. As explained in the analysis section below, the most appropriate variables for the analyses are ceramic weight, chert debris weight, rock weight, limestone weight, exotic item weight, chert tool count, and nonchert tool count, and floral and faunal counts. Matching counts and weights are useful for constructing indices of count and weight to compare debris types between selected features or feature categories.

Weight values in this study are coded and analyzed in tenths of grams, as typically tabulated in published reports, but results are often rounded to the nearest gram or kilogram for clarity. Unavailable data and feature superposition account for most of the missing values in the data. Some variables are not included in some of the published reports. For example, feature inventories are not published for the BBB Motor or Florence Street sites, and tool weights are seldom reported in any publications. Both counts and weights are coded where they are available.

Valid zero values are frequent among the debris variables, especially for rarities such as tools and exotic items. Feature metrics are also zero for some rare feature types. A few exterior features identified as stains, for example, had no perceivable depths.

All these variables are analyzed to provide a basis for interpretations. Feature interpretations are based on size, shape, location, and debris contents. Functionality of features is inferred from activities presumed to have been associated with their debris. Interpretations for buildings are based on their constituent feature elements and their debris contents, their arrangements, and their temporal and spatial interrelationships with other buildings. A household's feature configuration and debris contents are the main bases for interpretation of activities that occurred within the household. Distribution of households over the landscape is important for interpretations of communities in the regional system.

Chapter 4

Analysis
Patterns of Settlement in the Archaeological Record

This chapter examines the archaeological record for clues about how the daily lives of rural dwellers were organized to accommodate the interplay of complex social and cultural developments throughout the American Bottom during late prehistory. Four levels of analysis include the examination of artifactual debris distribution; feature design, arrangement, and content; building design and composition; and household organization. The analyses reveal patterns of behavior that reflect underlying frames of reference for rural dwellers during late prehistory.

The debris and feature analyses use data combined from multiple phases to derive general cultural patterns and to isolate biasing factors associated with some of the processes by which sites are formed. The debris analysis reveals shared patterns among the households that can be used to infer feature functionality, debris disposal, and other site formational processes. The feature analysis examines pits in terms of design, location, and content to demonstrate general patterns in the way people used domestic space. The building and household analyses focus on chronological developments so that changing processes can be seen in a regional perspective. Architectural modes in the ways that interior spaces were allocated are the focus of the building analysis. The household analysis combines the results of the other analyses to identify standards in the way that households were organized.

The analytical methods were carefully chosen to complement one another. The overall approach to analyzing the archaeological record is to apply methods specifically designed for each level of analysis and to use those results in the next level of analysis. No single set of measures is suitable for all the debris, feature, building, and household analyses. Although the results of each analysis are important to subsequent analyses, the analytical tools, such as typologies, are designed for specific purposes and are not applied in similar or direct ways to higher analyses.

In addition, the quantitative methods of analysis are innovative and tend to be exploratory rather than confirmatory (Hartwig and Dearing 1979). It is often more useful to depict the data graphically than to reduce them to summary statistics. The patterns that are important for interpreting data are made clear in the illustrated data distributions.

DEBRIS ANALYSIS

This debris analysis isolates some underlying dimensions in the way that debris was found to be scattered within the abandoned households. Two aspects of prehistoric lifeways are apparent from the distribution of debris. First, there were general habits in the ways that people discarded their refuse. Second, whether or not a site had been occupied before Mississippian times had an effect on the amount of debris that was found and on where it was found. The analysis was designed to reveal traditional Mississippian schemes for using domestic space; the results show some important effects of the ways that sites form. These effects bear on subsequent analyses in this study.

Debris values have been condensed from published inventories as discussed in Chapter 3. The measures used here make the sites comparable for examining spatial and temporal trends among sites (Table 5). Although most debris variables contained one or more very high values, or outliers, that skewed their distributions (Table 6), these outliers are omitted from some statistical measurements. Several other inappropriate values were omitted from the analyses because they represented an element of a feature's construction rather than its debris contents. Most notable among these are limestone slabs that lined the floors of a few structures and the bases of a few pits. Most debris outliers are from the Range and Julien site assemblages, suggesting that their occupations were extraordinary in some way. Other characteristics of these sites, revealed by subsequent analyses, reinforce one another to support a special interpretation for some Range or Julien site households.

A quantitative transformation was required because the debris data are bounded by zero, have no clear upper limit, and have many zero and low values, a few high values, and a few extreme outliers. Debris variables were transformed to approximate the normal distribution: first, the value of one was added to each quantity to remove fractional values less than one; second, each resulting value was logged at base ten. Exotics and tools, which had the most zeros, remained somewhat skewed even after transformation.

Weights rather than counts are appropriate for analyzing ceramic, chert, rough rock, and limestone. Ceramic and chert debris items are typically small and fragile, and feature inventories systematically include very small (less than 1

Table 5
Distribution of debris among sites.

Site	Ceramic Weight	Chert Weight	Rough Rock Weight	Lime-stone Weight	Exotic Item Weight	Chert Tool Count	Nonchert Tool Count
Carbon Dioxide	5.4	8.7	1.1	6.7	0.0	9	7
Range	19.0	9.0	2.1	248.4	0.4	54	40
Julien	117.0	37.7	64.8	240.2	1.8	302	212
Turner-DeMange	38.0	29.7	57.6	11.0	0.8	168	133
Robert Schneider	2.2	3.4	0.4	0.5	0.1	39	33
Total	181.6	88.5	126.0	506.8	3.1	572	425

Note: Weights are in kilograms. BBB Motor and Florence Street site inventories are not available.

cm) sherds and chips. Debris counts are therefore inflated disproportionately in relation to the weights. For this reason, counts may give a distinctly different picture of a feature's contents than weights would. Measurement by weight more usefully depicts the relative quantity of limestone and rough rock in a feature, because these items can be very heavy. The tool categories and exotic items have been counted rather than weighed because it is more important to know how many of these types of items were in a feature than to know their total weight.

Debris Distribution

The distribution of pit contents among the different types of features is crucial for interpretations of features and groups of features. Debris distribution varied widely in part because of the different sizes of the features making up the types (Table 7). For example, even if contents were not related to function, size alone would account for great differences between the inventories of postholes and structure basins. Feature size was therefore controlled in examinations of debris distribution.

If all debris had been distributed evenly, each feature would have contained an amount of debris in proportion to its size; large features would contain proportionately more debris than smaller features would contain. By the same token, each category of feature would contain a percentage of debris roughly equal to the proportion of total volume that the category had. However, structure basins, interior pits, and exterior pits, all of which represented different sizes, did not contain debris in amounts that were proportional to their volume.

Table 6

High outliers declared missing or removed from analysis.

Variable	Value	Comments
High Outliers Declared Missing in Some Analyses		
Range Site		
Limestone Count	648.0	Exterior pit 625; items in fill
Chert Tool Weight	239.4	Interior pit 323; 1 large hoe fragment
Chert Tool Weight	233.3	Exterior pit 523; 1 large hoe fragment
Nonchert Tool Weight	1,055.0	Interior pit 309; 2 large grinders
Faunal Weight	94.0	Exterior pit 630; items in fill
Julien Site		
Ceramic Weight	5,003.6	Structure 91; 9 complete vessels
Chert Tool Count	85.0	Interior pit 50; points and tools in pit fill
Exotic Weight	375.5	Structure 17; items in fill
Exotic Weight	280.5	Structure 2B; items in fill
Exotic Weight	312.3	Exterior postpit 43; items in fill
Faunal Weight	49.0	Structure; items in fill
Faunal Weight	44.4	Interior pit 88; items in fill
Faunal Weight	75.0	Exterior pit 150; items in fill
Turner-DeMange Site		
Chert Debris Weight	12,817.0	Exterior pit 48; 20 cached chert cores
Exotic Weight	456.9	Exterior pit 139; items in fill
Robert Schneider Site		
Nonchert Tool Weight	887.8	Structure 1; 9 grinders in fill
Values Permanently Removed		
Range Site		
Limestone Weight	14,017.1	Interior pit 17; 190 base flags
Limestone Weight	51,179.6	Circular structure 28; 125 floor flags
Limestone Weight	101,242.8	Circular structure 50; 434 floor flags
Julien Site		
Limestone Weight	27,621.7	Exterior pit 221; 60 base flags
Limestone Weight	17,000.0	Exterior pit 283; 56 base flags
Limestone Weight	61,344.4	Structure 3; 1 item on floor
Turner-DeMange Site		
Rough Rock Weight	29,130.0	Exterior pit 58; cached sandstone metate

Note: Weights are in grams.

A comparison of the proportions of total volume and total debris among feature types shows where debris was concentrated. For example, structure basins, which accounted for only one-eighth (12%) of the total number of features, represented two-thirds (66%) of the total volume but held only between 10% and 53% of the debris, depending on the debris type. Structure basins, therefore, held much less debris than the amount expected for their volume. Interior features, in contrast, represented only 8% of the total volume but held 20% to 34% of the debris, much more than expected. Exterior pits accounted for 26% of the total volume but held 32% to 54% of the debris, again more than expected.

A comparison of debris and volume proportions illustrates the relative degrees of concentration of the debris types among the feature categories. Figure 35 shows the relative amounts of debris per volume for each basic category of feature. The volume of each feature category is standardized to a value of 1.0, which would also be the expected value of each debris category if all debris were distributed evenly among all features. Interior features have about two-and-a-half times the amount of debris expected, except for exotics. Exterior features have between one-and-a-half and two times the amount expected, except for tools. Structure basins consistently have less debris than expected.

Table 7

Aggregate volume and debris for functional feature types.

Feature Type	Feature Volume	Ceramic Weight	Chert Weight	Rough Rock Weight	Lime-stone Weight	Exotic Item Weight	Chert Tool Count	Nonchert Tool Count	Faunal Item Weight
Structure									
Basin	246.7	38,923	29,962	37,056	58,676	1,583	235	186	64
Interior Pit									
General	27.8	19,825	15,493	27,568	35,260	260	174	100	126
Post	1.5	817	502	766	1,192	12	4	3	5
Hearth	0.5	349	56	21	673	0	2	2	7
Smudge	0.1	4	3	0	0	0	0	0	0
Misc.	0.2	302	2,581	10	172	0	2	0	0
Exterior Pit									
General	94.6	58,217	31,566	28,810	138,332	1,010	152	126	291
Post	0.4	69	80	86	73	312	0	2	N/A
Hearth	0.3	232	441	1,623	0	0	3	4	N/A
Misc.	0.1	8	4	922	155	0	0	2	N/A

Note: Weights are in grams; volume is in cubic meters. High outliers are included. BBB Motor and Florence Street site inventories are not available.

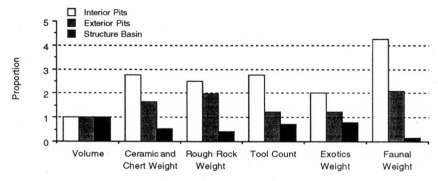

Figure 35. Volume and debris for basic pit types.

General refuse, made up of ceramic, chert, and rough rock (including lime-stone) was distributed similarly among the feature categories. Their graphs (Figure 35) nearly match one another in relative proportions, with each having its highest concentrations of refuse in interior pits and its lowest in structure basins. Tools, exotic debris, and faunal remains differ in their patterns of distri-bution from the more generalized refuse categories of ceramics, chert, and rough rock. Tools, which were concentrated in interior pits but not in exterior ones, are interesting because their distribution is often used to infer functional-ity of features and feature groups in terms of prehistoric socioeconomic activi-ties (e.g., Pauketat 1987; Prentice 1983, 1985). Exotic artifacts were the most evenly distributed among the feature types, but their highest concentration was in interior features. Faunal remains were dramatically concentrated in pits, es-pecially interior ones, at the expense of structure basins.

To see how debris was distributed among the hearth, smudge pit, posthole, and general (including miscellaneous) categories, volume and debris percent-ages were compared for the interior and exterior versions of each feature cate-gory (Figures 36 and 37). Among interior and exterior feature groups, the gen-eral category accounted for over 90% of the pit volume. This is true because postholes are small and hearths and miscellaneous features are rare. Smudge pits were so rare that they are not included in this analysis. Ceramics, chert, and rough rock tended to be evenly distributed among functional feature types according to their pit volume. Exceptions to this tendency are the features in the miscellaneous category: the nature of the category defies functional inter-pretations here.

The contents of exterior pits were less evenly distributed according to pit volume than the contents of interior pits. Except for a small percentage (0.8%), the total volume of exterior features was accounted for by general pits. Interior hearths were far more common than exterior hearths, but they con-

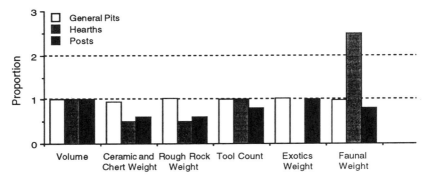

Figure 36.   Volume and debris for interior functional pit types.

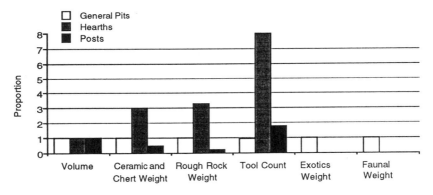

Figure 37.   Volume and debris for exterior functional pit types.

tained much less debris. Almost one-quarter (24%) of the exotic debris from exterior features was found in two pits with such high values that they were treated as outliers and were excluded from this proportional distribution analysis (Table 6); one was an exterior general pit at the Turner-DeMange site and the other was an exterior postpit at the Julien site. The example at the Turner-DeMange site appears to have been a large (1.3 m³) storage-type pit that was later filled with refuse. The Julien site example may constitute a dedicatory offering of exotic debris associated with the raising of a post.

Interior hearths and posts contained the expected number of tools, while exterior hearths and posts contained considerably more than expected. Interior hearth assemblages are dominated by faunal remains; exterior hearth assemblages are dominated by tools. Interior posts had a full range of debris types in sparse concentrations; exterior posts tended to lack exotic debris and faunal remains, although they contained abundant tools. Even though the sample has few hearths and exterior posts, the trends suggest that interior and exterior features functioned quite differently in their domestic settings.

To summarize, debris was concentrated more densely in pits than in structure basins. Interior pits had greater concentrations of all types of debris than did exterior pits. For each of these two pit categories, debris distributions provided little information because the general class of pits dominated the feature volume and debris data. General pits, both interior and exterior, are further subcategorized and analyzed in following sections. The interior and exterior classes of hearths and postholes had functional differences related to the use and disposal of tools, exotics, and faunal remains.

It is clear from this analysis that the basic feature categories (structure basins, interior pits, and exterior pits) must be understood in terms of the ways that debris is created, discarded, and redeposited before their prehistoric functions can be fully appreciated. Obvious functional types (hearths, postholes, and smudge pits) can give an adequate impression for only a small proportion of features and an even smaller proportion of debris.

Discriminant Analysis

Discriminant analysis reveals how strongly the debris contents of interior and exterior pits are patterned and which, if any, debris variables distinguish best between the feature categories. Different debris distributions were expected to be related to the sizes, shapes, locations, histories of usage, and debris discard behaviors associated with the feature classes. Potential data biases were recognized and controlled by subsampling and transformation of the data values.

To avoid an upward bias of the discriminant function's estimated effectiveness, a "split-halves" technique was used; a 50%, uniform, random sample of the selected Stirling phase features was used to create a discriminant function, and the remaining 50% was used to test it. If the cases used to create the function were also used to test it, an upward bias of effectiveness would have emerged (Morrison 1969:157), giving unduly optimistic results. Five separate analyses were conducted to reveal the effectiveness of the split-halves sampling procedure.

The sample for discriminant analysis included 222 Stirling phase pits selected from four sites (Table 8). A single phase was selected for analysis to control for possible chronological trends; the Stirling phase offered the largest and most diverse subset of features in the data set. Only features from spatially isolated clusters were selected to avoid contamination by the superposition of features from other phases. The debris data were measured as weights and counts per unit of feature volume to control for multicolinearity between feature types of different sizes and their contents. They were also transformed to common logarithms to approximate more nearly the normal distribution.

Table 8

Distribution of Stirling phase pits selected for discriminant analysis.

Feature Category	Range	Julien	Turner-DeMange	Robert Schneider	Total
Interior Pits	26	41	22	15	104
Exterior Pits	8	34	58	18	118
Total	34	75	80	33	222

A stepwise method of variable selection in the discriminant analysis was used with the Wilk's Lambda criterion for inclusion (Nie et al. 1975:447). Ceramic and chert debris weights were entered on the first step because they were most prevalent among features; they then were tested for exclusion in each succeeding step while chert tool count, nonchert tool count, rough rock weight, and limestone weight were entered or withheld according to the entry criterion. Exotic mineral weights were omitted from the analysis because they are rare and because in early runs of the analysis exotic debris never qualified according to the stepwise criterion for entry into the discriminant function.

Both the interior and exterior features were represented in each classification exercise, so the differences between prior probabilities of category membership were never extreme (Table 9). Because of this, the proportional chance criterion and the maximum chance criterion (Morrison 1969:158) are appropriate baselines from which to judge each function's effectiveness. The maximum chance criterion is the proportion of features that would have been correctly classified if all had simply been put in the largest category. The proportional chance criterion reflects the relative sizes of the two categories. The square of the canonical correlation can be understood as an estimate of the total variance explained by the function.

The discriminating power of the debris variables is stable, but not very strong, in its ability to distinguish between interior and exterior pits. In all five analyses (Table 9), the proportion of all pits correctly classified exceeded the proportional chance criteria, and in all but one analysis the proportion exceeded the maximum chance criteria. In only two instances did the proportion of correct classifications for a specific feature type fall below the prior probability. In these matters, all five of the analyses were almost consistently successful, although the proportions of correct classifications were not greatly in excess of either criteria.

The discriminant functions show that exterior features tend to contain large

Table 9

Discriminant analysis classification results.

Analysis	Feature Type	Number of Cases	Proportion Correctly Classified	Prior Probabilities	Proportional Chance Criteria	Correlation
1	Interior Pits	50	.50	.49		
	Exterior Pits	52	.71	.51		
	All Pits	102	.61		.50	.40
2	Interior Pits	40	.70	.38		
	Exterior Pits	64	.50	.62		
	All Pits	104	.58		.53	.33
3	Interior Pits	53	.51	.45		
	Exterior Pits	64	.61	.55		
	All Pits	117	.56		.50	.37
4	Interior Pits	49	.49	.45		
	Exterior Pits	61	.64	.55		
	All Pits	110	.57		.51	.40
5	Interior Pits	47	.34	.48		
	Exterior Pits	50	.90	.52		
	All Pits	97	.63		.50	.25

Note: The proportional chance criteria equal the interior prior squared plus the exterior prior squared; the maximun chance criteria equal the greater of the two priors.

quantities of ceramics, limestone, or rough rock; interior features, in contrast, tend to have large amounts of chert or chert tools. The best indicator variables, in descending order of importance, are ceramics, chert debris, chert tools, limestone, and rough rock. Nonchert tools and exotic minerals are not important enough to have been incorporated into the function according the stepwise criteria of selection. This may be because they are so rare, although chert tools, which did discriminate, were no more rare than nonchert ones. It appears that the distributions of nonchert tools and exotic minerals are not functionally related to pit location but that the distributions of chert tools and other debris categories are.

One important characteristic of the debris inventories is that each variable's distributions for interior and exterior pits were somewhat similar in terms of percentage of zero values, median, maximum, and skewness (Table 10). Such similarities tend to dampen a variable's potential to discriminate. Another important characteristic is the abundance of zero values. The rank of zero-value percentages coincides roughly with the inverse rank of a variable's strength to discriminate; that is, variables with more positive values tend to have greater discriminatory strength. Interesting exceptions are the variables for the two tool categories, chert and nonchert, which show similar percentages (77% of each variable's total). Chert tools were effective discriminators, but nonchert tools were not important enough even to be entered into the function. This suggests that the distribution of chert tools, few though they are, may be significant when viewed in the context of other debris categories and in specific groups of features.

Limestone and rough rock both characterize exterior pits, and it is reasonable to assume that this reflects some prehistoric use of these stones in the outdoors. It is less clear why ceramics should characterize exterior pits while chert debris and tools characterize interior pits. One possibility is that chert-working and tool use most frequently occurred indoors while ceramic pot use and breakage typically took place outdoors. Nonchert tools and exotic artifacts are not important discriminators between interior and exterior feature classes, but we have seen in the preceding analysis that they do have patterned distributions among functional pit categories of interior and exterior types.

Range Site Analysis

Although the analyses in this study are designed to examine broad trends, it is important to know what impact site-specific or idiosyncratic behaviors can have on patterns of debris distribution. A previous analysis of features and debris at the Range site (Mehrer 1982a) pointed out how the sequence of occupations at a multicomponent site and the habits of refuse disposal of its occupants can affect the distribution of the artifacts among the features. The Range site had a long and intense history of occupation prior to Mississippian times. No doubt there had been a considerable buildup of debris in long-abandoned pits and house basins, and probably a good deal of debris had accumulated at ground level.

Several classes of debris were analyzed for their distributions among a set of morphological feature types. The feature classes were structure basins, exterior pits, large interior pits, and medium-size interior pits. There were some small interior pits, but they contained so little debris and accounted for so little of the total feature volume that they are not mentioned further.

The structure basins accounted for over three-fourths (78%) of the feature volume but only less than a quarter (22%) of the total debris weight (Table 11). Exterior pits accounted for less than one-tenth (8%) of the volume but over half (53%) of the debris. Large interior pits accounted for a little over one-tenth (12%) of the volume and slightly more (18%) of the debris, but

Table 10

Logged debris density statistics for Stirling phase interior and exterior pits selected for discriminant analysis.

	Percentage of Zeros	Median	Maximum	Skewness
Ceramics				
Interior Pits	29	2.0	3.9	-0.2
Exterior Pits	15	2.3	4.3	-0.6
Chert Debris				
Interior Pits	25	2.2	4.5	-0.4
Exterior Pits	24	1.6	4.7	0.0
Limestone				
Interior Pits	78	0.0	4.9	1.8
Exterior Pits	59	0.0	4.8	0.9
Rough Rock				
Interior Pits	64	0.0+	3.6	1.4
Exterior Pits	50	0.0	4.2	1.0
Chert Tools				
Interior Pits	74	0.0	2.2	2.0
Exterior Pits	79	0.0	1.6	2.2
Nonchert Tools				
Interior Pits	79	0.0	2.5	2.8
Exterior Pits	74	0.0	1.8	2.1
Exotics				
Interior Pits	80	0.0+	3.0	3.5
Exterior Pits	89	0.0	2.9	3.7

medium-size pits, with less than 1% of the volume, had 5% of the debris, which is over seven times the expected amount of debris expected according to their size. Generally, medium-size interior pits and exterior pits contained much more than the expected amounts of debris; large interior pits contained approximately the amounts expected; and structure basins contained consistently less.

Table 11

Distribution of volume and debris among the feature categories of the Range site component.

| | Volume | | Debris | |
	(m3)	(%)	(kg)	(%)
Structure Basins	34.3	77.6	27	21.9
Interior Pits				
Large	5.4	12.1	22	17.8
Medium	0.3	0.7	6	5.0
Small	0.6	1.3	3	2.5
Exterior Pits	3.7	8.3	64	52.9
Total	44.3	100.0	122	100.1

The distribution of vessels, which were defined on the basis of refitted diagnostic rim sherds, was similar to that of the overall ceramic assemblage, but forty-five diagnostic Emergent Mississippian vessels had been disturbed and redeposited from a nearby Emergent Mississippian component of the site (Mehrer 1982a). However, the distribution of Emergent Mississippian pots among the Mississippian features was not similar to that of the Mississippian vessels. Structure basins received thirty-nine of the Emergent Mississippian vessels; exterior pits contained four; but interior pits held only two small Emergent Mississippian rim sherds that could easily have been redeposited by rodents. Structure basins and exterior pits had more Emergent Mississippian vessels than expected, while interior pits had less than one-third of the vessels.

This distribution of diagnostic Emergent Mississippian ceramics is important because it suggests that whenever Emergent Mississippian debris of any sort was disturbed and redeposited into Mississippian contexts, almost all of it was dumped into structure basins and exterior pits. It follows that the debris found in interior pits probably derived almost entirely from activities conducted within the Mississippian structures. This seems especially true for medium-size interior pits, which had very high concentrations of debris. These pits had over twelve times as many stone tools as expected, over six times as many ceramics, four times as much chert debris, and over five times as much limestone. Floral remains were notably low, totaling about one-fifth the amount expected.

Exterior pits had high values for both faunal remains and limestone (Table 12). These two debris types may be functionally related because limestone in pit fill tends to help preserve bones by altering the soil acidity. Equally important, limestone may have been intentionally thrown into pits with butchering offal to reduce the stench of decay, in much the same way that lime is often thrown into modern privies. The relatively high density of floral remains in exterior pits may reflect the same discard behavior or preservation factors as does the faunal and limestone distribution.

Table 12

Distribution of Range site debris types in proportion to the amount expected according to the total volumes of feature categories.

Debris Type	Structure Basin	Interior Pit		Exterior Pit
		Large	Medium	
Total Debris Weight*	0.3	1.5	7.1	6.3
Ceramic Sherds Weight	0.6	1.5	6.5	3.1
Ceramic Vessels Count	0.7	1.0	6.4	3.2
Lithic Tools Count	0.7	1.7	12.3	2.2
Chert Debris Weight	0.8	1.2	4.0	2.4
Limestone Debris Weight	0.1	1.4	5.3	8.0
Faunal Remains Count	0.1	0.4	1.3	10.6
Floral Remains Count†	0.9	1.0	0.2	1.6

*   Total debris includes ceramics, lithics, and miscellaneous debris, but not floral or faunal remains.

†   Floral remains values were calculated in proportion to float sample volumes rather than to feature volumes.

Note: Weights are in grams.

The basins of abandoned structures seem to have been filled rapidly with surface midden and prehistoric backdirt that included disturbed Emergent Mississippian feature fill. This is suggested by the absence of concentrated Mississippian debris, the presence of most of the Emergent Mississippian vessels in the assemblage, and the relative sparsity of faunal remains, which would have been poorly preserved in surface midden or disturbed fill.

Large interior pits were probably storage facilities that were filled with generalized Mississippian refuse after they ceased to function as storage pits. Like structure basins, large interior pits contained sparse concentrations of debris, and both types of features were probably filled quickly with backdirt to eliminate safety hazards and obstacles to the daily routine.

Medium-size interior pits held concentrated amounts of tool fragments, ceramics, and chert debitage but few floral remains and no Emergent Mississippian vessels. These features were probably refuse pits intended exclusively for rubbish from manufacturing and processing activities conducted within the structures. The fill zone configurations of these pits showed that they were cleaned and refilled repeatedly.

Exterior pits were probably storage facilities that were used as refuse dumps after their storage functions ended. They must have received at least some of the cleaned-up rubbish from the medium-size interior pits, along with charred remains of fires and decaying carcasses mixed with limestone to reduce odor. Coincidentally, the individual exterior pits that contained the most faunal debris were located at the northeast periphery of the household cluster, downwind of the structures, according to prevailing wind patterns. The recognizable patterns of features and debris in this component illustrate the range of activities and discard behaviors associated with a variety of functionally distinct facility types.

Results of the Debris Analysis

The debris analyses were designed to show what patterns are shared among rural settlements. It is important to distinguish patterns of behavior that characterize many of the households throughout the region from any that might characterize only individual sites or components. Sites and components must be understood in light of their own unique occupational histories.

Patterns of behavior are evident in the results of analysis, and the fact that several sites and time periods are represented strengthens inferences based on them. The results indicate strongly that structure basins and interior and exterior pits were constructed, used, and abandoned in different ways. Soil and refuse was deposited according to traditional habits of feature function and debris discard behavior. The trends help us understand debris discard behavior and site formation processes, but they do not reveal specific types of activities or types of activity areas within sites.

Hearths and postholes show interesting functional patterns of debris contents. Interior and exterior hearths appear to have been the foci of different types of intense debris-producing activity involving tools, exotic debris, and faunal remains. Interior postholes contained almost the expected quantity of exotic debris relative to their size. Exotic debris may have been part of dedicatory rituals conducted during the construction of buildings, and exotic residues may have been intentionally scattered nearby or into open foundation pits.

The combined results of the proportional distribution analysis and the discriminant analysis suggest that feature classes differ significantly in their contents. The results also suggest that variation within one feature category overlaps that of the others to such an extent that when features are considered individually, almost half of them cannot be correctly identified by their contents as either interior or exterior pits. In other words, the proportional distribution analysis isolated broad trends of debris distribution among feature types that are not identifiable at the level of features considered individually.

The Range site analysis showed that when old debris was incorporated into Mississippian contexts, it was concentrated in structure basins and exterior pits and not in interior pits. This indicates that assemblages from interior features are not likely to be contaminated by former occupations. Even though this result is based on a single component, it seems clear that the effects of previous occupations are not uniformly felt in all parts of a settlement. The broad trends show that pit features, especially interior pits, tend to receive more than their share of debris while structure basins tend to receive much less. The sparse contents of abandoned structure basins represent a discard behavior that is unlike behaviors associated with either interior or exterior pits.

People working indoors apparently put their castoffs into medium-size reusable pits dug inside their buildings. In the following analysis we will see that these were conveniently included in the floor plans. Although outdoor activities no doubt produced much of the debris found in exterior pits and abandoned structure basins, some exterior features probably received debris that was routinely cleaned up indoors and dumped outside.

Two major factors, discard behavior and occupational history, have been revealed as underlying dimensions of debris distribution that must be considered in highly specific interpretations of prehistoric activities or feature functionality. Also, habits of debris discard modify the contaminating effects of occupational history in the same sense that they influence the distribution of contemporaneous refuse.

FEATURE ANALYSIS

Feature analysis is designed to make distinctions among pit features on the basis of location, morphology, and content, and to suggest explanations for how features functioned and how their activities were organized. Pits are emphasized in this analysis because they account for most (about 90%) of the features in the study and because their functions are not often readily understood. Structures get thorough coverage in the building analysis that follows.

Among the 838 features in the analysis, there were several basic varieties of structures, interior features, and exterior features (Table 13). These classifications, as introduced in the debris analysis, were made on the basis of data, descriptions, and interpretations reported in the published reports (see Chapter 3). Two-thirds (563) of the features were considered to be either general interior or general exterior pits; others were interpreted as hearths, posts, smudge pits, burials, chert core caches, rock concentrations, or fortuitous depressions. As shown in the debris analysis, the general categories account for almost all the debris recovered in the sample.

Table 13

Distribution of basic and functional feature types among sites.

Feature Type	Carbon Dioxide	Range	Julien	Turner-DeMange	BBB Motor	Robert Schneider	Florence Street	Total
Structures								
Rectangular	4	12	28	14	20	4	3	85
Circular	0	3	3	0	0	0	0	6
Total	4	15	31	14	20	4	3	91
Interior Features								
General Pits	0	15	68	21	31	9	3	147
Hearths	0	2	11	0	4	4	1	22
Postholes	0	4	44	15	9	2	0	74
Smudge Pits	0	2	1	1	0	0	0	4
Miscellaneous	1	4	2	3	6	1	0	17
Total	1	27	126	40	50	16	4	264
Exterior Features								
General Pits	4	8	126	112	144	19	3	416
Hearths	0	0	3	2	0	0	0	5
Postholes	1	0	3	5	9	0	0	18
Smudge Pits	0	0	0	0	0	0	0	0
Burials	0	0	0	0	19	0	0	19
Miscellaneous	0	0	5	0	19	1	0	25
Total	5	8	137	119	191	20	3	483

Structure basins were expectedly larger than other features in most dimensions, but they were not deeper (Table 14). Many, roughly one-third, of the structure basin metrics were missing because structures tended to be shallow enough that one or more basin limits were often obscured by plow disturbance. In contrast, floor measurements were missing in only two cases (Table 15) because the wall foundations that bordered the floors consistently extended well below the plowzone. Fortunately, floor measurements are more revealing indicators than basin metrics because they delimit the usable area within the shelter.

Table 14

Metrics for basic feature categories.

	Length	Width	Depth	Volume
Structures (N = 91)				
Minimum	2.5	1.7	.0	.00
Median	5.0	3.1	.3	3.61
Maximum	8.4	6.3	.5	17.26
Valid n	65	65	73	49
Interior Features (N = 263)				
Minimum	.2	.2	.0	.00
Median	.6	.4	.3	.03
Maximum	2.6	1.7	1.1	2.26
Valid n	262	262	258	246
Exterior Features (N =446)*				
Minimum	.2	.2	.0	.00
Median	1.1	1.0	.3	.21
Maximum	3.2	2.5	1.1	2.62
Valid n	439	437	435	419

Note: Length, width, and depth are in meters; Volume is in cubic meters.
* Burials and exterior miscellaneous features are excluded from values.

Interior features were generally smaller than exterior ones. Although their coded depths were similar (Table 14), it must be remembered that the depths of exterior pits exclude the upper 20 to 30 cm portion of pit fill destroyed by plowing, while interior pits, which originated at floor levels, were seldom disturbed. So it appears that exterior pits as a class were dug prehistorically to depths roughly 20 to 30 cm deeper than interior pits. Exterior pits also tended to be longer, wider, and greater in volume than interior pits.

Exterior features were more numerous than interior ones at all sites except the Range and Florence Street sites (Table 13). The Florence Street site's Sand Prairie phase component, with only three structures and seven pits, was very small, yet it had an elaborate mortuary area nearby—a fact that may relate to

Table 15

Metrics for rectangular and circular structures.

	Basin				Floor		
	Length	Width	Depth	Volume	Length	Width	Area
Rectangular Structures (N = 85)							
Minimum	2.5	1.7	0	0	2.3	1.5	3.4
Median	5.1	3.1	.3	4.0	4.8	2.9	14.8
Maximum	8.4	6.3	.5	17.3	7.5	5.6	42.0
Valid n	61	61	68	45	83	83	85
Circular Structures (N = 6)							
Minimum	3.0	2.0	.1	.2	1.0	1.0	.8
Median	3.2	3.0	.2	2.0	2.6	2.6	5.0
Maximum	3.6	3.6	.5	3.6	3.0	3.0	7.2
Valid n	4	4	5	4	6	6	6

Note: Length, width, and depth are in meters; volume is in cubic meters; area is in square meters.

the disproportionate representation of basic feature types. (The Florence Street mortuary features are not included in this study.) The Lohmann and Stirling components at the Range site were not especially small, but they were situated in an area of several intense previous Late Woodland and Emergent Mississippian occupations. Some exterior Mississippian features lacking significantly diagnostic artifacts may have been inadvertently relegated to earlier components. This likelihood does not significantly alter the results of analysis or their interpretations.

Locational Analysis

A typology of feature locations was devised as a way to examine pits that were situated alike. Pits in the corners of floors, for example, could be grouped this way so that other characteristics they might share could be examined. The locations of interior features were coded according to a scheme of relative positions in the floors of rectangular buildings (Figure 33). Only a few interior pits were unassignable in this way. Because each quarter of the floor is a mirror image of the others, many of these idealized interior locations had four places in a rectangular floor plan (for example, corners). Locations on the axes, however, had only two places each, and the center-point of the floor at the intersection of the axes had only one spot per building. Raw feature counts for the different locations are therefore not directly comparable. A systematic adjustment of the feature counts is needed to yield comparable values for all the idealized locations: values on both the central axes are multiplied by two and the value at the center-point is multiplied by four to match the probability of the other locations.

Exterior pits were coded according to their position relative to a nearby structure (Figure 34). Pits were assigned codes only where there was a reasonably clear choice. A total of two hundred exterior pits were categorized in this way; the remaining exterior pits could not be coded because their associations with individual structures were ambiguous or absent. Many of the unassigned pits were close to two or more buildings for which their locational codes would have differed. If a pit could be coded the same for two nearby structures, however, the code was assigned, even though one specific structure was not implied.

All exterior zones were not represented equally in the coding scheme, since rectangular structures have two short walls and two long walls but four corners. Also, the size of each zone depends on the length and width of the structure. For a structure two meters wide and three meters long, for example, the areas of the "near" zones have a ratio of 8:12:12.6 square meters. The "far" zones have no definite outer limit; their relative proportions are dominated by the far-corner zone, which increases geometrically as it expands away from a structure, while the wall zones expand only additively.

An adjustment to the exterior feature distribution counts is needed to obtain comparable values for zones of different sizes. Because the results are intended to show broad trends, two factors can be standardized. First, the buildings are assumed to be one-and-a-half times as long as they are wide, an estimate that accommodates the buildings in the study. Second, the arbitrary outer limit of the far zone is assumed to be the width of two buildings away from the structure. According to these standards, the near- and far-short-wall values are multiplied by 1.50 and the far-corner values are multiplied by 0.33. This reduces the effect of different-size zones on feature distribution counts, making them directly comparable. The adjustments are approximations only, but they are comprehensible; as the results will show, because the trends are so strong, further refinement of these adjustments is unwarranted.

The distributions of interior pits over floor areas (Figures 38A and 38B) show broad trends. The adjusted results (Figures 39A and 39B) have high values on the long axis near the center of each floor. From the center outward, values decline to moderately low zones flanking moderately high corner values.

Interior hearths (Figures 38C and 39C) were concentrated around the center of the floors. Four smudge pits have no obvious pattern (Figures 38D and 39D). Adjusted values for interior posts were concentrated at the center and adjacent to the long axis away from the center, but all other zones were very low in value. The miscellaneous category pits were sparse but evenly distributed.

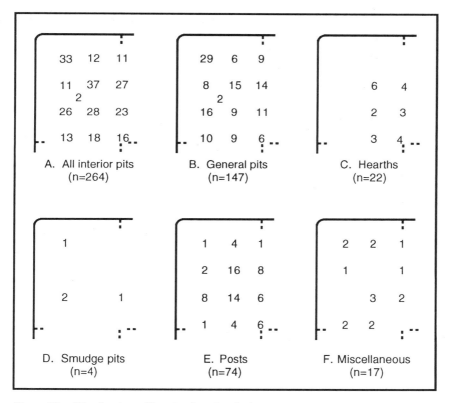

Figure 38. Distribution of interior functional pit types.

Exterior pits appear to have been placed relative to the walls of buildings rather than to the corners. Adjusted values for the distribution of exterior pits (Figure 40) show high values near the long walls and both near and far from the short walls. The zone far from the long wall showed notably low values as did both corner zones. There were too few coded exterior posts to reveal any patterned distribution. Only two of the five exterior hearths were coded, and these were both near long walls.

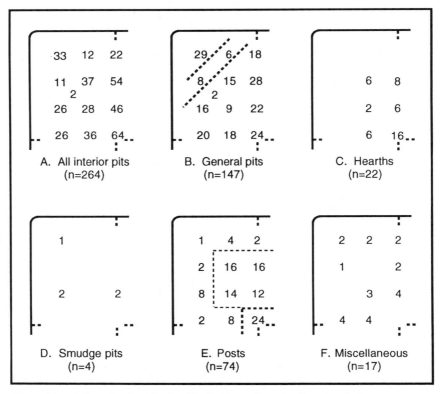

Figure 39. Adjusted values for the distribution of interior functional pit types.

The analyses that follow are necessary to define important distributional patterns that might imply behavioral or functional interpretations. This is especially true for the general pit categories for which there are no obvious functional interpretations.

Morphological Analysis

Categories such as structures, interior pits, exterior pits, postholes, and hearths are based on location, gross morphology, and functionality. Furthermore, the functional categories account for only a small portion of all features, which leaves most features in the general class. In order to recognize prehistoric functional types, it was necessary to further refine feature variability; therefore pits were considered according to construction elements incorporated into their original designs. An operating assumption here is that the location and gross morphology of each pit is related directly, although not in a detailed or

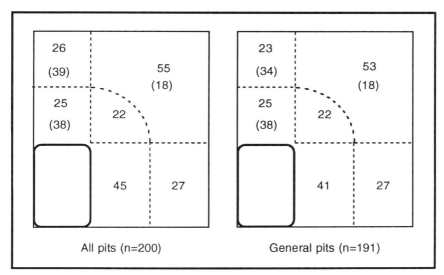

Figure 40.   Distribution of exterior pit types. Adjusted values are in parentheses.

precise way, to its primary prehistoric function. For example, postholes were by design smaller, shallower, and arranged differently than storage pits; and these types of pits represent the two extremes in a wide range of pit sizes, shapes, and arrangements.

A cluster analysis of pits was designed to reflect trends of primary feature function in terms of locational and morphological variables. Only pits with complete morphological and locational data were used. Excluded from the cluster analysis were pits with missing values for length, width, or depth, and any others considered incomplete because of superimposition by other features or other disturbance. Exterior pits were not excluded because of truncation by the plowzone, although interior pits defined as being below, rather than even with, the floor level of their structure were excluded. On these bases, 137 pits were excluded, leaving 232 interior and 379 exterior pits for the cluster analysis (Table 16). These features are adequate in number and variability for analysis and interpretation.

Cluster analyses were performed on interior pits and on exterior pits, each analysis using length, width, and depth as variables. Pits are often compared in terms of length, width, and depth, so the analyses are conceptually straightforward; all the variables are scaled the same, and the three-dimensional Euclidian space of the analysis is that of everyday experience. The BMDP2M program was used with a centroid-linkage algorithm that measures the distance between variable averages in Euclidian space (Dixon 1985). This method avoids the problems associated with single, multiple, or complete linkages (for

Table 16

Number of features selected from each site for cluster analysis.

Sites	Interior Pits	Exterior Pits	Total
Carbon Dioxide	1	5	6
Range	26	8	34
Julien	117	111	228
Turner-DeMange	31	108	139
BBB Motor	42	129	171
Robert Schneider	15	18	33
Total	232	379	611

a discussion, see Aldenderfer and Blashfield 1984; Hodson 1969, 1970; and Sneath and Sokal 1973).

The cluster analysis resulted in twenty-three morphological pit types differentiated on the basis of their lengths, widths, and depths (Table 17). The types will be useful when the feature composition of buildings and household clusters are considered. The morphological types must be considered not as functional types but rather as a shorthand way of referring to salient characteristics of feature design and construction. Measurements within morphological types tended to be normally distributed because of the nature of centroid-linkage and the distribution of pit metrics themselves. Scattergrams (Figure 41) show the relative shapes represented by the types. Types with five or fewer members tended to be deep or narrow (Table 17). Small pits were the most numerous.

Functional feature types are widely but unevenly represented among both interior or exterior morphological types (Tables 18 and 19). Although there were more exterior pits than interior pits, there were more interior hearths and many more interior posts. Interior postholes were naturally concentrated in the morphologically smaller categories, but exterior posts ranged to somewhat larger in size. The gross size categories of large, medium, and small were derived from the three dimensions of length, width, and depth rather than from the single dimension of volume. These categories are convenient for grouping the many morphological types, and they do correspond to the distribution of functional types (Tables 18 and 19). It must be remembered that the large, medium, and small categories are different sizes for interior and exterior pits (Figure 42). It is important that the relative size categories of interior versus exterior pits remain independent for interpretational reasons because the volumes of exterior pits lack the upper 20 to 30 cm of fill lost in the plowzone.

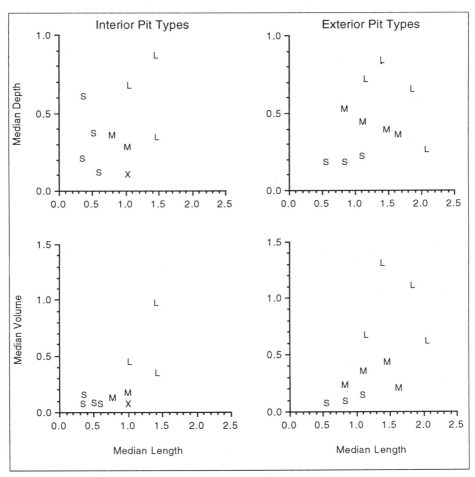

Figure 41. Morphological pit-type metrics (S = small; M = medium; L = large; X = unassignable floor depression).

Note that the morphologically small interior types are dominated by postholes (Tables 18 and 19). Indeed, almost half of the small interior features have been interpreted in the original site reports, but relatively few of the medium and none of the large interior features have been so well understood. Once again, the general category is widely distributed among the morphological types, suggesting that significant variation within the category might be characterized in useful terms after further analysis. This seems especially notable for the categories of medium and large features, where there have been few functional interpretations.

Table 17

Median values for the metrics of morphological pit types.

	Volume	Length	Width	Depth	L:W Ratio	Number of Pits
Interior Pit Types (N=234)						
IP3	.01	.33	.25	.20	1.17	81
IP1	.01	.58	.44	.11	1.28	29
IP7	.02	1.02	.47	.10	2.00	2
IP4	.03	.34	.30	.60	1.10	4
IP2	.05	.50	.41	.36	1.21	37
IP9	.10	.80	.66	.35	1.16	18
IP8	.12	1.04	.90	.26	1.18	22
IP6	.34	1.46	.98	.34	1.41	5
IP11	.44	1.04	.89	.67	1.10	19
IP12	.96	1.45	1.28	.86	1.10	15
IP5	N/A	.96	.32	.66	3.00	1
IP10	N/A	.76	.72	.65	1.06	1
Exterior Pit Types (N=379)						
EP33	.01	.54	.38	.16	1.25	56
EP31	.06	.84	.66	.18	1.24	48
EP36	.12	1.09	.93	.12	1.15	63
EP39	.19	1.54	.59	.19	2.30	4
EP32	.21	.85	.69	.51	1.15	9
EP35	.34	1.14	1.00	.34	1.11	71
EP38	.42	1.47	1.24	.42	1.13	57
EP40	.59	2.04	1.76	.59	1.15	20
EP37	.63	1.15	1.00	.63	1.09	24
EP41	1.08	1.84	1.54	1.08	1.23	18
EP34	1.28	1.39	1.30	1.28	1.08	9

Note: Volume is in cubic meters; length, width, and depth are in meters.

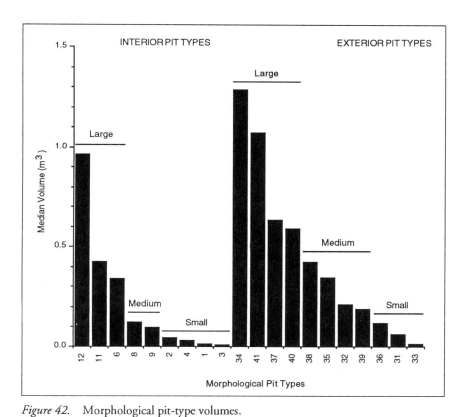

Figure 42. Morphological pit-type volumes.

Table 18

Distribution of interior pits among functional and morphological types.

	Size Categories of Morphological Feature Types			
Functional Feature Type	Large (IP6, 11, 12)	Medium (IP8, 9)	Small (IP1, 2, 3, 4)	Total
General	30	22	52	104
Hearth	0	2	10	12
Smudge Pit	0	0	4	4
Posthole	0	0	61	61
Miscellaneous	0	2	6	10*
Total	30	26	133	191

* Two large, very shallow, Type IP7 floor depressions fit no size category.

Table 19

Distribution of exterior pits among functional and morphological types.

| Functional Feature Type | Size Categories of Morphological Feature Types | | | Total |
	Large (EP34, 37, 40, 41)	Medium (EP32, 35, 38, 39)	Small (EP31, 33, 36)	
General	58	87	94	239
Hearth	0	1	3	4
Posthole	0	3	4	7
Total	58	91	101	250

As noted in the debris analysis, if debris were distributed evenly throughout the fill of all features, then the amount of debris contained in a feature, or a whole category of features, would be proportional to its volume. This expectation is only partly realized in the distribution of debris among the size categories of interior and exterior morphological pit types. Among interior pits (Figure 43), the distribution of debris per volume was relatively smooth; large and medium categories had a bit more debris than expected; the debris types varied somewhat for the medium and small categories. Medium and small pits had more than their share of tools and exotics. Among exterior pits (Figure 44), the large-size category had consistently low values, while the medium-size category had consistently high ones. The small-size category was remarkable because it contained relatively high values for rough rock, tools, and exotic minerals. The distribution of tools and exotic items among exterior pits matched that of interior pits; there were high values for medium and small features only. Furthermore, within each morphological category of features, trends in the distribution of debris by percentage were generally stable.

The distribution of interior pits according to their size categories and their idealized floor locations is shown in Figure 45. The size categories differed from one another in their patterns of floor distribution. The large pits are concentrated at the midpoints along the walls, in the corners, and in the center of the floor. Medium-size pits are concentrated along the axes near the center of the floor and in the corners. Small pits are concentrated primarily at the center or away from the axes.

Concentrations of large pits indicate a tendency for them to be situated at the periphery of the floor, especially at the corners and midpoints of the walls. This is emphasized by the fact that the mid-short-wall locus and the one adjacent to it on the long axis are closely related; pits were assigned to a "wall" zone

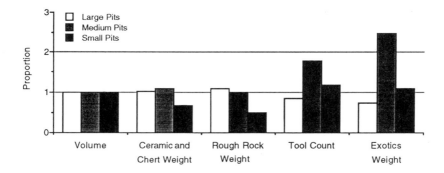

Figure 43.   Volume and debris for interior morphological pit types.

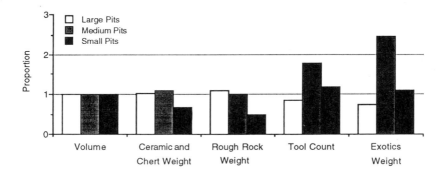

Figure 44.   Volume and debris for exterior morphological pit types.

only if they were very near to or actually abutting the wall; if pits were more than several centimeters away, they were assigned a locus away from the wall. It seems that placement of a large pit near the center of a short wall was less than precise; perhaps because of the oblong shape of the building, a pit could be a bit farther away from a short wall without interfering with open floor area in the middle of the structure. In contrast, the rather high adjusted value for large pits at the center of the floor is offset by the fact that there were actually only two large pits found at floor centers.

The pattern for medium-size pits contrasts with that for large pits, except for another concentration in the corners; these large and medium pit distributions will be important in the building analysis in the next section. The distribution of small pits is interesting since many of them have previously been interpreted as postholes. Indeed, the basic trends of small pit distribution match

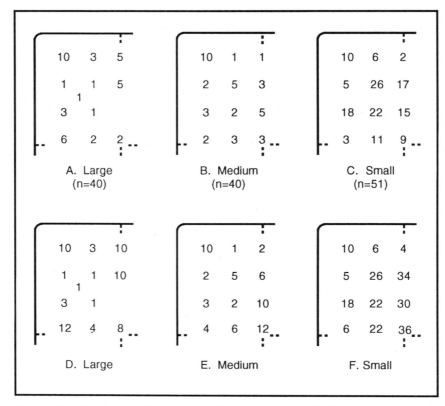

Figure 45. Distribution of interior morphological pit types (A, B, and C show actual values; D, E, and F show adjusted values).

closely the trends for recognized postholes (Figure 39). Their tendency to fall on or near the long axes suggests that many of these features held auxiliary roof supports in mid-floor or racks and benches that perhaps extended from the walls.

Exterior pit types were distributed in patterns (Figure 46). Morphological categories of large exterior pits were found most highly concentrated near the long walls of buildings and were moderately concentrated far from the long walls and near the corners. Morphological categories of medium-size pits were found highly concentrated both near the long and short walls and were moderately concentrated far from a short wall. Categories of small pits were highest both near and far from a short wall and were moderate near the corner and long walls. The number of hearths and posts was so few that well-defined patterns for these were not clear.

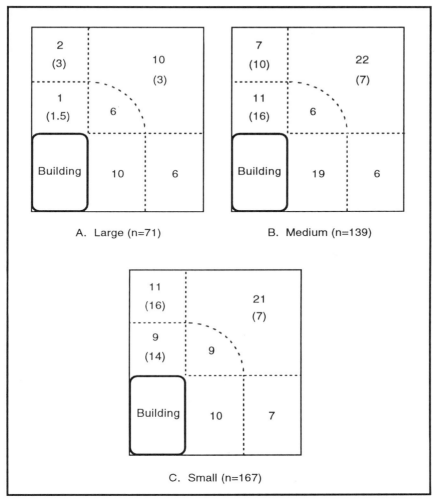

Figure 46. Distribution of exterior morphological pit types. Adjusted values are in parentheses.

Results of Feature Analysis

One general trend indicates that pits were placed according to their size. Small pits were concentrated in the middle of the floor; large pits were concentrated at the periphery, especially in corners and the midpoints of walls; medium-size pits were concentrated both in the very center of the floor and in the corners. Pits of different sizes tended to have different concentrations of debris. Medium-size interior pits, as a category, had almost twice (1.8 times) as many tools as expected for their size. This contrasts with the category of large interior pits, which had fewer tools (0.8 times) than expected. It seems reasonable to infer that many medium-size pits functioned as waste bins to receive concentrated debris from tool-related activities and that large pits did not. Indeed, the categories of large interior and exterior pits held consistently low amounts of debris, which indicates that they received mostly soil. Prehistoric people may have filled them rapidly with excavation spoil or sparse midden in an effort to remove dangers to traffic and increase the usable open areas in and around buildings.

The distribution of pits of known functional types—that is, those previously interpreted in the descriptive site reports—suggests functional interpretations for other similar pits that have not been previously interpreted. For example, the placement of the small pits was similar to that of known postholes, suggesting that many of the small pits were actually postholes. Some of them perhaps held central supports for the ridge poles of the buildings' roofs. Concentrations of tools and exotic items in interior and exterior small pits reinforce a notion that was suggested in the debris analysis for exotics found in postholes. Many small interior and exterior pits were probably foundation elements for buildings or other facilities. Their exotic debris and tool contents may have been associated with them in such ritual contexts as dedicatory ceremonies.

The feature analysis was designed to reveal prehistoric styles of pit design and patterns of pit use that were widely shared throughout the region. The results show that feature shape, placement, and content are interrelated with one another because pits were designed and used in specific ways that make sense functionally.

BUILDING ANALYSIS

The building is one of the basic units of settlement analysis. A building is defined here as an aggregate group of features made up of a structure and its interior facilities. A structure is represented by the remains of its subterranean basin, its floor at the base of the basin, the wall foundations at the edge of the floor, and any auxiliary roof supports located in the floor area. Interior facilities include pits, hearths, isolated postmolds, and benches or partitions represented by postmold patterns. Buildings are complex architectural constructs with stylistic, technological, functional, social, demographic, and economic implications. They are useful as units of analysis because they are spatially and chronologically discrete shelters for people, goods, and activities and because they are important parts of households.

There are ninety-one buildings in the sample (Table 20). Architectural patterns of design and use are defined on the basis of building shape and the composition and arrangement of interior facilities. Size and foundation type were not generally used as typological criteria, but there are some strong and inter-

Table 20
Distribution of buildings among sites by phase.

Site	Edelhardt Phase	Lohmann Phase	Stirling Phase	Moorehead Phase	Sand Prairie Phase	Total
Carbon Dioxide	0	4	0	0	0	4
Range	0	7	8	0	0	15
Julien	0	0	12	14	5	31
Florence Street	0	0	0	0	3	3
Turner-DeMange	0	2	11	1	0	14
BBB Motor	16	0	4	0	0	20
Robert Schneider	0	0	4	0	0	4
Total	16	13	39	15	8	91

esting correlations between these two variables and some of the types, which will be discussed in their turn. As units of analysis, buildings are typed architecturally and then analyzed quantitatively according to the composition of their associated pits, sites, and phases.

Lohmann phase buildings at the Range site (Buildings 19, 32, 33, 38, 51, and 316) were originally interpreted as Stirling phase features (Mehrer 1982a). Subsequent reformulation of the Mississippian phase chronology (Milner et al. 1984), analysis of other Mississippian components at the Range site (Hanenberger and Mehrer, in preparation), and analysis of other Mississippian settlements (Mehrer 1983, 1986a, 1986b) strongly indicate the reassignment of these buildings to the Lohmann phase. Five of the buildings are early in a sequence of superimposition that represents at least five separate episodes of structure abandonment and replacement at the core of the Mississippian occupation (Figure 47). Building size, shape, location, and orientation demonstrate occupational continuity during the Lohmann to Stirling transition.

In the present study, building qualities are compared and contrasted chronologically among the phases, but subphase chronology is not ignored. During its use-life, a building often required the repair or replacement of structural elements and the reuse or replacement of abandoned interior facilities. Examples of this might include a sequence of rebuilt wall foundations or a sequence of superimposed interior pits. It should be remembered that a building's functions may have changed during its use-life and that few architectural configurations can be interpreted as snapshots of prehistoric design or use; superstructures and interior facilities were often rebuilt, redesigned, abandoned, and reused according to the whims of the inhabitants. Because these facts demand methodological consideration, individual cases, patterns, and trends are

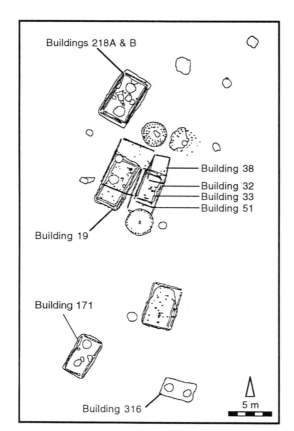

Figure 47. Mississippian households at the Range site.

not interpreted simply. In light of the great potential for confusion, the patterns that are finally observable are noteworthy.

Because individual cases were examined for evidence of subphase chronology, the repair and replacement of walls were treated differently than the superposition of pits. Where wall foundations had been replaced, separate buildings are defined and often designated by feature numbers with alphabet suffixes (e.g., Buildings 218A and 218B). When interior facilities in such a sequence could not be confidently assigned to one or the other building, they were assigned to the latest one. However, when a building was not fully redesigned but was merely repaired or enlarged, a single pit may have been interpreted as having functioned during the use-life of both buildings. This was important for buildings that were categorized according to their configurations of interior pits. However, after a building was defined, the superimposition of pits within it was often ignored when it was assigned to a building type. The full use-life of a building, or the full record of its occupancy, was thereby considered in its typological assignment.

Building Typology

The purpose of creating a building typology is to highlight patterns of architecture that seem to be expressions of prehistoric design or use. Two separate schemes were required, one for the Emergent Mississippian Edelhardt phase and another for the Mississippian phases. Fundamental building qualities that required separate typologies include building size, shape, foundation type, and configurations of interior pits. Each building type is described below.

Emergent Mississippian Buildings

The Emergent Mississippian period is represented by the Edelhardt phase component of the BBB Motor site. This component had sixteen structures and thirty-three interior pits. As a group, these structures were qualitatively different from the later Mississippian ones in their construction technology, size, and general trends of interior pit configurations. Edelhardt phase structures had posthole rather than wall-trench foundations, they were smaller than later structures, and their interior pits tended to be smaller than those of later phases. That is why they were categorized independently of Mississippian buildings. The Edelhardt phase buildings had distinct and repeated patterns of floor plan layout that were readily categorized, so the limitation of having only a single component for the Emergent Mississippian period is discounted for present purposes.

The arrangement of interior pits was critical in the definition of Emergent Mississippian building types. In the feature analysis described above, Edelhardt phase pits were typed morphologically using the same criteria—length, width, and depth—as those of later phases. Thirty Edelhardt phase interior pits were classified into nine morphological pit types. Only extremely rare pit types are not represented in the Edelhardt phase; the rare types include only six Mississippian postpit and posthole features (Table 17; pit types IP4, IP5, and IP10). It is important to notice, however, that large, deep interior pit types (IP6, IP11, and IP12) were rare during the Edelhardt phase.

The sixteen Edelhardt phase structures from the BBB Motor site were classified into five categories based on the interior configurations of their pits (Figure 48). Four Type EM1 buildings were relatively large (9–12 m²). Each had only a few small pits or none at all. Two Type EM2 buildings were also relatively large (9 m²), but each one had a pair of interior pits in one lateral half of the floor area. The pits in one house compared favorably with those in the other. Their volumes ranged from .09 m³ to .29 m³ (mean = .19 m³). Three Type EM3 buildings tended to be only slightly smaller than the first two types, though one was relatively large (10 m²). Type EM3 buildings are characterized by four superimposed pits. Though much of the floor area in each building

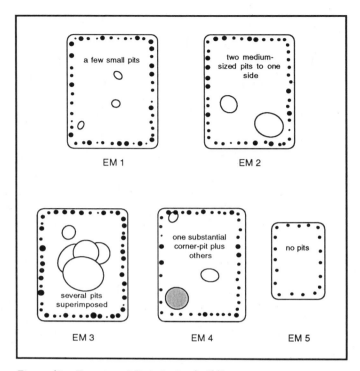

Figure 48.   Emergent Mississippian building types.

was thus occupied, few pits could have been used simultaneously. One pit in each of these buildings was about 60 cm deep, while the others ranged from 15 to 35 cm deep. One of the buildings had a floor level hearth area near the center of the floor. Four Type EM4 buildings were all smaller than those above, but they ranged considerably in size (5–8 m²). All had at least one substantial pit (30–50 cm deep) in a corner; two of the buildings also had one or two other pits. On the basis of floor area and floor plan, the quartet of EM4 buildings could logically be subdivided into two pairs. The four, however, are a coherent group and are classed together as examples with one substantial corner pit and mostly open floor area. Three Type EM5 buildings were all relatively very small and lacked any substantial floor pits. None had any interior facilities.

Emergent Mississippian buildings were relatively small rectangular structures with posthole foundations and clearly definable patterns in their floor plans. Interiors tended to be free of isolated postholes and small pits, probably because the small buildings did not need extra support for their roofs. Large pits were rare, but they were important parts of two building types. The trends for the Edelhardt phase make instructive contrasts with those of the following

Mississippian phases, even though data are available from only a single Emergent Mississippian component.

Mississippian Buildings

Seventy-four Mississippian structures were divided into seven distinct architectural categories (Figure 49) distinguished from one another by floor-plan size, shape, and arrangements of large and medium-size interior pits. Four types of large rectangular buildings were characterized mainly by their arrangements of large pits. Smaller pits, present in most rectangular buildings, were often arranged in coherent patterns. Relatively large circular buildings often had benches and hearths but never had substantial pits. Small buildings of either rectangular or circular shape seldom had pits. Arrangements of postholes and postmolds sometimes suggested interior roof supports, racks, dividers, and benches, but because the evidence for these furnishings is more often suggestive than definitive, only the clearest cases will be mentioned.

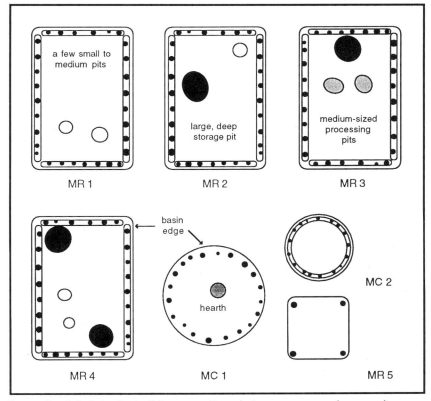

Figure 49.   Mississippian building types. Foundation types vary and are not diagnostic of building types (M = Mississippian; R = rectangular; C = circular).

There are five types of rectangular buildings. Type MR1 rectangular buildings (Figure 49) had either no pits or only a few relatively small ones. The most salient characteristic of Type MR1 structures is the absence of large interior pits. A few also lacked basins or floors, which indicates that plowing may have destroyed some of their small interior features (had large pits been present, they would not have been completely destroyed). Thirty-five examples were part of ten components, including all but the Moorehead phase at the Turner-DeMange site (Tables 21 and 22). Type MR2 rectangular buildings had one large pit in the middle of the floor adjacent to a long wall, plus one or more medium or small pits in lateral floor areas. Ten such buildings, representing all the phases and all but two sites, are known from six components. Type MR3 rectangular structures had large pits near a short wall but had either no other pits or only a few medium-size ones in the middle of the floor. Six of these buildings were part of four components at the Range and Julien sites. Type MR4 rectangular buildings had large pits located near corners. Often there were multiple large pits and a few medium-size or smaller pits scattered over the floor. Fourteen such structures were found at five components. Type MR5 rectangular buildings, which were very small (ca. 4.5 m²) and nearly square, lacked substantial interior features, although one such building did have a single large pit. There were only three MR5 buildings, all from the Julien site. One had a wall-trench foundation; one had only four small corner postholes; another had no evidence for a foundation.

Two distinct patterns of circular buildings were found, even though there were only six circular structures in the study. Type MC1 circular structures

Table 21

Distribution of Mississippian building types among sites.

Site	MR1	MR2	MR3	MR4	MR5	MC1	MC2	Total
Carbon Dioxide	4	0	0	0	0	0	0	4
Range	5	3	4	0	0	3	0	15
Julien	13	3	2	6	3	1	2	30
Turner-DeMange	9	2	0	3	0	0	0	14
BBB Motor	1	1	0	2	0	0	0	4
Robert Schneider	1	0	0	3	0	0	0	4
Florence Street	2	1	0	0	0	0	0	3
Total	35	10	6	14	3	4	2	74

Note: MR = Mississippian rectangular; MC = Mississippian circular.

Table 22

Distribution of Mississippian building types among phases.

Phase	MR1	MR2	MR3	MR4	MR5	MC1	MC2	Total
Sand Prairie	6	1	0	2	0	0	0	9
Moorehead	3	1	1	5	2	0	1	13
Stirling	16	6	4	7	1	4	1	39
Lohmann	10	2	1	0	0	0	0	13
Total	35	10	6	14	3	4	2	74

Note: MR = Mississippian rectangular; MC = Mississippian circular.

(Figure 49) had posthole foundations and at least one interior element such as a hearth, an interior bench, or a prepared floor. In contrast, there were only two Type MC2 circular structures; much smaller than the MC1 circular structures, these contained wall-trench foundations but lacked interior elements. Even though Type MC2 buildings were very small, they had substantial wall-trench foundations that suggested massive superstructures (Milner 1984a).

Results of the Building Analysis

Important results of the building analysis include temporal trends, site-specific trends, and organizational aspects of interior space. Temporal trends are the most obvious results. Edelhardt phase buildings incorporate architectural innovations in the form of patterned arrangements of a variety of interior pits, even though the structures are similar in size and construction to those of earlier phases (Kelly 1980:86; Milner 1984b:21). Patterned arrangements of interior pits are recognized for the Mississippian period, but none of the individual Edelhardt phase floor plan arrangements seem to be "ancestral" to any of the later configurations.

Basic building design and technology changed with the shift from Emergent Mississippian to Mississippian traditions. There was a new overarching scheme of Mississippian structural design and construction, and within this scheme are obvious architectural distinctions based on floor plans. During Mississippian times there was a trend of first increasing and then decreasing architectural complexity. A lack of diversity in the Lohmann phase is followed by a peak of complexity in the Stirling phase and a gradual decline of variety in the subsequent Moorehead and Sand Prairie phases (Figure 50). It might seem that the architectural diversity is a function of the number of buildings per phase because the pattern of diversity roughly parallels the number of buildings per phase (Figure 51). Note, however, that while the Moorehead phase has roughly the same number of buildings as the Lohmann phase, it has over twice (233%) as many different types of building. Note also that the Sand Prairie phase has fewer buildings than the Lohmann phase but the same number of types (three). It therefore appears that the number of buildings and their diversity are two independent expressions of underlying sociocultural and demographic phenomena (this and other important trends are examined in Chapter 5).

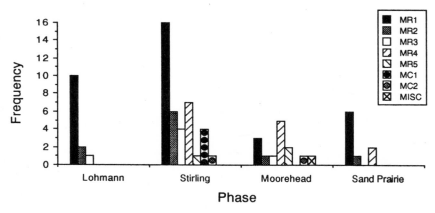

Figure 50. Mississippian building types by phase.

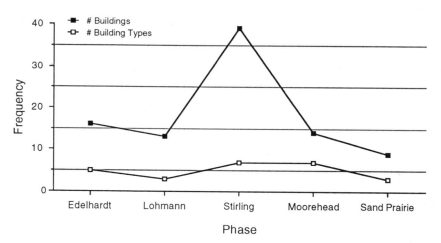

Figure 51. Distribution of buildings and types among phases.

Rectangular buildings were found to uphold previous notions of chronological trends in size and shape (e.g., Gregg 1975a:133; Milner et al. 1984; Porter 1974b). That is, buildings got larger and more square in shape through time. For buildings in the sample, the median area rose steadily through time, but the range of sizes fluctuated (Figure 52). Rectangular buildings tended to become consistently more square through time, but, once again, the range fluctuated (Figure 53). The range of length-to-width ratios for rectangular buildings fluctuates in the same chronological pattern as the number of architectural types. Remember, however, that the length-to-width ratio was not a criteria in the architectural typology. The variety of architectural types and the length-to-width ratio of floors seem to be independent of one another, yet both were expressions of a more fundamental trend of architectural variability.

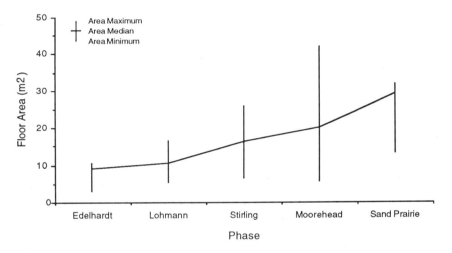

Figure 52.   Rectangular structure floor area by phase.

In addition to chronological trends, there are also site-specific patterns. The Stirling phase component at the BBB Motor site offers a useful insight. Stirling phase Building 87 at the BBB Motor site was difficult to classify because of its unique and complex arrangement of superimposed interior pits. The floor plan is similar to, but larger than, the Edelhardt phase EM3-type structures that predated it at the site. Building 87 is interpreted as a temple, so the floor plan design may be an intentional reflection of "ancient" Edelhardt phase traditions at the site (Emerson and Jackson 1984). Moreover, this building was one of the few Stirling structures to have a posthole foundation, again recalling ancestral Edelhardt phase architecture. Some buildings at the Range site are so similar to one another that they could have been built and occupied by the same

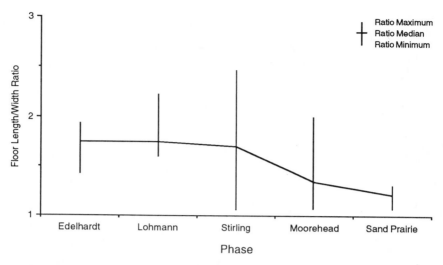

Figure 53. Rectangular structure shape by phase.

family. At the center of the occupation area (Figure 47), a superimposed sequence of similar MR2 buildings (Buildings 19 and 16) spans the Lohmann
and Stirling phases. A set of three MR3 buildings (Buildings 218A, 218B, and
171) nearby are also remarkably similar to one another. Buildings 218A and
218B represent a single structure basin with a sequence of two MR3 constructions, the second oriented 180 degrees to the first. Each of these two in turn
resembles Building 171. Taken together, all three buildings are nearly identical
in their placement of large pits, medium pits, floor depressions, and even a peculiar pattern of three postholes that flanked pits in the floor. Similar MR3
buildings at other sites did not match these three so precisely. The site-specific
patterns at the Robert Schneider site are characterized by a somewhat limited
range of variability. Three out of four buildings at this site contained large pits
that were smaller than usual, which were situated tightly in corners, along with
one other rather small but deep pit and a few postholes elsewhere.

The BBB Motor, Range, and Robert Schneider sites appear to have architectural patterns that relate to site-specific occupational continuities, such as
family or other ancient traditions, that overlay any underlying temporal, stylistic, or technical affiliations. Occupational continuity cannot be inferred for the
BBB Motor site according to our present chronological understanding, however, because of the absence of a Lohmann phase occupation between the Edelhardt and Stirling phases. This reemphasizes the notion of expression of "ancient" tradition in temple architecture, but it also raises the question of
whether or not the fleeting trends of the Lohmann phase, only fifty years long,
would necessarily have been clearly expressed at this mortuary/temple com-

plex, or at any other site, even if it were occupied continuously throughout that time.

Among the buildings in the analysis, a variety of interior facilities were noted that were not used as criteria for sorting the building types. These include hearths, benches, prepared floors, auxiliary roof supports, and post patterns that probably related to partitions, racks, shelves, or other furnishings. The large circular buildings (Type MC1) were notable in this regard because they often had hearths, benches, prepared floor surfaces, and a posthole placed near the center of the floor. Otherwise, MR1 buildings had no interior pits. Rectangular Type MR2 buildings often had a set of postholes or small features near the long axis of the floor flanking the large pit (e.g., Figure 22). An open portion of floor area may have been a design element of rectangular Type MR3 structures, in which pit features were often concentrated in the middle and at one end of the floor, leaving the other end open except for a floor depression that was probably not a facility. Partitions are not obvious, perhaps because the buildings are so small. An interior partition no longer than the width of a building would have required only a few insubstantial supports. Structures were so small, though, that they could not have permitted much subdivision. Interior wall trenches, where present, often paralleled a structural wall and are understood here to be bench supports rather than interior partitions. One interior wall trench in Building 15 at the Robert Schneider site, however, may have been part of an extended entryway rather than a partition or bench.

There are several aspects of the results that bear on social, economic, and evolutionary interpretations for the region. Trends in building size may seem to be related to demographic aspects of regional population growth, but while the size of buildings tended to increase steadily through time, the population of the region fell drastically during the last 250 years of the period (population trends are discussed in Chapter 5). Another factor that may be related to increased structure size is the addition of numerous and large pits to the floor plans of buildings during Stirling phase times (Collins 1987).

It is not clear why buildings became more square over time, but the reasons may have been technical rather than aesthetic. To enlarge a common building design, it may have been easier to widen it rather than to lengthen it because of the nature of construction materials. For example, the length of ridge poles, which extend along the peak of a house's gabled roof, may have been a limiting factor. If locally available trees were not large enough or were not otherwise suitable to yield increasingly longer ridge poles, people may have had to widen their traditional layout to increase its size without lengthening it.

The variety of interior facilities and their arrangements may relate to the changing opportunities and obligations of the evolving social and economic systems. New types of activities may have required specially designated spaces. New social roles may have required specialized buildings for new or enhanced activities. Clearly, the organization of space was changing in subtle but persistent ways. These and other analytical results are further considered in a discussion of regional context that follows.

HOUSEHOLD ANALYSIS

The term *household* indicates the domestic context of daily family life. Considering the developmental cycle of a family and the impermanent nature of prehistoric building materials used in the region, household facilities, including structures, can be expected to have been readily adapted to the family's changing needs. Embodying a complex set of phenomena and being a naturally "organic" unit, the household is expected to reflect the changing needs of society. The assignment of features to households for the analysis generally followed the definitions of feature clusters in the site reports, but modifications were often necessary to accommodate assumptions of household occupancy. Clusters of features spanning two or more phases, for example, were divided into separate single-phase households.

To derive an approximation of the set of facilities that could have been used simultaneously during a household occupation, maps were made without those features that had been abandoned and superimposed upon by others, thereby deriving a maximal configuration of features. This simple, exploratory method removed "noise" in areas of repeated feature construction to help reveal underlying patterns of spatial organization. It was useful for investigating spatial trends in the arrangement of features because it reduced the complexity resulting from the abandonment and rebuilding of protracted occupation. However, multiple rebuilding is itself important in the analysis and results.

A typology of household arrangements was constructed to illustrate trends in the variation among households. Individual households were examined for spatial patterning of buildings and pits in terms of morphological feature types, pit volume, and debris contents. Ceramics, chert debris, rough rock, and limestone were considered in terms of their feature densities (grams per cubic meter of feature fill). Rare items such as tools and exotics were noted by count and weight per feature. The distributions of debris categories within each household were also examined.

Mortuary artifact assemblages were not used to represent nearby households in the analysis because grave goods were not relevant to the ongoing activities of the inhabitants. Graveyards must have served more than one family, since each household did not have its own burial plot. Presumably the dead of most households were interred in distant, possibly communal, spots, such as the ones at sites in this analysis.

Sites with different occupational histories are not directly comparable in terms of specific quantitative measures of debris density distributions. Dense accumulations of durable refuse such as chert, limestone, and ceramics can be expected for components with intense prior occupation, while sparser accumulations can be expected for ones with little or no prior history. For example, the Stirling phase occupation at the Robert Schneider site had sparse collections for all debris categories, while the Stirling phase occupation at the Range site had very dense accumulations. The Robert Schneider site had been occupied only briefly before Stirling times, but the Range site had a long history stretching back to Archaic times.

In addition, debris density values for individual features had to be considered in light of a feature's volume, because for very small features the presence of any debris sometimes translated into dense concentrations per cubic meter of fill. Such cases cannot be compared in a simple way with medium or large pits, where enormous amounts of debris would have been required to create equally dense concentrations per unit volume. With small pits, the debris densities tended to be either zero or very high, so the relative size of the feature and the actual amount of debris had to be considered together, along with its debris density for interpretations of concentrated debris distribution; simple density values or frequency values interpreted without consideration of such aspects as feature size and occupational history would have been misleading.

Occupational history also affected the composition of features for some households because of uncertainties at multicomponent sites where a few features lacked phase designations due to their lack of sufficiently diagnostic artifacts. Such features were tentatively considered possible members of more than one household, but during the analysis the evidence often suggested which household they belonged to and therefore indicated a phase designation.

At the Range site, however, there may have been a few Mississippian pits that contained redeposited Emergent Mississippian diagnostic artifacts but that lacked Mississippian diagnostics. If such pits existed, they were included in an Emergent Mississippian component and were not available for consideration here. This potential bias at the Range site has no significant effect on the final results or interpretations, because there are more important characteristics of the Mississippian occupations there.

Household Typology

For each household in the sample, the volumes, debris inventories, and debris densities of all features were examined for spatial patterns. Because of the complex interrelationships of factors at each household, inferences of spatial patterning were made on the basis of the relative debris densities for features within a household. These densities were considered in terms of the size and composition of the household, its occupational history, its features, and their volumes. Given the long time span of the sample, the patterns that emerged are strikingly consistent. Occasional deviations from the recognized patterns merely highlight the potential range of configurations that were not implemented. Each phase had distinguishing characteristics.

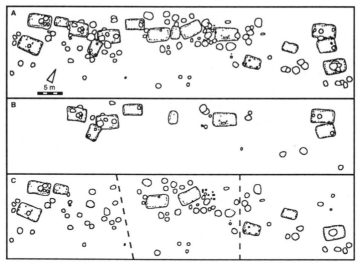

Figure 54.   Edelhardt phase households.

Table 23

Summary of Emergent Mississippian households.

| Household | Frequency of Building Types | | | | | Total Floor Area |
	EM1	EM2	EM3	EM4	EM5	
West	1	1	2	1	1	45
Central	3	0	0	1	1	39
East	0	1	1	2	1	36

Note: Areas are in m^2; EM = Emergent Mississippian.

Edelhardt Phase Households

The Edelhardt phase component of the BBB Motor site had the largest and most dense arrangement of features and households in the study (Figure 54; Table 23). Emerson and Jackson (1984) defined three clusters of features and clearly distinguished them from the Stirling phase occupation at the site.

Superimposition of pits and structures indicated that some of the features had been abandoned and filled and their locations had been reused during the

Edelhardt phase. In an effort to reveal spatial patterns and to isolate household patterns in the site layout (Figure 54A), features that had been superimposed by later Edelhardt phase features (Figure 54B) were eliminated from a work-map to show the maximal configuration of features (Figure 54C) that could possibly have been in use at a single time toward the end of the occupation. Of course, the resulting map includes many features that may have been abandoned and filled but not subsequently superimposed. The intention here is to systematically remove confusion from the site pattern in areas where activities were most intense. The results suggest community planning in the spacing and location of different types of buildings. The households were identified as dense clusters of features that were separated by relatively clear zones.

The central household (Figure 54C) has a pair of EM1 buildings and is flanked on either side by triads of buildings in the eastern and western households. Each triad includes one EM3 building, one EM5 building, plus one other: an EM1 building in the western household and an EM4 building in the eastern household. At the center of the central household is an EM5 building (Figures 54A and 54B) only slightly superimposed by one pit. This small structure may actually have served with the other two buildings during much or all of the central household's use-life. Each of the other two households had a similar small building associated with it (Figure 54C).

The distribution of exterior pits is most dense for the central household and somewhat less dense for those flanking it. Most of the pits were of the small or medium types. Seven large pits were distributed evenly over the site area, with two or three in each household cluster suggesting that each was important to a household's routine. There were no large interior storage pits comparable to the Mississippian ones. Three buildings had two or three pits placed just outside of a short wall. Whether or not this was intentionally planned is unclear, but it appears to be unique to the site. Considering the dense and seemingly unstructured exterior pit configurations, these building and pit combinations may simply be coincidences.

The Edelhardt phase households were close to one another and had dense concentrations of exterior features. The arrangement of building types suggests that each family used several simultaneously. Exterior pits are dispersed evenly over the area immediately surrounding the buildings, but there are so many of them that the overall effect is that of a dense profusion without the strikingly patterned pit clusters that will be noted for subsequent phases.

Lohmann Phase Households

There are six Lohmann phase households from the Carbon Dioxide, Range, and Turner-DeMange sites. The Turner-DeMange and Carbon Dioxide sites had relatively simple occupational histories, so their households are positively defined (Figure 55; Table 24). Because of the intense occupational history at the Range site, no exterior pit features can be assigned to its Lohmann phase component with certainty.

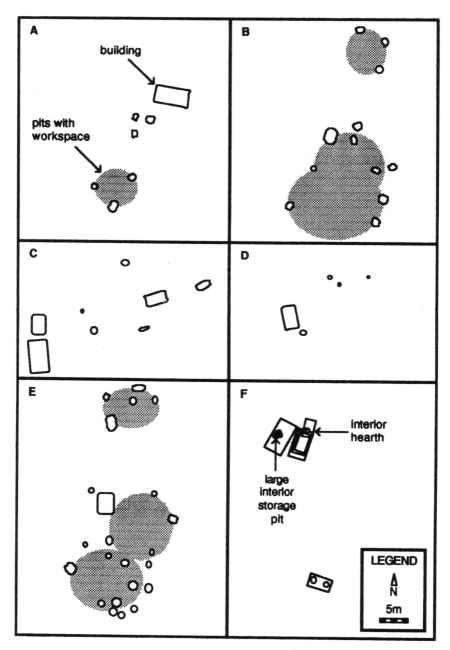

Figure 55. Lohmann phase households.

Table 24

Summary of Mississippian households by site and phase.

Household	Type	Frequency of Building Types							Total Floor Area	Interior Storage Volume
		MR1	MR2	MR3	MR4	MR5	MC1	MC2		
Lohmann Phase										
RAN-1	LC	4	2	1	0	0	0	0	77	1.7
CO2-1	LA	3	0	0	0	0	0	0	26	0
TUR-1	LB	1	0	0	0	0	0	0	10	0
TUR-2	LA	1	0	0	0	0	0	0	11	0
TUR-3	LB	0	0	0	0	0	0	0	0	0
CO2-2	LA	1	0	0	0	0	0	0	8	0
Stirling Phase										
RAN-2	Node	1	1	3	0	0	3	0	108	3.6
JUL-1	Node	4	1	0	0	0	1	1	88	1.8
BBB-1	Node	1	0	0	1	0	0	0	32	3.0
BBB-2	Node	0	1	0	1	0	0	0	26	1.2
JUL-2	SB	1	1	0	0	1	0	0	44	.7
JUL-3	SA	0	0	1	0	0	0	0	16	1.1
JUL-4	SC	1	0	0	0	0	0	0	10	0
JUL-5	-	0	0	0	0	0	0	0	0	0
TUR-4	SB	0	2	0	0	0	0	0	31	1.7
TUR-5	SA	4	0	0	2	0	0	0	99	.5
TUR-6	-	2	0	0	0	0	0	0	21	0
TUR-7	SA	1	0	0	0	0	0	0	8	0
ROB-1	SB	1	0	0	1	0	0	0	46	.5
ROB-2	SA	0	0	0	1	0	0	0	12	.4
ROB-3	SC	0	0	0	1	0	0	0	18	.7
Moorehead Phase										
JUL-6	Node	0	1	1	3	2	0	0	125	5.6
JUL-7	Node	1	0	0	1	0	0	0	61	2.0
JUL-8	-	2	0	0	0	0	0	0	45	0
TUR-8	-	0	0	0	1	0	0	0	19	.8
JUL-9	-	0	0	0	0	0	0	1	1	0
JUL-10	-	0	0	0	0	0	0	0	0	0
Sand Prairie Phase										
JUL-11	Node	2	0	0	2	0	0	0	93	2.6
FLO-1	Node	2	1	0	0	0	0	0	69	1.2
JUL-12	-	1	0	0	0	0	0	0	32	0
JUL-13	-	1	0	0	0	0	0	0	29	0

Note: Areas are in m^2; volumes are in m^3. Storage volume includes only large storage pits. CO2 = Carbon Dioxide; RAN = Range; TUR = Turner-DeMange; JUL = Julien; ROB = Robert Schneider; BBB = BBB Motor; FLO = Florence Street; MR = Mississippian rectangular; MC = Mississippian circular.

Three basic organizational patterns are evident. The first pattern, designated LA, consists of one to three buildings with only a few exterior pits, many of which were small and contained little material, and one or two larger pits that held a great deal of material in dense concentrations. Both households at the Carbon Dioxide site and one at the Turner-DeMange site (Figures 55A, 55C, and 55D; Table 24, CO2-1, CO2-2, and TUR-2) fit this pattern. The second pattern, LB, contains numerous widely scattered exterior pits. One such household at the Turner-DeMange site (Figure 55B; Table 24, TUR-3) resembles the first pattern superficially, as there are three pits that contained abundant debris and many others with sparse debris. This household lacked evidence for an associated structure, although there probably was one originally. A second household at the Turner-DeMange site (Figure 55E; Table 24, TUR-1) resembled the first household, but it did have a building. It also had numerous tools, plus a cache of chert cores and a cached sandstone metate, all of which were distributed widely among the pits in a manner not observed at the other Lohmann site households (Table 25). Presumably these tools were used in daily activities, since there is no previous occupation nearby from which they could have been redeposited. In both the first and second patterns, there are small groups of pits arranged around what seem to have been work spaces.

The third pattern, designated LC, was seen only at the Range site (Figure 55F; Table 24, RAN-1), where the Lohmann phase occupation, lacking pits, may be incompletely defined. The Range site was unique among Lohmann households with its complex sequence of structure superposition, its large deep interior pits in two buildings, a small building with a prepared hearth pit, and its occupational continuity with the succeeding Stirling phase. Lohmann phase building assignments were made on the basis of ceramic assemblages that lacked Stirling phase diagnostics; the buildings themselves had traits typical of both the Lohmann and Stirling phases. Only three buildings could have stood at any one time. Building 38 was especially small and lacked interior features other than the prepared hearth pit (Figure 47). It may have been a predecessor of the Stirling phase circular structures that had hearths but no other pits. The fact that the Stirling household at the Range site had three such circular buildings reinforces this notion, especially in view of the occupational continuity between the Lohmann and Stirling phases.

The main characteristic of Lohmann households is that they were relatively isolated from one another. Other important characteristics are the dispersed nature of exterior pits with their work spaces, the lack of substantial interior pits, a small number of tools (except as noted above) and exotics, and a tendency for a few exterior pits to contain the main portion of the household material. The recurring pattern of exterior pits arranged around a small open area is also found in later phases.

The divergent nature of the Range site's Lohmann phase household is interesting because of its continuity with the subsequent Stirling phase household,

Table 25

Summary of household inventories.

Households	Number of Features	Total Volume (m³)	Ceramic Weight (kg)	Chert Weight (kg)	Lime- stone Weight (kg)	Rough Rock Weight (kg)	Tool Count	Exotic Item Weight (g)
Lohmann Phase								
TUR-1	31	18.9	4.1	14.2	3.2	4.3	53	143
RAN-1	10	8.8	3.5	2.1	9.6	0.5	26	59
CO2-2	2	3.3	2.0	0.5	1.4	0.2	12	0
CO2-1	8	5.8	3.5	0.3	5.3	0.9	4	9
TUR-3	12	1.3	3.8	0.4	1.8	1.2	5	0
TUR-2	8	2.0	1.5	0.1	0.2	0.8	3	1
Stirling Phase								
RAN-2*	37	34.7	15.5	7.0	71.8	1.6	67	376
JUL-1*	43	43.3	6.1	3.5	3.5	6.2	36	274
TUR-5	58	42.5	10.3	7.6	1.2	11.2	108	642
JUL-5	5	4.4	2.7	0.4	2.7	0.7	3	22
JUL-4	6	2.4	1.0	0.1	0.1	0.0	1	0
JUL-2	31	18.6	2.4	1.0	13.6	0.8	6	13
JUL-3	24	5.3	2.9	2.41	3.6	1.1	7	1
TUR-7	22	10.2	7.3	2.4	0.9	5.1	35	24
TUR-4	15	21.6	7.0	3.9	2.3	4.7	75	21
TUR-6	5	7.3	2.0	0.4	1.1	0.5	7	0
ROB-1	19	5.3	2.0	0.7	0.0	0.3	21	77
ROB-2	12	1.2	0.2	0.1	0.5	0.0	9	15
ROB-3	6	0.9	0.1	0.1	0.0	0.0	12	18
Moorehead Phase								
JUL-6*	62	50.6	17.0	13.5	53.0	33.7	166	573
JUL-7*	20	31.6	2.4	3.4	4.1	5.6	140	54
JUL-10	4	0.7	0.4	0.1	0.1	0.0	0	38
JUL-8	13	3.2	1.2	0.3	0.3	2.0	4	3
JUL-9	2	0.1	0.0	0.0	20.4	0.0	1	0
TUR-8	7	7.3	1.3	2.1	0.2	3.2	21	11
Sand Prairie Phase								
JUL-11*	39	36.2	9.8	11.1	11.6	8.6	117	785
JUL-13	6	3.4	0.3	0.1	1.9	0.3	3	0
JUL-12	1	0.0	5.0	0.4	5.3	2.5	7	0

Note: * designates nodal households; CO2 = Carbon Dioxide; RAN = Range; TUR = Turner-DeMange; JUL = Julien; ROB = Robert Schneider.

which figures prominently in the following analysis. The Range site's Lohmann phase household seems to foreshadow its successor because they both had unusual configurations.

Stirling Phase Households

There are fifteen Stirling phase households from the Range, Julien, Turner-DeMange, BBB Motor, and Robert Schneider sites (Table 24). Most are comparable to earlier households (Figure 56), but four are considered to be nodal points (Figure 57). Nodal points, or nodes, are households with additional special purpose facilities. The notion of small nodal settlements was introduced by Riordan (1975) and later discussed by Muller (1978) in reference to the Kincaid settlement system in southern Illinois. The concept became useful in the American Bottom after work there uncovered the numerous small settlements in this study (Milner and Emerson 1981; Emerson and Milner 1981, 1982). Two different types of nodal points are distinguished in the following analysis. Civic-ceremonial nodes are more complex than other households. They have accumulations of exotic debris, contain more buildings of distinctive types, and are laid out differently (Figures 57A and 57B). Mortuary/temple nodes have a pair of rectangular buildings with exterior pits and a graveyard; exotic paraphernalia may also be present (Figures 57C and 57D).

Ordinary households occurred in three configurations (Figure 56). The type SA configuration is defined by single buildings with approximately fifteen to twenty exterior pits arranged a comfortable distance away in loose patterns. There are four examples, one each at the Julien and Turner-DeMange sites (Figures 56A and 56B; Table 24, TUR-7, JUL-3), and one each at the Turner-DeMange and Robert Schneider sites (TUR-5 and ROB-2, not illustrated). At one end of the buildings in this pattern are clusters of pits around small open areas approximately three to six meters wide. Occasionally pits seem to occur in pairs in which one pit is substantially larger than the other. Toward the other end of the building, an outside area is dominated by a large, shallow pit containing sparse debris. The large pit at the Julien site was lined with limestone slabs. Tools were widely scattered among the pits, but unusually dense concentrations of debris were found in one or two exterior pits of medium or large size.

Two examples from the Julien and Turner-DeMange sites (Figures 56A and 56B) illustrate this Type SA pattern clearly. The third example, from the Turner-DeMange site (Tables 24 and 25, TUR-5, not illustrated), was much less clear because of repeated structure abandonment, replacement, and superposition by later pits and buildings. Although six buildings were included in this third household cluster of features, only two or three could have been in use at any one time, since there were three stages of construction involving superimposition of buildings and pits. Comparison with the other households at the Julien, Turner-DeMange, and Robert Schneider sites suggests strongly that only two buildings were in use at any one time and that not all the pits were in

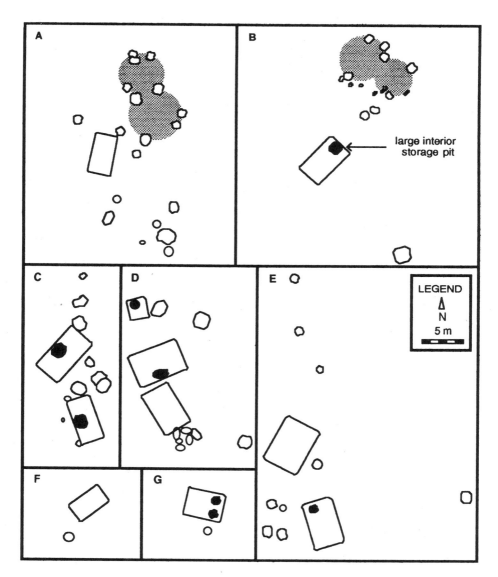

Figure 56. Stirling phase ordinary households.

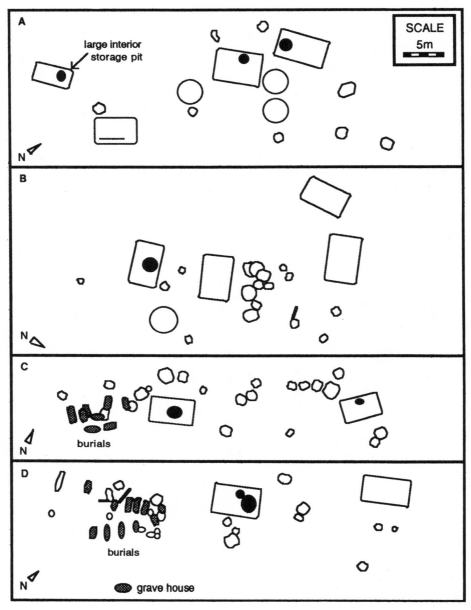

SCALE
5m

A

large interior
storage pit

N

B

N

C

burials

N

D

burials

N

grave house

Figure 57. Stirling phase nodal households.

use simultaneously. In this way, the patterns evident at three undisturbed households provide a suggestion for interpreting a household arrangement complicated by abandonment, reuse, and reoccupation of the area.

Nevertheless, this somewhat complex household (TUR-5) had a very large total floor area (Table 24) and unusually high totals for ceramics, chert, tools, and exotics. It also had several unusual exterior posthole arrangements that may represent an unspecified outdoor facility. The repeated superimposition of features, in addition to the numerous pits, tools, and exotics, makes this household resemble a nodal point, although it had only three buildings in use at one time and apparently no communal buildings resembling nodal points.

A fourth example of household Type SA at the Robert Schneider site (Tables 24 and 25, ROB-2, not illustrated) had fewer pits and consequently less clearly defined patterns of arrangement, which was consistent with the overall tendency of occupation at that site. The Robert Schneider site had relatively few pits and sparse debris and may have been occupied only briefly.

There are three examples of the Type SB household configuration, one each from the Julien, Turner-DeMange, and Robert Schneider sites (Figures 56C, 56D, and 56E). This configuration is defined by a pair of closely spaced buildings with several exterior pits clustered near the outside walls. The spacing of the exterior pits is notably different from that of the Type SA configuration described above and from that of the Lohmann phase households. Tools were found in all but one of the buildings, in most of the interior pits, and in many of the exterior pits.

The Type SC household arrangement has a single structure with one exterior pit nearby. The only two examples are from the Julien and Robert Schneider sites (Figures 56F and 56G). There were twelve tools and a small amount of exotics associated with the Robert Schneider site building, including two medium-size pits, and very few remains in the exterior pit. At the Julien site, a single tool was found in the building, which lacked substantial-size pits, and the exterior pit had relatively sparse debris. Each household had an isolated pit (not illustrated) some fifteen to twenty meters away from the building. At the Robert Schneider site, the distant pit contained no material; at the Julien site the distant pit had been disturbed by a later building, but it contained seven tools and a trace of exotic materials. It may be that these settlements were of limited purpose or duration; few pits were dug and scant debris accumulated in exterior pits.

Among the Stirling phase households, there were only two that did not readily conform to one of the three patterns. One such exception is a household at the Turner-DeMange site (Tables 24 and 25, TUR-6, not illustrated) that does not fit a pattern. At this household, two widely spaced buildings were oriented at right angles to one another. A single large shallow pit approximately fifteen meters away was comparable in shape and debris contents to the large pits of the Type SA household arrangement; it had high concentrations of limestone and two tools. Another exception is a group of exterior pits at the

Julien site that was not associated with a building (Tables 24 and 25, JUL-5, not illustrated) and therefore could not be assigned to any defined household.

For each of the household patterns, a standard number of buildings was consistently matched with a particular arrangement of exterior pits, confirming that the overall configurations were not merely coincidental. Also, the Type SA household configuration (Figures 56A and 56B) included small outdoor work zones with pit facilities arranged around their periphery in a pattern similar to that of the Lohmann phase.

Even though such regularities confirm that the household patterns are prehistoric designs and not artificial constructs of the analysis, household types did not consistently incorporate specific building types. In this way, the building types seem to have been independent of the standard household configurations. Perhaps the two organizational realms of building and household were related to different prehistoric systems. For example, architectural styles may have been aesthetic expressions while household configurations were economic arrangements, or vice versa.

No striking patterns were apparent for the distribution of ceramic, chert, rough rock, or limestone debris among the various-size interior or exterior pits. Tools were widely distributed among the pits and house basins in any household, but exotics were rare and present in only a few features or in limited quantities. Only one household, the Robert Schneider site Type SB cluster, had widely distributed exotic debris, but even here the largest quantities were found in a single house basin (49 g) and a single pit (27 g) within it. The sparse distribution of exotic debris among ordinary households, however, contrasts importantly with that distributed among the nodal points described in the discussion that follows.

There were two examples of Stirling phase civic-ceremonial nodes—one at the Range site and one at the Julien site (Figures 57A and 57B). Each was situated on the highest point of local topography, where pit and structure superposition indicated several stages of construction and rebuilding (Figures 57A and 57B show maximal configurations). Each may have had three or four rectangular and one or more circular buildings in use simultaneously. Small open areas partially enclosed by buildings may have served as courtyards.

The Range site node (Figure 57A) had many tools and exotic debris items distributed widely among the structure basins and pits (Table 25). There were also extraordinarily high amounts of limestone in many of the features. It seems likely that limestone was redeposited from earlier contexts and represents centuries of accumulation. The Range site nodal component was preceded by a Lohmann phase household, with which it appears to have been linked by continuous occupation. Some of the tools and exotic debris might have been redeposited from earlier centuries, but many were characteristic or diagnostic of the Mississippian tradition. There was no cluster of exterior pits here, but this seems to be a factor of the site's occupational history, which may have obscured the nature of some of the Mississippian pits.

The Julien site nodal point (Figure 57B) was isolated from intense previous occupation and included a dense cluster of exterior pits in its central area. Tools and exotic debris were only slightly less abundant than at the Range site, which may be a factor of their different occupational histories (Table 25). Limestone was much less abundánt, since there was no immediate natural source. Although this nodal point had only a single Type MC1 circular building, it also had a smaller Type MC2 structure (not illustrated) that had fallen into disuse during the occupation and then been superimposed by a large rectangular building.

Circular buildings occur only in the Stirling civic-ceremonial nodes, where activities were different than those of other households. The small circular buildings (Type MC2) may have been above-ground storage bins or granaries (Milner 1984a), but the larger ones (Type MC1) were almost surely multifunctional meeting houses and sweatlodges (e.g., Mehrer 1982a, 1983, 1986a, 1986b).[1]

Two temple/mortuary nodes were found at the BBB Motor site (Figures 57C and 57D; Table 24, BBB-2, and BBB-1). Each had a pair of rectangular buildings with exterior pits and a graveyard nearby. A unique feature interpreted as a "grave house" was associated with one of the burial plots (Emerson and Jackson 1984:215). This structure had a wall trench set into a basin much too small (0.6 m^2) to have sheltered the living. It seems to have been an important facility associated with the mortuary program conducted at the site. In each of the temple complexes, there were several large and medium-size pits but only a few small ones, which were found mainly near the burials. One of the temple buildings (Building 87), which had several interior pits and a posthole foundation, resembles the Emergent Mississippian Type EM3 buildings to such an extent that it appears to be an architectural legacy of those times, perhaps a metaphorical link to the "ancient" origins of ongoing traditions and hence to the ancestors buried nearby. Complete inventories were not available for features at the BBB Motor site, but the list of exotics—including numerous small items, debris, and the intricately carved Birger and Keller figurines—is extraordinary (Emerson and Jackson 1984; Emerson 1982; Prentice 1986).

The salient characteristics of the two temple complexes include burials, a grave house, figurines, abundant exotics, and interior hearths. These two households have been interpreted as temples largely on the basis of their similarities with complexes known from the ethnohistoric Southeast (Emerson and Jackson 1984:341). No other Stirling phase household in the sample had clusters of burials or such fine ritual paraphernalia. Even without burials and ritual items, however, the BBB Motor site feature arrangements would not resemble typical households.

In summary, the Stirling phase households, the most numerous of all the phases, demonstrate the most patterned variety in their composition and arrangement. Following the Stirling phase, the number of households decreases but considerable variety is maintained.

Moorehead Phase Households

There are five Moorehead phase households from two components at the Julien and Turner-DeMange sites. Two relatively complex arrangements at the scenes of intense activity are interpreted as civic-ceremonial nodes; three others are interpreted as ordinary households (Figure 58). The most complex node (Figure 58A; illustrated as a maximal configuration; Table 24, JUL-6) included a pair of rectangular buildings adjacent to a zone of complex superposition involving several structures and numerous pits; there could have been as many as three buildings in use simultaneously. The zone of complex superposition was in the western third of the occupation area, which held one large rectangular building and three or four small ones (Type MR5), plus five large interior pits, three large exterior pits, a medium-size exterior pit, and an exterior hearth; all were superimposed in a sequence of at least five construction episodes. The maximal configuration, as illustrated, includes two large rectangular buildings and one small one, an exterior hearth pit, and numerous other exterior pits ringing a pair of small open areas.

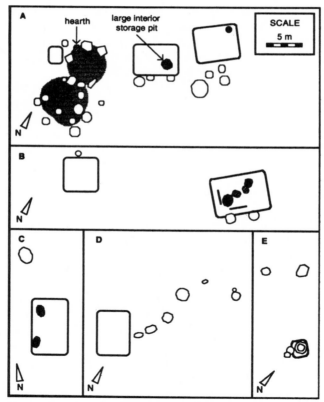

Figure 58. Moorehead phase ordinary and nodal households.

The other nodal household in the Moorehead phase (Figure 58B; Table 24, JUL-7) had only two buildings and four exterior pits. One of these buildings, an extremely large structure (42 m² of floor area), had numerous interior pits and hearths and a pair of interior wall trenches indicating an interior fixture. These two buildings had a total of 140 tools and 54 grams of exotics and other debris. The unique interior configuration of the large building suggests that a wide (approximately 1 m) bench at least partially surrounded the central floor area and prevented pits from being placed near the walls. No postmolds mark the area of the bench on the sides opposite the interior wall trenches. The size and configuration of this building, with its bench, its numerous hearths, pits, and tools, and its exotics, mark the household as the scene of unusual activities. This node was approximately 75 m from the complex Moorehead phase node previously discussed, so there may have been in some way an association. It is unknown, however, whether they were contemporaneous or sequential.

Three other relatively simple households involved only one building at a time and possibly one or more exterior pits (Figures 58C, 58D, and 58E). The building at the Julien site (Figure 58C) had a sequence of two structures that occupied the same basin. A set of nearby Mississippian exterior pits contained no diagnostics and so had no secure phase assignment; these pits are suggested here as possible accompaniments to the building. A building at the Turner-De-Mange site (Figure 58C) had two substantial interior pits containing a total of seven tools and one equally large exterior pit with two tools. This household superimposed a complex series of Stirling phase households, so there is the possibility that Moorehead phase pits without suitable diagnostic materials were assigned to the Stirling phase. This possibility is intriguing, because the set of exterior pits accompanying the rather simple Julien site Moorehead phase household (Figure 58D) lacked sufficiently diagnostic materials, too, but there were no nearby Stirling features from which Stirling phase diagnostics could have been redeposited. It appears that families at both of these two simple Moorehead phase households may have discarded relatively few diagnostic artifacts into exterior pits.

A final unusual Moorehead phase household (Figure 58E) consisted of a single, very small rectangular basin with a substantially deep circular wall trench at its base and two superimposed exterior pits adjacent to it. A few other nearby exterior pits of undetermined phase were in the context of a Stirling phase household. The nature of these Moorehead phase features is unclear since there appears to be no associated domicile. This structure could have been a special facility, perhaps a granary for one of the households a short distance away.

The Moorehead phase households had considerable variety, even though there are only five of them. They range from multistructure complexes to a set of features that barely qualifies as a household, but there are two main patterns. The first pattern shows evidence of continuing, complex, pit-related activities, either outside or inside buildings. Exterior pits ring small clear areas as in earlier phases, and dense accumulations of tools and exotics associated with unusual buildings recall similar combinations from the Stirling phase nodal points. The second pattern is relatively simple, involving single structures with few exterior pits. The very small building (Figure 58E) with its circular wall trench is an enigma.

The two complex households are interpreted here as civic-ceremonial nodes similar to those of the Stirling phase. The architecture has changed, but the complex series of rebuilding in the first household and the large, elaborate building in the second are more similar to Stirling phase nodes than they are to the other Moorehead phase households. These nodes also have more floor area, interior storage capacity, tools, and exotic items than ordinary households (Tables 24 and 25).

Sand Prairie Phase Households

There were only four Sand Prairie phase households in the study sample; three at the Julien site, one at the Florence Street site. Perhaps the most interesting of these households is the one at the Florence Street site, where a pair of buildings was accompanied by a mortuary plot (Figure 59B; Table 24, FLO-1). This combination is reminiscent of the Stirling phase component at the BBB Motor site, but the Florence Street site lacked comparable exotic materials or figurines. The graves at the Florence Street site did have a few exotics, though, including fragments of embossed copper, crystal, and galena as well as numerous ceramic vessels, including plates, bottles, effigies, and other ceramic forms. Another interesting complex household is at the Julien site, where a maximum of three buildings could have been in use at one time (Figure 59A; a maximal configuration is illustrated; Table 24, JUL-11). These three buildings bordered a courtyard marked by an outdoor activity area with a few pits. The building with five large deep pits in the floor periphery had been rebuilt once during the Sand Prairie phase (Milner 1984a). This household had numerous tools and abundant exotic debris (Table 25). Two other Sand Prairie phase households were found at the Julien site (Figures 59C and 59D; Table 24, JUL-13 and JUL-12). These were extremely simple; each was a single building without interior features. Only one had exterior pits.

Although the Sand Prairie phase has only a few households, each one is notable for either its simplicity or its complexity. More complex arrangements are seen in the Stirling phase, but it is remarkable that with only four Sand Prairie households, a mortuary complex and a civic-ceremonial nodal point are represented. All four are located along approximately 400 m of high ground, and they may all have been parts of the same local community.

Results of Household Analysis

The household analysis has isolated and defined recurring themes of domestic spatial organization. With regard to domestic themes, nodes are considered

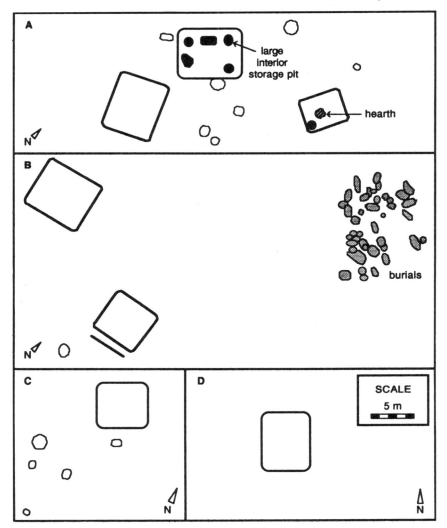

Figure 59.   Sand Prairie phase ordinary and nodal households.

primarily domestic settlements but with overlays of communal functionality. The themes include modes of interhousehold spacing. Note, for example, the contrast between the close spacing of Edelhardt phase households and the relatively isolated Mississippian ones. Outdoor activities also seem to have been organized in several recurrent patterns, the most notable being the small clear areas ringed with pits occasionally arranged in radiating pairs. The number and spacing of buildings and exterior pits per household varied among a few well-defined patterns that were found at several sites.

For example, the building pairs that are tightly clustered with exterior pits (Figures 56C, 56D, and 56E) contrast with the single structures that are accompanied by expansive exterior work areas (Figures 55A, 55B, 55E, 56A, and 56B). Other well-defined patterns are the domestic-scale community centers or nodes that are established in the Stirling phase and that persist thereafter. These nodal points are characterized by community-related facilities such as sweatlodges, meeting houses, and mortuary facilities, by numerous domestic structures, and by the long-term use of house plots demonstrated by repeated episodes of building repair and replacement.

The stability of household locations seems to have increased through time. In several instances, dwelling construction sites were repeatedly reused, resulting in wall foundations that were nested within one another or that overlapped in complex series of superimpositions. It seems clear that precise building spots were established and maintained for long periods and that they were immediately surrounded by yards that were continuously or recurrently used. This has implications for the changing relationship between families and the land they used. Apparently, neighborhoods, as at the Julien site, and even what is the equivalent of house lots within them were permanently established and probably continuously occupied. This seems incompatible with a pattern of periodic abandonment and reoccupation of settlements associated with swidden or slash-and-burn agriculture. Wolforth (1989), however, makes a case for shifting settlement caused by soil depletion. He also points out that nodal households, which tend to have more episodes of building repair and replacement than ordinary households, representing more stable long-term occupation, may not have had to abandon their depleted gardens because they relied on the surplus of their lower-status neighbors.

The results of the household analysis, like those of the building analysis, show chronological trends of rising and falling population and complexity of spatial order. The Stirling phase had the largest number and the most variety of households, but even though subsequent phases had fewer households, they maintained both nodal and ordinary family-size settlements. Household patterns were replicated at several sites, showing that they were planned according to widely shared norms of spatial organization. Patterns recognized in some of the well-defined households helped clarify patterns in other, less well-defined ones that were obscured by prolonged occupation or superposition of other components. Patterns of household organization have been shown to be peculiar to specific phases, and the patterns change from phase to phase in ways that are interpretable in a regional context. These interpretations are discussed in the next section.

Chapter 5

Interpretation
Summary and Settlement Model

The thesis of this work is that the parallel social, economic, and political processes of the rise and fall of complex society during late prehistory in the American Bottom were accompanied by regional settlement trends that involved even the smallest rural habitations. Specifically, socioeconomic developments modified rural status roles or divisions of labor in ways that can be recognized in trends of spatial organization at rural households. The question addressed here has asked, in what manner and to what degree were rural households involved in the regional processes that had such obvious results at the temple-towns? The purpose has been to trace these regional developments as they were experienced at small sites through an examination of facilities and debris. Two assumptions made in the study have been that the archaeological record reflects in a sufficiently useful way the behavior of the people and that their behavior conformed to traditional norms common throughout the region. Three working hypotheses have been that 1) concentrations of features and debris correspond to spatially organized activity areas, 2) distributional patterns can be used to infer models of social interaction, and 3) changes in spatial organization reflect changes in social organization.

The summary that follows includes ethnohistoric comparisons to illustrate the nature of some basic interpretations. Next, a settlement model places the findings in a coherent framework to provide an understanding of the context of Cahokia's changing hinterland farmsteads. The results and model are fitted against recent results of analysis at Cahokia and other sites in the region to demonstrate the wide applicability of the model. Patterned events at small sites are evaluated in terms of indigenous, regional cultural trends because during late prehistory the American Bottom was not subject to overbearing foreign influences.

SUMMARY OF RESULTS

Interpretations of the results of this study are often straightforward and the socioeconomic implications are often clear because the sample represents a substantial portion of the region's small rural settlements. The effects of site formational processes have also been identified and taken into account. Widespread regional patterns are distinguishable from idiosyncratic or site-specific ones.

The results can be interpreted in terms that are applicable elsewhere, but the construction and activity patterns they represent are somewhat peculiar to the region. This is not wholly unexpected, because settlement patterns are known to exhibit both general trends and highly specific regularities. For example, even though cross-cultural similarities of debris discard and site formation have been delineated for certain classes of ethnoarchaeological sites, microsettlement studies have identified archaeological patterns that are correlated to ethnicity.[1]

The analyses have shown that 1) debris is distributed in uneven patterns among the basic feature types; 2) features of different types tend to be arranged differently; 3) buildings conform to several modes of design; 4) households conform to various modes of spatial organization; 5) modes of household spatial organization changed through time; and 6) changes in the rural setting paralleled regional cultural trends. Each of these results is treated individually in the discussion that follows.

Debris Distribution

Two underlying dimensions characterize the results of the debris distribution analyses. One dimension is primarily an aspect of debris discard, the other is primarily an aspect of site formation processes. Concerning the underlying dimension of debris discard, the various feature types had different patterns of debris concentration. Among the basic categories, interior pits tended to have the highest debris densities, exterior pits had somewhat less, and structure basins had the least. These patterns represent debris discard habits—an important aspect of almost any research question regarding prehistoric behavior in terms of artifact or refuse distributions.

Morphological categories of feature types also showed different concentrations of debris. Small and medium-size interior pits tended to have more tools and exotics than expected for their volumes. Small and medium exterior pits also tended to have more tools and exotics than expected, but in addition they tended to have more than their expected amounts of ceramics, chert debris, and rough rocks. One inference from this trend is that small to medium pits received primary refuse from daily activities and were routinely cleaned out; another is that large pits were filled rapidly with soil that was relatively free of artifactual debris. These notions of activity-related debris discard behavior pertain to the way that work is carried out (Binford 1983:144–192, 1987:497–504; South 1977a, 1977b).

The second underlying dimension is that the entire occupational history of a site has an effect on the final distribution of a component's debris and even its composition of features. Debris from previous occupations was redeposited into Mississippian contexts at sites with intense prior occupations. This was especially true for exterior pits and abandoned structure basins. The Range site is an example where diagnostic Emergent Mississippian ceramics were found concentrated in abandoned Mississippian structure basins and exterior pits. Nondiagnostic tools and debris must have been redeposited there also, but there is no way to identify them or to control for their presence. In addition, Mississippian exterior pits lacking Mississippian diagnostics but containing Emergent Mississippian diagnostics may have been relegated to earlier components. Occupational history represents an underlying dimension that is important to research strategies dealing with debris distributions, but it can be unrecognized and unaccounted for (e.g., Prentice 1985; Pauketat 1987).

Distributional patterns can also be interpreted in terms of commonsense habits of debris discard. Indoor-activity refuse appears to have been deposited initially in interior contexts. Much, if not all, of the debris found in interior pits is in primary context in the sense that it was produced by activities carried out within the building. Because buildings were permanent facilities, periodic cleanups of indoor refuse (for example, the cleanup of small, often-used refuse pits) probably resulted in the secondary redeposit of much indoor debris into outdoor surface midden or abandoned exterior pits and structure basins.

Floor-level accumulations of debris in burned structures are rare in the study sample, but they do seem to have patterned floor distributions (e.g., Mehrer 1982a:186–196; Milner 1984a:44–48). Such accumulations of debris, representing snapshots of prehistoric activity, may reflect typical situations or an unknown type of special circumstance. These moments frozen in time are likely to be strongly idiosyncratic. That they represent highly unusual circumstances is supported by the fact that they are so rare. They can best be understood as special cases rather than as especially well-preserved examples of normative patterns. They bear little on our understanding of the more generally available patterns of interior pit accumulations that comprise the bulk of our evidence for indoor behavior.

Outdoor activity refuse was probably deposited primarily at ground level and in the same abandoned pits and house basins that finally received some portion of the indoor refuse. Exterior features, especially abandoned house basins, tended to have relatively sparse accumulations of debris, probably because they were filled rapidly with soil and other bulky material.

"Hut-rings" were reported during the latter part of the last century, before the extensive plowing of some sites (e.g., Thomas 1894:118, 140, 156), indicating that houses were originally ringed by low soil embankments that were probably composed of relatively clean backdirt removed during the original basin excavation. Upon abandonment, much of this dirt must have eroded back into the basins, contributing to the sparseness of their debris assemblages and coincidentally redepositing any refuse from former occupations that had been disturbed by building construction.

Large open holes, such as defunct storage pits, would have been hazards to the safe conduct of daily routines. The dangers of falling in may have prompted their rapid filling. An ethnohistoric account of the Pawnee supports this reasonable interpretation:

> All over the village there were abandoned cache pits, and, although the women tried to throw their old sweepings into them in order to fill them up, they never quite succeeded and from time to time someone that was not very familiar with the particular part of the village fell in. On this occasion as Brave Shield's group [several adult women] was going along they came to an old cache pit and the group separated, walking around it. But Grieves-the-Enemy was so preoccupied with her singing that she fell straight in. She yelled as loud as she could, but everyone was singing so loud that no one could hear her. Finally when the next party came passing that way and the men began to walk around the pit, they heard the old lady yelling and got a ladder so that she could climb out. "I was singing for Brave Shield when I fell in and they never heard me," she said. The men asked her, "Are you hurt?" "No, I just hit my knees," she said. "That's good!" (Weltfish 1977:297).

The Spatial Arrangement of Features

Dissimilar types of pits were arranged differently. Patterns were recognized on the basis of data combined from all the phases. Interior pits were situated according to their morphological and functional characteristics. Hearths were found placed away from the walls and near the center of the floor. Most postholes were found toward the center of the floor, where they probably held auxiliary roof supports and furnishings such as racks, dividers, or platforms. Postholes near the walls may have held makeshift wall buttresses or furniture legs. Morphological categories of large interior pits were focused in peripheral floor locations near the midpoints of the walls and the corners. Categories of medium-size pits were found mostly in the central floor area, but also in corners. Many of the uninterpreted small pits were probably postholes; their location, contents, and size often matched those of recognized postholes.

There were also trends of outdoor feature placement. Exterior pits tended to be placed near buildings and adjacent to walls more often than to corners. Large pits tended to be placed near long walls, but small pits were focused along short walls; medium-size pits were found in both areas. These trends represent patterns that are better understood in the household context, which is addressed in the discussion that follows.

Storage is an important economic function associated with pits, and several aspects of this study relate to it. A pit feature's storage function is difficult to interpret unambiguously, but evidence indicates that there were different kinds of storage facilities, including small caches, large bulk-storage pits, and probably structures used as granaries or storehouses. Pits are emphasized below, but the point is to highlight trends in their distribution and not to "discover" Mississippian storage facilities.

Patterns of large storage pit placement changed through time. For several hundred years before the study period, pits were invariably placed outdoors. Interior storage did not become important until the Stirling phase, when pits of substantial size appear in the larger types of rectangular building. Design elements of rectangular buildings, storage pits were most often placed in a corner or at the midpoint of a wall (Figure 49).

Storage of commodities such as maize and other cultigens was presumably an important aspect of the yearly routine. Experimental replication of storage pits (Reynolds 1974), ethnohistoric accounts (Fletcher and LaFlesche 1972; Weltfish 1977), and archaeological evidence (Milner 1983, 1984a; Strong 1935) reinforce interpretations of storage functionality for certain classes of pit features.

Experimental studies have shown that underground pits can be used successfully to store food and seed grain for extended periods (Reynolds 1974). A desirable combination of traits for a storage pit is a large volume with a relatively small orifice. Cylinder or bell shapes are thus more appropriate than bowl shapes for grain storage. A small orifice seals better with less chance of admitting either water or air. Live grain in storage uses air until none is available, whereupon it goes dormant, prolonging seed fertility. A tight seal is therefore important not only for keeping out rain and pests but also for keeping out air.

Ethnohistoric accounts of large storage pits on the Great Plains detail their use (Weltfish 1977:67–69, 268–271, 297; Fletcher and LaFlesche 1972:98–99). There is mention of the importance of the pit seal both for preservation of the contents and for hiding pits from intruders who might steal their contents. Storage pits on the Great Plains were much larger than any in the American Bottom, but each served several nuclear families in an environment with seasonally limited resources. As previously noted, they were large enough that someone who fell in would need help to get out.

An account of the Pawnee returning from their summer encampment to their earthlodge settlement details storage pit maintenance and use:

> The following morning the South Side family rode up to the lodge, dumped their goods outside, set up the beds, and laid the mats. Then they brought in the

rest of their things, and the house was crowded with parfleches of dry meat, corn, beans, and everything they had gathered. The women talked of storing them in the cache pit. Grandma and Old-Lady-Grieves-the-Enemy told about how they had looked over the pit when they first got home from the hunt and cleared off some mold that had developed on the grass lining and that it was now clean and ready to be filled. After the pit was filled this time, it would not be open until the middle of November when they were ready to go off on the winter hunt. It did not do to open the pit more than once a month at the most. Otherwise, if one opened it often, a storm might come up and water might leak in. In the wintertime there was less danger of this. From time to time one would hear that a certain woman had not put enough earth on the lid of the pit and water had leaked in, with the resulting tragic consequence that all her corn was destroyed—the bags and everything having turned moldy. . . . Two years of hard work and the security it could bring destroyed by one careless oversight. In the Pawnee way of life, vigilance could seldom be relaxed!

The storage pit was built nearby when the earth lodge was constructed. It was an indispensable part of the earthlodge economy. The usual size was about 10 feet deep. It was bell-shaped, with a narrow neck and a round [flat] bottom about 10 feet in diameter. The north side of the pit was for the use of the people who inhabited that side of the earth lodge, and the south side for the South Side families. In the case of an exceptionally important public figure, the household might have two cache pits. The bottom was covered with clean sand and on top of this some sticks as a sort of grating and these covered with grass. The walls were lined with thatch grass fastened in place with sticks that were shored up against it. (Weltfish 1977:267–268)

Mats were also stored in the pit for future use, indicating that nonfood items were also preserved in this way (Weltfish 1977:270).

Such durable items as tools and pots have been recovered archaeologically from a number of pits in contexts that suggest they were stored but never retrieved (for a Central Plains example, see Strong 1935:78, 129, 157). In the present sample there are examples ranging widely in size from both the Julien site and the Turner-DeMange site (Milner 1983, 1984a). Favored locations for small caches were along interior walls. However, large storage pits, presumably designed for the bulk storage of grain, implements, and other commodities, are of interest here because they were economically important to families and to the development of the regional system.

Mississippian houses, residence groups, and storage pits were smaller than those on the Central Plains. Large storage pits at Mississippian sites are numerous, whereas the Central Plains accounts speak of a single cache pit serving a multifamily household. Several Mississippian storage pits seem to have served in the same way that a single, large Central Plains pit did. Also, a limited resource base on the Central Plains may have required extensive commodity storage, while the rich environment of the American Bottom may have required relatively less storage capacity.

The Architectural Patterns of Buildings

In size and complexity Late Woodland buildings represent an early stage in the continuum of architectural change that extended through Emergent Mississippian and Mississippian times. Late Woodland Patrick phase domestic buildings tend to be smaller than their successors, and they rarely have interior pits. Five Edelhardt phase building types owe much to their forerunners in size, shape, and technology, but they have greater variety of interior facilities. Seven Mississippian building types include large and small varieties of both rectangular and circular shapes. Only the large rectangular ones regularly had storage or processing pits, which were often in patterned arrangements. It is easy to imagine that the rectangular floor plans relate to the organization of daily routines. The small varieties of both shapes rarely had any interior facilities, and they seem to represent small storehouses. The relatively large circular buildings, in contrast, seem to have had more specialized or nondomestic functions. They often had central hearths, peripheral benches, and prepared floors but never had any substantial pits. These types of buildings are sometimes interpreted as sweatlodges or hot houses (e.g., Mehrer 1982a; Milner 1984a:33; Pauketat 1991:224–226; Pauketat and Woods 1986; Porter 1974a:70–74; Yerkes 1987).

Early travel accounts from the Southeast mention circular buildings of three types—rotundas, winter lodges, and general purpose dwellings—that were found in different contexts and functioned in different ways. The most striking is the large rotunda, which was often noted as a communal shelter and meeting house (Williams 1930:450–452; Bushnell 1919:69; Swanton 1946:387–389). Smaller circular winter lodges protected householders during cold weather, while other nearby buildings served other domestic needs. In some places a single round house was the only dwelling used.

Households from the early Historic period often incorporated several buildings, each designed for a distinct purpose. The best examples of these buildings come from the Creek Indians (Bartram 1909), although there are others (Swanton 1946:806). The total number of buildings in a household depended on the relative economic situation of the family. The most elaborate layout, for a well-off family, had four buildings: one for a kitchen and winter lodge; a second for a summer lodge and reception hall for visitors; a third for a granary and storehouse; and a fourth for a warehouse for trade goods (Bartram 1909:55–56). Kitchens or winter lodges were sometimes circular (Bartram 1909:56–57; Swanton 1946:400, 401, 403, 410).

The relatively large circular buildings (ca. 3 m diameter) in this analysis appear well-suited to ceremonial and domestic functions. Their small size, compared to the size of rotundas, fits in the domestic context, but their central hearths, benches, prepared floors, and general lack of utilitarian pits indicate that they had specific nonutilitarian functions that were probably analogous to the civic-ceremonial functions of the rotundas and town houses of ethnohistory. Archaeological examples of circular buildings in and around the region are discussed in the next section.

Circular buildings are only one aspect of trends in domestic architecture. Temporal shifts in the nature of rectangular floor plans seem to relate to changing requirements of daily life. The details are enigmatic, but broad trends are clear. For example, the proliferation of interior storage and utility pits during the Stirling phase must reflect some change in domestic economy or society, since interior pit-related activities were not common before. Families may have taken more responsibility for their surplus production if communal storage was declining in popularity. Families may have favored the privacy that interior storage afforded if status relations with their neighbors were changing as part of the increasingly complex social order. The simultaneous proliferation of standard floor plans, apparent in the building types, must also mean that the number and types of common activities or roles for buildings increased, since it seems unlikely that all the various building types functioned in the same ways. Circular buildings have the most obvious indicators of special functionality. Differences between the various types of large rectangular floor plans are not as easy to interpret, but the storage of bulk commodities was absent from some and organized according to several different standards in the others. Some elaboration of social and economic roles is indicated because not all the new building types are strictly utilitarian and not all types are found in each household. Some of the smallest rectangular and circular buildings were probably storehouses or granaries, since they are too small to shelter people comfortably. The larger circular buildings seem unrelated to economic functions. The large rectangular buildings sheltered at least part of the families' stores, some utilitarian activities, and presumably the family itself.

Increasing family size might have been a cause for the trend of increasing building size, but extra living space for larger families need not have been put under a single roof. Social conditions related to complex new demands on domestic life or technological innovations may have stimulated the construction of larger and more various buildings. Indeed, simply the addition of a large, deep interior storage pit to a family's facilities may have created the need for a larger structure.

Changes in architectural styles have been known to accompany changing worldviews. For example, the Georgian architectural style that became popular in New England by 1760 was a material reflection of the change from a medieval to a Renaissance worldview. The spatial arrangement of Georgian architecture is balanced and symmetrical, part of the Age of Reason, while its medievally derived predecessor was not, being "essentially organic" (Deetz 1977:38–43). An architectural pattern must be understood not as the effect of a single cause but as part of a complete material complex and as an expression of complex worldviews (Cunningham 1973:234–235).

An example of an architectural solution to a worldview problem is documented for the Muller Range area in the highlands of New Guinea, where most of the settlements are dispersed households that only occasionally are situated near enough to one another to be considered hamlets (Steensberg 1980:127). Here a household includes at least two buildings a short distance from one another, a "man's house" and a "woman's house." One man, however, decided to build a "joint house" for his wife and himself because a religious leader, a "local indigenous Catholic priest," impressed upon him that a husband and a wife should live under one roof (Steensberg 1980:137). The new joint house had two rooms, a "man's room" and a "woman's room" that had no interior doorway between them. The new building was also centered on the former man's house in such a way that the old hearth could still function in the new man's room. This architectural solution accommodated a new religious notion with longstanding traditions, and it was implemented in reference to the former household arrangement.

There is no mention of other families being similarly pressured, but there is no reason to believe this was an isolated example. The design solution effectively doubled a building's occupancy, its functionality, and its rooms in a way that would be visible archaeologically. In this one instance, a dramatic design shift was made by a single household to accommodate both outside influences and established tradition. Of course, the architectural solution also involved changing the whole organization of the household settlement.

The Spatial Organization of Households

All the strains of variation in feature and debris distribution and building design were brought together in the household analysis. Each phase had widely shared characteristic spatial configurations related to the development of regional society.

Household organizational complexity intensified over time, as did architectural complexity. Simple households were characterized by a few buildings each, and some had planned outdoor activity areas. Higher-order nodal points included mortuary/temple household complexes and households oriented toward civic-ceremonial activities. Mortuary/temple nodes were characterized by burial plots and in one instance by elaborate ritual paraphernalia. Civic-ceremonial nodes, larger than ordinary households, were characterized by abundant exotics and more buildings, some of which were specialized.

The classic example of household composition and variability in the Southeast comes from Bartram (1909:55–56):

> The dwellings of the Upper Creeks consist of little squares, or rather of four dwelling-houses inclosing a square area. . . . Every family, however, has not four of these houses; some have but three, others not more than two, and some but one, according to the circumstances of the individual, or the number of his

family. Those who have four buildings have a particular use for each building. One serves as a cook-room and winter lodging-house, another as a summer lodging-house and hall for receiving visitors, and a third for a granary or provision house, etc. The last is commonly two stories high, and divided into two apartments, transversely, the lower story of one end being a potato house, for keeping such other roots and fruits as require to be kept close, or defended from cold in winter. The chamber over it is the council. At the other end of this building, both upper and lower stories are open on their sides: the lower story serves for a shed for their saddles, pack-saddles, and gears, and the other lumber; where the chief of the family reposes in the hot seasons, and receives his guests, etc. The fourth house (which completes the square) is a skin or ware-house, if the proprietor is a wealthy man, and engaged in trade or traffic, where he keeps his deer-skins, furs, merchandise, etc., and treats his customers. Smaller or less wealthy families make one, two, or three houses serve all their purposes as well as they can.

The Lower Creeks or Seminoles are not so regular or ingenious in their building. . . .

Their private habitations consist generally of two buildings: one a large oblong house, which serves for a cook-room, eating-house, and lodging-rooms, in three apartments under one roof; the other not quite so large, which is situated eight or ten yards distant, one end opposite the principal house. This is two stories high, of the same construction, and serving the same purpose with the granary or provision house of the Upper Creeks.

The Cherokees, too, differ greatly from the Muscogulges, in respect to their buildings. . . .

Their private houses or habitations consist of one large oblong-square log building, divided transversely into several apartments; and a round hot-house stands a little distance off, for winter lodging-house.

Bartram describes different household organizations based on family status and on regional or tribal traditions. Distinct architectural patterns are assigned functionality and standard household layouts are indicated. Although no attempt is made on the basis of this analysis to rank all the households in the study according to the number of buildings they have, it is reasonable to isolate the largest households, which share other distinguishing characteristics, because they are different enought from the others that they indicate their inhabitants' special role in the locality. There is no inference of formal leadership, but there is indication that families in nodal points were more wealthy, more prominent, or more influential than their neighbors.

Temporal Trends of Spatial Organization

Hinterland modes of spatial organization shifted through time in trends of pit arrangement, building design, and household organization. Exterior pit arrangements in the Edelhardt phase were characterized by dense clustering with little obvious patterning. In the Lohmann and Stirling phases, specific patterns of outdoor pits were associated with certain styles of household organization. Subsequently, Moorehead phase and Sand Prairie phase outdoor pits had little patterned variety.

There was an architectural trend ranging from relatively little variation and lack of interior bulk storage in the earlier phases to more variation with abundant interior storage in Stirling phase times and then to considerable variety but less interior storage in later times. Apparently, a rural settlement hierarchy developed with the appearance of nodal households as focal points of dispersed communities.

Small aggregations of households characterize the Edelhardt phase. The households were laid out so close to one another that spatial boundaries between households are not readily distinguishable. Likewise, exterior pits are numerous but appear in no obvious patterned arrangements. Such small groupings of rural families are unknown later in the Mississippian period, when rural households became more isolated on the landscape and exterior activity areas become more clearly defined than before with small work areas surrounded by pits.

The Stirling phase is a time of settlement diversity. Isolated households incorporate interior storage pits and patterns of household organization that are readily distinguishable from those of earlier phases. At this time nodal households emerged as centers for community activities that helped to integrate the local "neighborhoods."

Again, the highlands of New Guinea provide a useful example of the role of the nodal households and their potential for integrating influences. The Grand Valley Dani settlements (Heider 1966, 1979) are commonly laid out as compound clusters, with two to five compounds sharing inner fences and a common outer one. There are in addition a few exceptional single compounds at the edges of these neighborhoods. In this case the compound clusters are not hamlets, because there is no compound cluster leader. The compound is the basic settlement unit, but neither the compound, nor the cluster, nor the neighborhood is a political level. There are only two hierarchical levels in the political system, "confederations," which incorporate a few hundred to one thousand people, and "alliances," which incorporate several thousand people (Heider 1979:62–64). The social system is not stratified and leadership is provided by what is known in the society as Big Men, individuals who have the power to persuade but not to coerce. Indeed, the Dani are so egalitarian that "almost every man can be called *ab goktek* [Big Man]" (Heider 1979:66).

Individuals move from one compound cluster to another as often as every few weeks. Houses and even entire compounds stand empty for up to one or two years. There are many more houses and compounds standing at any given time than are in use. A population estimate based even on standing structures would be in error by about one-half. Furthermore, fences and ditches are for irrigation, drainage, and pigs, not defense. Such settlements would be interpreted differently by an archaeologist, for whom the Dani furnish a cautionary ethnoarchaeological tale (Heider 1966).

The American Bottom Mississippians were not Grand Valley Dani, but even in a hierarchical Mississippian social system the "neighborhood" level of integration, as proposed here for the nodal point households, may have been one of persuasion rather than of coercion. The role of nodal point householder, which seems to have begun during the Stirling phase, was probably not a formal leadership role.

Later, during the Moorehead and Sand Prairie phases, as rural population decreased and temple-towns declined, nodal and nonnodal households were still present. The role of the farm family seems to have changed, though. Interior storage pits were the hallmark of self-sufficient families in earlier phases at the peak of socioeconomic complexity, but at the end of the regional sequence, only nodal settlements had them.

Hinterland Settlements in Regional Context

Trends of rural household organization during late prehistory paralleled those of the temple-towns more closely than previously thought. For example, in the early 1970s, differentiation among isolated farmsteads and hamlets was unknown because of insufficient excavation data. These types of settlements were thought to have dwindled in number as the mound centers grew in size in a process of population nucleation (Fowler 1974; Fowler and Hall 1978:564; Harn 1971).

It is clear now that as the mound centers were evolving, so were backwoods settlements. Dispersed rural communities occupying prime ground along waterways came to be focused in some ways on a few households that served integrative community functions. Household spatial organization developed general standards of activity area configuration. Domestic architecture in the hinterlands diversified to fit several design standards appropriate to specific household roles.

During the Mississippian period, a number of building spots were consistently reused, with buildings reconstructed or replaced within precise limits. Some of these building spots were stable from one phase to the next. This is evidence for a degree of settlement stability unknown in previous times. If family rights to the land had become more stable during this time, there may be a relationship between this stable form of settlement and the appearance of private storage and the dispersal of families over the countryside. The underlying dimension of these trends may be increasing rural sedentism in association with the increasing sedentism seemingly apparent in the large towns.

A new niche in the regional system was filled by the rural households of the Stirling phase. Their distinctive characteristic is their relative independence from communal economic affairs that their spatial organization depicts. A fair estimate of their relative independence in the regional context might be comparable to the example of the Atoni of Indonesian Timor (Cunningham 1973:205):

> The house . . . is the residential, economic, and ritual unit at the base of Atoni society. It is inhabited mainly by an elementary family, which eats and sleeps there, and guests are entertained in the house. There are no communal houses for lineages or hamlets. Grain from the fields of a household is smoked on racks over the hearth and stored in the attic. There are no communal granaries for local lineages or hamlets, and there is a minimum of economic cooperation between households. There is, however, obligatory participation in life-cycle activities and ritual for agnates, affines, and hamlet-mates, and a general agreement on the value of aid within the hamlet in the time of need.

In the American Bottom evidence for private family storage is abundant. Although there seems to have been communal storage, there is no evidence in the region for rural communal dwellings, although there are small-scale communal ritual shelters. The families at this time appear to be well integrated with one another socially and economically, though they are substantially independent.

Toward the end of the Mississippian period, much settlement variety and complexity was lost in the hinterlands, but the two-tiered hierarchy persisted. The picture of rural life in the region is less clear than that for earlier phases because of population depletion. It is clear, however, that the organization of rural life during these final stages did not simply revert to that of pre-Mississippian times.

REGIONAL SYNTHETIC MODEL

This section synthesizes the results of analysis in a model that develops the implications of household roles in an integrated regional settlement system. The study sample includes only sites at the lowest levels of a multitiered site hierarchy ranging from large multimound towns to relatively isolated single-family dwellings. The model is based on the study sample, so it is most applicable to the American Bottom where numerous late prehistoric habitations formed a settlement system that was apparently bounded at least in some tenuous ways by the limits of the floodplain environment (Milner 1986:235) because the lay of the land and the natural resources of the uplands are quite different from those of the floodplain (Woods 1986).

The following discussion emphasizes the archaeological data in a regional context of time, relative social power, centralization, coordination, and settlement pattern. The chronological axis in the diagram (Figure 60) is based on recent revisions of the regional chronology (Kelly 1990a, 1990b; Kelly et al.

1984a, 1984b; Milner et al. 1984) from the beginning of the Late Woodland Patrick phase through the Mississippian period. The vertical axis of the diagram is an approximate scale of relative social power as reflected by settlement patterns. An assumption is that the social rank of a site is related to its size, which indicates in a general way its relative degree of control over resources. This should not be confused with a hierarchy of sites with relative control over one another; although possible, it is not inevitable that many variously sized settlements will have control over one another in direct proportion to their relative sizes. Sketches of community plans for the earliest phases, which were not included in the analysis, illustrate the history of settlement patterns prior to the time under study. Branching lines trace the diversification of settlement types as they rise, bifurcate, and fall through time, representing trends of social power for the ranked settlement levels.

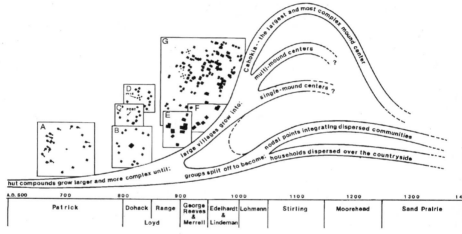

Figure 60.   Chronological trends of settlement pattern and social power.

The highest level of settlement complexity in the region grew from small conglomerates of families in the Late Woodland period to the formalized layouts of the Emergent Mississippian hut compounds, then to the large town-and-mound centers of the Mississippian period (Figure 60). Beneath the highest level at each stage of development, there were hierarchical sublevels. Topics for the discussion of chronological units include settlement hierarchy, community planning, household organization, domestic architecture, private storage, and their implications for relative social power.

Late Woodland Predecessors

There was an ongoing process of settlement nucleation and intensification during the Late Woodland period (Kelly 1990a; Kelly et al. 1984a, 1987). By

Patrick phase times, buildings were semisubterranean pit houses occasionally laid out with some degree of formal planning (Figure 60A; Range site). Buildings were smaller and more numerous than before, often with a "ramp" extension of their rectangular basins, which gave them a characteristic keyhole shape known elsewhere in the Midwest (e.g., Binford et al. 1970; Wagner 1986). Basins dug to make subterranean floors and sturdy walls with many posts represent a new high level of labor and material investment. Superpositioning of structures and pits indicates a prolonged occupation with continued investment of labor and materials. These settlements were not temporary; they demonstrate the continuity of a large corporate social group, such as a lineage, and its dedication to a permanent residential district. There were three types of buildings for the Patrick phase, all with posthole foundations. Two were semisubterranean pit houses, one keyhole shaped and the other rectangular. A third type was a large posthole construction without a subterranean floor. A Fish Lake site example, interpreted as a ceremonial building, accompanied several keyhole structures in a community plan that was not completely revealed by excavation (Fortier et al. 1984b). Similar buildings at the Range site are interpreted as communal structures or men's houses (Kelly 1990a:74; Kelly et al. 1987:178, 423). Furthermore, private interior storage pits are unknown. Interior features of any sort are extremely rare among all the buildings except for the large rectangular communal ones, where there were a few substantial pits of unknown function (Kelly et al. 1987:176–178; Fortier et al. 1984:38–43).

Various Patrick phase pit and structure configurations at the Range site are interpreted as single or multiple-family homesteads, hamlets, or large multi-family villages. An important aspect of the village is an open area encompassed by the dwellings, representing some type of communal space (Kelly et al. 1987:213). The two largest known villages had a maximum of twelve and thirty families each (Kelly et al. 1987:425). Patrick phase villages were less formally planned than their Emergent Mississippian successors. They were prototypes for a plan of village life that would eventually develop into a multitiered settlement hierarchy.

Patrick phase villages seem to mark the beginning of permanent, communal settlement in the region, because there have been no earlier hut compound layouts discovered there. It seems probable that in such a settlement several families coordinated with one another on a relatively egalitarian basis, with no one person or family having a great deal more social power than another. Subsistence emphasized native domesticated plants. Maize was present but not of primary economic importance. The social structure may be interpreted on the basis of the settlement layout as an acephalous local group (Johnson and Earle 1987). There would have been little social control in the form of central leadership. Community members would have granted social power to one another reciprocally. Kelly (1990a, 1990b) interprets the Range site Patrick phase community in terms of household clusters and a possible moiety division. The compound occupants make a relatively large corporate group, such as a lineage, that was relatively sedentary and permanent on the landscape. Such a group may have had a headman who influenced the course of events in the community, but the group probably split up seasonally and at other times because of disputes.

Emergent Mississippian Period

During the Emergent Mississippian period, community plans developed with increasing complexity into a rather formal hut compound arrangement (Kelly 1990a, 1990b). The Dohack (A.D. 800–850) and Range (A.D. 850–900) phase hut compounds (Figures 60B, 60C, 60D; Range site) often had several groups of buildings arranged evenly around a courtyard and centered on communal facilities, either four storage pits and a central pole or a large building (Kelly et al. 1984b).

Later, during the George Reeves and Merrell phases and the Lindeman and Edelhardt phases, an existing settlement hierarchy is apparent (Figures 60E, Robinson's Lake site; 60F, George Reeves site; 60G, Range site). The simple hut compound formula was no longer suitable; some villages were too large and others were too small. Consequently, the largest ones—for example, the Lindeman component of the Range site (Figure 60G; Kelly et al. 1984b:149, Figure 43; Kelly 1990a:104–105, Figure 42)—were complexly organized nucleated villages with multiple courtyards. The smallest ones, including those at the George Reeves, Robinson's Lake (Figures 60E and 60F), and Marcus sites, needed little formal planning (Emerson and Jackson 1987; McElrath and Finney 1987; Milner 1984b).

Subsistence was a key factor in regional developments. The addition of maize to an already flourishing agricultural complex was an important new source of energy flowing into regional systems at this time. Extra energy requires more complex organization to control its production, distribution, and consumption (Adams 1975, 1977). Population growth, settlement complexity, and a broadening agricultural resource base are important characteristics of the Emergent Mississippian period. Small settlements probably represent the process of community fissioning, in which a few families split from a village and relocate. The evidence for population increase during this period is clear at the Range site, for example, and regional estimates have been made (Kelly 1992:187–189).

The Emergent Mississippian trend from simple hut compounds to complex villages signifies a shift in the underlying character of socioeconomic institutions. The hut compound represents a group of families affiliated with one another as a small centralized group where real power or authority is lacking. The communal storage facilities that marked the centers of the courtyards indicate that food production, storage, and probably consumption was to some extent a communal affair. Flannery (1972:48) discusses the political situation of hut compound settlements:

With respect to intensification of production, however, compounds come off more poorly than villages, for the compound is a real commune in which, as we have seen, storage facilities are shared openly, and there is no reward for intensification. Indeed, the reverse is often true: among Bohannan's Tiv, for example, the compound head prevents profit-taking by anyone wanting to plant more yams than he needs, or so many that his own planting and harvesting would prevent him from participation in communal labour for the compound. Disparities of land, wealth, and material goods between members of a compound are almost non-existent, and there are social institutions which prevent them from arising.

Flannery also considers that the relatively small size of hut compound settlements is a reflection not of agricultural potential but of political weakness (Flannery 1972:47–48); among the Tiv the average number of individuals per hut compound is about twenty (Bohannan 1954:61). Each building in a hut compound does not serve a whole nuclear family, as demonstrated by David (1971) for the Fulani. Often a hut shelters only one man or woman and perhaps some children; serves as a visitor's lodge, storehouse, or meeting house; or provides some other use. This notion of multibuilding families is suitable where structures are as small as the Late Woodland and Emergent Mississippian ones.

Early in the Emergent Mississippian period, hut compounds were smaller in total area than their Late Woodland Patrick phase predecessors. The central courtyards were more well-defined by the regular placement of houses around the periphery. As Kelly (1990a,1990b) points out, the Emergent Mississippian hut compound layouts had areas devoted to specific purposes. At the center of the courtyard there was almost always some sort of communal complex, either a large building or a set of four large, deep storage pits flanking a central pole that probably held important community emblems. Sets of earth ovens were occasionally grouped together in a part of the courtyard area. The largest house in the perimeter sometimes had an open area devoid of pits in front of it in the courtyard. This space may have been dedicated to rituals overseen by a leader with some centralized authority who may have lived in the large house. Such rituals have served to integrate the families in the community and reaffirm their collective identity. This type of community plan seems to indicate that the corporate group had a higher degree of centralized social control than previously known in the region. Communal storage indicates a centralized concern for risk management. A strong leader is not necessary to the function of communal storage, but it might be expected that someone in the community, a respected person, could have stepped forward to help settle disputes about the dispersal of communal stores. What is seen here is not the sharing of food by one family with others but the allocation of food to a central coffer and the dispersal made on behalf of the community as a whole. The difference lies in the innovation of weakly centralized power, or the control of the dispersal of food as an energy source. This is the time, early in the Emergent

Mississippian period, that maize quickly became a major staple food. Corn became ubiquitous, occurring in almost every feature. This is important with regard to energy capture and control—control of energy is social power—and there is now a greatly enhanced potential for social power.

Late in the Emergent Mississippian period there was a qualitative and quantitative difference in the types of community layouts (Kelly 1990a, 1990b). During the George Reeves and Lindeman phases there were some of the same elements as in the earlier Dohack and Range phase communities, but there were more of them and there were larger examples. The large, complex villages at the Range site had multiple plazas and several small courtyards with multiple communal storage complexes. There were also multiple large communal buildings to serve the many families of the one hundred-plus domestic structures in the village. These large villages seem to represent agglomerations of smaller groups, such as those represented by the Dohack and Range phase community plans. There is a degree of centralization apparent in such a complex community plan, which indicates the focusing of authority by several small groups on one individual or family. The leadership could have been as tenuous as a headman or a Big Man society (Johnson and Earle 1987) or it could have been as strong as a simple chiefdom. The size of the complex villages does not call for a simple chiefdom, but the political situation twenty to fifty years later, in Mississippian times, may indicate that there were simple chiefdoms in operation late in the Emergent Mississippian period.

Edelhardt Phase

The Edelhardt phase occupation of the BBB Motor site represents a special case of small-scale social organization late in the Emergent Mississippian period that contrasts sharply with the contemporaneous complex villages at the Range site several kilometers to the south. The Edelhardt phase occupation of the BBB Motor site was moderate in size, and, though it was not a hut compound, it was patterned in its arrangement. The layout seems suited to a few affiliated families living apart from others but perhaps tied socially to a village at some distance. Storage pits, though not new to the region, were elements in the development of Emergent Mississippian community plans. They often marked the hubs of hut compounds in early phases when communal storage was central to community life. In the more complex communities of the final phases of this period, storage pits occupied only a few of the multiple courtyards. Communal storage facilities are not evident at smaller settlements, but private ones are, in the form of relatively small interior storage pits and small Type EM5 buildings, which were probably family storehouses.

Domestic architecture evolved smoothly during the Emergent Mississippian period. Edelhardt phase buildings clearly had their roots in earlier traditions, but an important new element for this phase is the patterned arrangement of utility pits within some buildings representing a new kind of permanently assigned activity space. Among these interior facilities, the most interesting single type is a relatively small form of bulk-storage pit that seems to indicate some form of subsistence autonomy for single-family groups. This type of interior facility became much larger and more popular in later times.

Private family storage of bulk food commodities may have been an important outgrowth of a new political economy based on surplus maize production in the context of increasingly large-scale centralization of social power. As centralized goups grew in size to incorporate increasingly larger numbers of families, the daily or yearly routines of individual families would have, of necessity, come under less scrutiny from central leaders who had to manage much larger groups than did leaders who lived one hundred to two hundred years before. Families, such as those at the BBB Motor site, who lived at some distance from nucleated villages, where the leaders presumably resided, might have had to rely on family storage to a greater extent than their counterparts in nucleated villages who could depend on communal storage.

To summarize, trends toward complex social organization are apparent in the new regional settlement hierarchy, in population nucleation, in communal storage, in private storage, and in patterned permanent allocation of domestic activity areas. All of these trends were elaborated even more in the subsequent Mississippian period. During the Emergent Mississippian period there was the development of maize as a newly important economic resource. This addition to the subsistence base was a crucial addition to the amount of energy available from the environment. This created the need or opportunity for more complex social organization to channel the surplus energy.

Mississippian Period

The most salient characteristic of the Mississippian period is the hierarchical settlement pattern with several sizes of town-and-mound complexes and a variety of small sites. This pattern is a logical consequence of prior trends, but it was a dramatic shift. Monumental temple-mound architecture was a new kind of grand-scale public statement at towns where resident populations reached previously unknown sizes and densities. Although large mound sites do sometimes have considerable Emergent Mississippian scatters of surface debris, there are no known cases of Emergent Mississippian mounds (Kelly et al. 1984b:156). Some archaeologists, however, argue that Monks Mound at Cahokia was begun as early as A.D. 900 (Benchley 1974; Reed, Bennett, and Porter 1968; Skele 1987).

A few known sites indicate the variety of large-scale settlements. At this time the Cahokia site flourished as a regional center. The elaborate Mound 72 burials there included elites and retainers, a fact that clearly demonstrates complex society during the Lohmann phase (Fowler 1974, 1975). A well-planned residential district has also been revealed here by recent excavations at the Interpretive Center Tract-II (Collins 1990). The Lohmann site had a single mound. The full extent of the site is unclear because parts of it have been destroyed by modern development. Excavations uncovered a number of buildings peripheral to the main site area (Esarey and Good 1981:152; Esarey and Pauketat 1992). The Lunsford-Pulcher site, with twelve mounds in the southern portion of the study area, may have been one of the temple-towns constructed during the Lohmann phase (Freimuth 1974; Griffin 1977; Griffin and Spaulding 1951). Excavations have been limited at Lunsford-Pulcher, so any chronological assignment of the mound group is tentative. However, a circular structure of the Type MC1 characteristic of the following Stirling phase was uncovered there recently (1976–1977; Kelly 1993).

With the shift from Emergent Mississippian to Mississippian times, the nucleated villages of the Lindeman phase disintegrated, with some families apparently moving to the growing temple-towns and other families dispersing over the landscape to build family-size homesteads. The best example is at the Range site, where George Reeves and Lindeman phase nucleated villages containing well over one hundred structures each (see Figure 60E; Kelly 1990a, 1990b; Kelly et al. 1984b:149) had been abandoned by Lohmann phase times, when the site was reoccupied by four isolated homesteads (Hanenberger and Mehrer, in prep.; Kelly 1990a:106–107; Mehrer 1982a). The abandonment of the Lindeman village and the construction of the Lohmann households must have been closely timed, because the phases are each only fifty years long.

The situation was different away from the floodplain. The Knoebel site (Bareis 1976; Stephens 1993), located in the uplands about fifteen miles east-southeast of Cahokia, maintained an established community pattern during the transition from Emergent Mississippian to Mississippian times. The community had two groups of buildings situated opposite one another across a courtyard marked by a central pole. The plan is reminiscent of hut compounds from early Emergent Mississippian phases in the American Bottom, but the courtyard is not encircled and does not have communal storage pits. Knoebel is clear evidence that American Bottom settlement trends are not identical to those in the adjacent uplands, where natural and social conditions must have been considerably different.

A new high level of regional centralization was achieved, at least within the floodplain, when Mississippian temple-towns coalesced apparently out of the combined populations of abandoned Emergent Mississippian complex villages. This seems to demonstrate a new powerful centralizing force that extended throughout the floodplain and influenced many villages. At present it is impossible to know whether the centralizing force had multiple "centers" simultaneously represented by the several temple-towns in the American Bottom or if it had a single center represented by the Cahokia site.

Lohmann Phase

Early in the Mississippian period the settlement hierarchy developed rapidly until there were mound centers and dispersed communities of isolated farmsteads (Fowler 1974). So far there are no nucleated nonmound Mississippian villages known in the American Bottom such as there are in nearby regions (e.g., Price and Griffin 1979). There is also no evidence for a type of community organization intermediate in level between the new temple-towns and the isolated households, such as will be seen for the succeeding Stirling phase. This was probably a time of accelerating population growth; it was certainly a period of continuing population nucleation.

Regional centralization of power at temple-towns proceeded at the expense of village-level organization. This trend is apparent in the nucleation of temple-towns, the absence of small rural villages, and the isolation of individual farmsteads. As during the preceding Edelhardt and Lindeman phases, there were two basic settlement types, both exaggerated versions of earlier ones. Large sites had monumental public earthworks, and small sites were even more isolated on the landscape than before. For example, the two Lohmann households at the Carbon Dioxide site are spaced more widely apart than the three crowded Edelhardt households at the BBB Motor site. The Dohack phase component of the Dohack site (Stahl 1985:166) and the Merrell component of the Radic site (McElrath et al. 1987:25) are other less-isolated examples of small Emergent Mississippian settlements for comparison.

Lohmann does not represent a smooth transition from Edelhardt to Stirling phase times, and in many ways the isolated Lohmann phase farmsteads are a distinct break from the patterns of preceding phases. At small Lohmann phase sites, the buildings were larger, the households were more isolated, and the outdoor activity areas were more clearly delineated than in earlier phases. Some outdoor activity areas were made up of small rings of exterior pits flanking open spaces. There are no small Lohmann phase storage-type buildings, such as those noted for the Edelhardt phase.

The patterned allocation of interior space to pits, as seen in the Edelhardt phase at the BBB Motor site, seems to have been lost in the Lohmann phase, when the patterning of exterior pits becomes characteristic. However, the earliest evidence for hierarchical order among isolated households may be at the Range site, where a Lohmann household was occupied continuously into the Stirling phase, when it developed into a nodal point.

The Olszewski Borrow Pit site (Hanenberger 1986:46–53) compares favorably with the analyzed Lohmann components. The main building there lacked substantial storage features, although it did have a large, deep posthole interpreted as a wooden mortar foundation. The Olszewski component is noted specifically as being similar to the Carbon Dioxide component (Hanenberger 1986:53), even in the fact that a single large, deep exterior pit contained considerable amounts of debris, which is a common element of Lohmann phase households.

A dimension of social power underlies the transition from Emergent Mississippian settlement patterns to Mississippian ones, when intermediate-size villages were lost as people moved either to large temple-towns or to isolated households. This trend toward both larger and smaller settlements indicates a polarization of social power as temple-towns became regional social centers and isolated families gained additional autonomy. While social elites assumed control over regional and temple-town matters, village affairs degenerated into household affairs. That is, as temple-town authority waxed, village authority waned, and considerable autonomy was left to those living in the hinterlands, who were dispersed over the landscape. This autonomy is understood here in terms of the ways that families would have gained increasingly direct control over their domestic affairs simply by virtue of their new isolation. That is, they seem to have no longer been under the direct and constant observation of a village leader or chief as was the case for families in the complex villages of Emergent Mississippian times. Isolated Lohmann phase households probably coordinated with one another on a relatively egalitarian basis even though they were each under the centralizing influence of the nearest temple-town. In this way it is clear that the dispersed communities of Lohmann times lacked centralized leadership, at least until the transition to Stirling phase times.

Stirling Phase

The shift from the Lohmann phase to the Stirling phase brought increasingly complex social power to both temple-towns and households. Evidence for this is seen in a three-part ranking of temple-towns according to size and number of mounds (Fowler 1974). Cahokia is unique, with over 120 mounds covering at least 10 square kilometers. Medium-size multimound centers include the St. Louis group, the East St. Louis or Metro East group, the Mitchell site, and the Lunsford-Pulcher site. There were also single-mound centers, such as the Lohmann site, as well as diversity among isolated households, as will be discussed below.

Population estimates have been made for the Lohmann through Sand Prairie phases (Milner 1986) based on the number of buildings for each phase, the number of persons estimated per structure, and the duration of the phases. A growth estimate for the Lohmann to Stirling phase shift was 104%, according to a simple building count, but 153% if the number of family members is assumed to have increased with building size (Milner 1986:232–233).

The Lohmann to Stirling phase transition at the Range site is characterized by continuous occupation, and a precise distinction between the phases at Range cannot be made. The ongoing processes of building and household repair, replacement, and enhancement show trends typical of the region for building size, shape, floor plan, and construction technique, but the trends are out of step with one another as they move gradually from early patterns toward later ones. This should not be unexpected for the brief transition from one phase to another during continuous occupation. The Lohmann component foreshadows the Stirling phase node in its unusual arrangement, structure rebuilding, and topographical situation. This supports the notion that social distinctions among isolated households began late during the Lohmann phase.

As isolated households emerged as basic settlement units in a dispersed community plan, they developed private storage facilities, maintained relatively isolated positions on the landscape, and developed a hierarchy among themselves based on the civic and mortuary ceremonialism that helped to integrate them as a community. These trends reach their apex in the Stirling phase.

Stirling phase farmsteads are the most complex in this study. A new type of nodal household with communal facilities served the ritual needs of nearby families. These nodal points represent a new level of dispersed community integration that was missing during the Lohmann phase, intermediate between the level of temple-town organization and that of isolated households.[2]

Daily life for the isolated farm families would have been relatively free of the authoritative notions of regional elites, more so than daily life for town dwellers. Regional elites must have had a considerable effect on the religious, economic, and social climate of the dispersed communities, but many daily matters at isolated farmsteads were probably not closely regulated. Likewise, a community leader of dispersed rural families must have had limited control over family affairs.

The Stirling phase is marked by an abundance of private storage for most of the isolated households and by the great diversity of building and household types. This degree of diversity in architecture and household organization matches the well-known diversity of other aspects of material culture (for example, ceramic and lithic styles) and the complex social hierarchy. Abundant private storage facilities for households indicate a substantial degree of potential autonomy over domestic subsistence matters and a need for privacy. In a discussion of the "visibility of surplus consumables and relations of inequality," Root (1984:150–152), dealing mainly with egalitarian societies, notes that although all societies produce surpluses, the visibility of a surplus depends on the regularity of its production and the disposition of its storage. The morphology and arrangement of storage facilities have implications for the ways that social inequalities are masked. The difference between private family storage and communal village storage implies different social scales for coordinating production and concealing inequalities in production. In another sense more appropriate to the present problem, differences of material wealth or well-being between individuals within families are obscured by pooling the family's resources; differences between families are obscured by private family storage (Root 1984:149). Flannery (1972) notes that village life, as opposed to life in hut compounds, is the beginning of the family-based economic unit, because private storage indicates a substantial degree of economic autonomy. This notion is extended here to families living in dispersed rural communities scattered between the temple-towns. Nodal households demonstrate that social power in dispersed communities was at least weakly centralized. Private storage and dispersed community plans indicate each family's direct control of its productive potential.

The purely economic aspects of household storage are relevant to the notion that redistribution of food was important in the regional socioeconomic system. If there was a coordinated system of food tribute and redistribution, it seems that households at the lowest order of settlement were prepared to store their own commodities. Of course, exterior storage pits were a long-standing tradition by Stirling times, and their use continued. Exterior communal storage is not as readily evident during Mississippian times, but above-ground granaries, which are not readily visible to the archaeologist, probably played the role at temple-towns that large, deep pits once did in the centers of Emergent Mississippian villages. Indeed, the small circular Type MC2 buildings in this analysis and at other sites have been interpreted as granaries (Milner 1984a).

The added element of privacy demonstrated by interior storage pits is interesting. A need for privacy may have been associated with the rapidly increasing social hierarchy. The new hierarchical social system was developing in the context of an ancient tradition of relative egalitarianism, as implied by the settlements of the Emergent Mississippian period. The daily realities of a rapidly emerging social hierarchy might have been at odds with people's understanding of traditionally more egalitarian social and economic roles. Clearly even isolated farm dwellers had access to exotic goods and elaborate cult items, although these were concentrated at the nodal points of the dispersed communities. Independent accumulation of wealth may have been a somewhat covert process for most householders.

Small Stirling phase sites from the region that were not included in the analysis often resembled those included in the analysis. Lab Woofie (11-S-346) was an unplowed Stirling phase site with two buildings and twenty-four exterior pits on the steep bluff slope overlooking the American Bottom floodplain to the west (Prentice and Mehrer 1981). The buildings were similar to Types MR1 and MR3 and were arranged with exterior pits in a pattern resembling Stirling homestead Type A, but with two structures instead of one. Twelve of the twenty-four pits and probably one of the buildings at this site would have been destroyed without a trace by a 30-cm plowzone. Deep pits that would have survived such a plowzone were peripheral to a short wall of a building, where five pits form a ring around a small clear area.

At the Olszewski Borrow Pit site (11-S-465; Hanenberger 1986), a Stirling phase structure with two large storage pits fits none of the defined architectural patterns. It does, however, reemphasize the importance of interior storage pits during Stirling times. The Olszewski site also had a Type MR1 building that lacked storage pits and a small (6.78 m²) square MR5-type structure.

The Bluff Shadow site (11-Mo-562; Hargrave 1982) had an architectural feature that included one structure and an associated exterior wall trench in an unusual configuration, which suggested a rectangular wall-trench basin structure with an attached room at ground-level. This case points out the considerable range of architectural possibilities available to rural householders, who most often built within a rather narrow range of variation.

Buildings at a number of sites conform to the types defined in the building analysis. The Labras Lake site (Yerkes 1987:85) had Types MR2 and MR3 rectangular buildings that were very similar to those of the nearby (3.5 km) Range site (Mehrer 1982a). Labras Lake also had two small circular buildings that closely resemble the type MC2, but their foundations were not as substantial as those at the Julien site.

A central cluster of features at the Labras Lake site seems to be a nodal point; it had five rectangular buildings and two small circular Type MC2 buildings (Yerkes 1987:86). Four of the rectangular buildings were Type MR2 structures and one was Type MR4. One of the MR2 structures was a precisely located replacement of an earlier one, an example of the structure superposition characteristic of the nodal points at the Range and Julien sites. There were also a number of "storage/refuse" pits (Yerkes 1987:84–94). Two other structures are situated peripherally about forty meters away near the limits of excavation.

Yerkes (1987:156–185) uses microwear traces on lithic tools from the Labras Lake site to identify some of the activities associated with several of the structures there. It seems that hide-processing, shell-working, and agriculture-related tasks were unevenly distributed among the buildings. For example, hide and bone/antler scrapers and meat knives were found throughout the site's buildings, but a cluster of three centrally located houses had the only drills and saws at the site. This differential distribution of functional tool types supports the notion that buildings and pits can represent activities and that some activities in these farmsteads were widespread and some were focused in certain areas. It also supports the notion that even these nodal points were primarily subsistence related and not fully specialized social centers.

What is known of the Lily Lake site (Norris 1978) compares favorably with the results of the present analysis. Most of the nine buildings there are Types MR1, MR2, and MR3, as defined in the household analysis, so interior storage facilities are abundant. Superpositioning and differences in foundation type suggest that only four or five of the structures were actually in use at any one time. The Stirling component here may extend beyond the limits of reported excavations (Norris 1978). None of the household patterns defined previously is evident.

Circular buildings, although rare, are hallmarks of the Stirling phase, and they characterize the civic-ceremonial nodes as a new level of social organization that falls between the temple-towns and the isolated households. A brief survey of circular buildings in the Midwest and Southeast yielded fifty-four examples from eighteen sites (Table 26). Building sizes clustered at the 3 m to 5 m (47%) and 6 m to 7.5 m (19.6%) diameter ranges. All but four of those in the 3 m to 5 m range were found in the American Bottom region. One very small (<2.1 m) building at the Powell Tract and another at the Kincaid site were probably granaries or small steam baths such as those at the Julien and Labras Lake sites. None of the ten large (10–18 m) buildings were from the American Bottom. Large, rotunda-scale circular foundations have been uncovered at Cahokia, but documentation of them remains unpublished (e.g., Wittry 1961).

Table 26

Distribution of architectural variables of circular structures.

Site (State)	Diameter	Foundation	Fireplace	Reference
Cahokia (Ill.)				
Sub-Mound 55	5.0	w	c	Smith 1973
Tract 15A	4.0	w	c	Wittry and Vogel 1962
"	3.0	w	-	
Powell Tract	3.0	w	-	O'Brien 1972b
"	3.0	w	-	
"	3.0	w	-	
"	3.0	w	-	
"	2.0	w	-	
Sub-Mound 33	4.0	w	c	Moorehead 1923, 1929
"	3.0	p	c	
Mitchell (Ill.)	7.0	w	?	Porter 1974b
	6.0	w	c	
	3.5	w	c	
	3.5	w	c	
Lunsford-Pulcher (Ill.)	4.1	w	c	Charles Bentz, pers. comm.
Julien (Ill.)	3.5	p	c	Milner 1984a
	2.0	w	-	
	1.0	w	-	
Range (Ill.)	3.0	p	c	Mehrer 1982a
	3.0	p	c	
	2.5	p	c	
Labras Lake (Ill.)	1.9	w	c	Yerkes 1987
	1.7	w	-	
Orendorf (Ill.)	15.2	?	?	Esarey and Conrad 1981
Mansker (Ill.)	3.0	w	c	Piesinger 1972
	3.0	w	c	

Foundation type seems to vary independently of structure size, but all the very small round buildings (<2.1 m) had wall trenches and all the large ones (>15 m) were unknown. Interior furnishings were highly variable, but there were often centrally located fireplaces and no interior pit features of significant size or content. Two of the buildings at the Range site had prepared floors. The only other prepared floors were in the Lunsford-Pulcher site building, the Macon site earthlodge, Cahokia's sub-Mound 55 structure, and probably the Cherry Valley site earthlodge. Benches were not common, but two of the three Range site

Table 26. *Continued.*

Kincaid (Ill.)	1.5	?	?	Cole et al. 1951
	?	?	c	
	?	?	?	
Lambert-St. Louis	4.6	p	–	Blake 1955
Airport (Mo.)	4.6	p	–	
	4.6	p	–	
Crosno (Mo.)	6.5	w	c	Williams 1954
Lilbourn (Mo.)	3.5	w	c	Cottier 1977a, 1977b
	5.0	w	–	
Angel (Ind.)	11.0	w	–	Black 1967
	10.0	w	c	
Cherry Valley (Ark.)	10.0	?	c	Morse and Morse 1983
Hiwassee Island (Tenn.)	14.5	w	c	Lewis and Kneberg 1946
	13.5	p	c	
	10.5	w	c	
	10.5	p	–	
	7.5	p	–	
	6.5	p	c	
	6.0	w	–	
	1.0	w	–	
Town of Chota (Tenn.)	18.0	?	c	Faulkner 197
	7.0	?	c	
	6.0	?	c	
	?	?	c	
Jonathan Creek (Ky.)	6.9	p	–	Webb 1952
	4.8	p	–	
	2.7	p	–	
Macon Plateau (Ga.)	13.0	?	c	Fairbanks 1946

Note: Diameters are in meters; w = wall trench; p = posthole; c = central; – = absent; ? = unknown.

buildings had interior posthole patterns, indicating peripheral benches. The Macon site earthlodge had a molded clay peripheral bench with individual seats, but this unusual building also had an elaborate eagle-shaped platform.

Some elements noted archaeologically were documented ethnohistorically by Adair (Williams 1930), Bartram (1909, 1928), and others cited in Swanton (1946) and Bushnell (1919). While avoiding interpretations based on ethnographic analogies, it is appropriate to compare the ethnohistorical and archaeological examples. Rotundas noted by the early travellers were rather large

(10+ m), and they often had single or multiple central support posts, peripheral benches, and central hearths. They served as meeting houses for local leaders on a regular basis, housed ceremonies on special occasions, and sheltered villagers in extremely cold weather. They were often called hot-houses by visiting Europeans. Little is known historically about the functions of the smaller winter lodges except that they were parts of domestic households.

The sizes of the round archaeological buildings might seem to indicate their function either as large communal rotundas or as small domestic winter lodges. Archaeological data confirm this in a limited sense only. While the larger (8+ m) archaeological examples are likely counterparts to historical rotundas because of their size and amenities, medium-size buildings (6–7 m) at the Hiwassee Island site were clearly part of a civic-ceremonial complex. Likewise, although the small size of the American Bottom circular buildings might seem to indicate domestic functions, they lacked storage or work-related facilities. Their shapes and hearths, however, indicate that they were designed to generate and to retain heat. Each may have served as foul-weather shelter or steam bath as the occasion demanded, but like their larger counterparts, they may have housed some of the rituals and ceremonies that integrated their local communities.

Dispersed communities delineated in the analysis were linear arrangements (cf. Butzer 1982:230–234) paralleling local topography or waterways, which were no doubt transportation and communication routes. Although dispersed, the communities were not amorphous. Rather, they were loose associations of households in the sense that physical proximity is a metaphor for social ties between households. Of course, there may have been many strong ties between households, even though they were separated by a few hundred yards of backwater lakeshore, but the weakness of the community-level power structure is expressed in the dispersal of households and in the composition of the households themselves.

These small communities and households maintained regional and extraregional contacts through exchange networks that furnished them with exotic raw materials and wealth items. Small sites were clearly integral parts of regional and interregional systems. Town and mound complexes, in contrast, were nucleated around temples and therefore seem to have had relatively strong community ties. Social power at mound centers was such that considerable energy was expended there, at least on public projects such as mound building. Whatever the nature of social power operating within the mound centers, it influenced daily life there more than at isolated farms some distance away. Similarly, whatever the level of community concern about everyday matters among the town dwellers, concern about rural dwellers would have been dampened by their remoteness.

Moorehead Phase

Regional population declined during the Moorehead phase. Milner's (1986) Moorehead phase population estimates, based on countryside households, indicates that population decreased to 38% to 40% of the Stirling phase levels. The present study uses a slightly different sample of households than Milner's study, but the decline is readily seen; there was less than one-third (31%) as many Moorehead phase buildings (only 12) as Stirling phase buildings (39); likewise, there was less than one-third (28%) as many Moorehead phase households (5) as Stirling phase ones (18). Moorehead phase buildings tended to be larger than Stirling ones, but even if families were comparably larger, it was not enough to offset the decreasing number of buildings and households (Milner 1986).

The nature of public construction activity also changed with the Moorehead phase, at least at Cahokia. Evidence from excavations on the summit of Monks Mound (Reed, Bennett, and Porter 1968) indicates that although the final earthen stages of the mound had been applied in the Stirling phase, no buildings were ever placed upon them. Moorehead phase activity continued on the first terrace of Monks Mound, however, where ceremonial buildings were constructed and stages of a secondary mound were added (Benchley 1974:70–76, 1975; Walthall and Benchley 1987).

Archaeological evidence at large sites does bear on the model of rural households. Mound center buildings are generally different enough from those of the small sites to show that some building types are characteristic of either temple-towns or isolated households. Many of the common building designs detailed in this study are peculiar to small sites, but other rare types, some of them very large, are found only at mound centers.

Few details on the architecture of Mississippian buildings at the Cahokia site have been published, until recently (i.e., Collins 1990; Pauketat 1991, 1994). In a following section addressing the Cahokia site trajectory, recent results from the Cahokia site are considered in some detail as they relate to the trends evident in the countryside. Collins's and Pauketat's analyses were conducted with the advantage of the currently refined chronology, making them directly comparable to the results in this analysis.

However, at the Powell Tract, twenty-three rectangular buildings have been classified by size and type (O'Brien 1972a). In contrast to the small sites of this study, pits in Powell Tract buildings were relatively rare, and large interior storage-type pits were all but absent. Most buildings ranged in size from 10 m^2 to 35 m^2, which is well within the range of rural household dwellings examined in this study. Four of the Powell Tract buildings were 50 m^2 to 60 m^2 in size and one was 178 m^2—all much larger than the rural houses.

Household configurations comparable to those at rural sites were not identified at the Powell Tract (O'Brien 1972a). The Powell Tract's location in Cahokia, a major civic-ceremonial center, makes comparisons between it and the rural households unproductive. However, it is clear that rural households were not simply conglomerated to form the fabric of the Powell Tract occupation. The spatial configuration of buildings and building types is quite distinct from that of rural settlements, although the structure arrangements at the Powell Tract are not completely clear because of the considerable superimposition of buildings.

The Mitchell site has been interpreted as dating to the early half (A.D. 1150–1200) of the Moorehead phase (Porter 1974b). Major excavations were focused on the mound and plaza area rather than on the residential districts, and the excavated areas were restricted in size, so no discussion of households is possible. Some of the rectangular buildings were similar in size to those of small isolated households, but others were much larger than any at the smaller sites. There were no examples of the building types MR2, MR3, or MR4 that incorporated large interior storage facilities. Interior storage pits at the Mitchell site were very rare. Indeed, there were only two possible cases, and each of these may have been an exterior pit superimposed by a later building.

Although regional population was decreasing, the social system did not collapse abruptly. Considerable variety was maintained among the Moorehead phase buildings and household organizations, even though the top of the regional hierarchy was dwindling (Figure 60). Private storage was still common at isolated households, but circular buildings were absent in the study sample. Even among the five analyzed Moorehead phase households, two appear to be civic-ceremonial nodes: one is characterized by intense rebuilding and superposition; another containing abundant exotics was dominated by an exceptionally large building with peripheral benches and interior pits that seems to have been a meeting house of some sort.

One thoroughly investigated American Bottom site, the Lawrence Primas site (11-Ms-895), was not in this analysis but does support the above interpretation (Pauketat and Woods 1986). Two late Moorehead phase or early Sand Prairie phase buildings were excavated there. One of the buildings was a relatively large (34 m²) rectangular wall-trench construction and the other was a rather small (7.5 m²) oval posthole building. The larger of the two buildings contained a single large interior storage-type pit that had been filled, redug, and partially refilled when the structure burned to the ground. This left a living-floor scatter of tools, debris, and small caches of artifacts that strongly suggest separate male and female work areas at the floor edges, especially in the corners, and a more general activity space in the central floor area focused around a central hearth. This burned structure yielded exotic materials in the form of six galena cubes and a siltstone elbow pipe. Nearby, a smaller posthole building with only an interior hearth depression was interpreted as a sweatlodge (Pauketat and Woods 1986). The sweatlodge and the exotic minerals characterize the Lawrence Primas site as a civic-ceremonial node in the manner of the Stirling phase nodes at the Range and Julien sites, which had circular (Type MC1) buildings and exotics.

The Lawrence Primas site is important for its evidence of presumably sex-role related work areas and agricultural and hunting implements inside the main building. Thus, there is no evidence of full-time craft or ritual specialization at this nodal household.

Although the Moorehead phase appears to have been a time of regional decline in social complexity, the mound centers remained active and rural households retained their dispersed community organization. Interior storage facilities and community nodes persisted in a modified fashion even though rural populations were shrinking.

Sand Prairie Phase

The Sand Prairie phase was a time of accelerating regional decline in population and settlement system. Milner's (1986) estimates indicate a population reduction ranging from 34% to 37% of Moorehead phase levels, or only 13% to 15% of Stirling phase levels. This low population may have made it impossible to maintain the upper levels of the social hierarchy. Evidence seems to indicate that temple-towns may have fallen into disuse. For example, there was little or no construction of ceremonial facilities on Monks Mound at Cahokia, and there was for the first time dense accumulations of refuse and possibly some pit features put there, indicating a domestic occupation by nonelite inhabitants (Benchley 1974:161–172; Walthall and Benchley 1987). At the same time there is evidence that regional integration was breaking down in rural areas. Floodplain mortuaries (Milner 1984c) of the time appear to have been serving smaller, relatively autonomous rural communities, in contrast to the bluff-edge mortuaries of Moorehead phase times that appear to have served larger groups of interrelated communities. This is taken as evidence of societal segmentation associated with the decline of Cahokia's integrating influence in the region.

The number and variety of buildings in this study reaches a final low point in the Sand Prairie phase, but there are still two clearly distinguishable types of isolated household. In a total of only four households, two qualify as nodal points. One node is characterized by three structures, one of which was rebuilt and had numerous interior storage pits with abundant exotics and tools. The other node includes a mortuary area with numerous burials and many grave offerings.

Small Sand Prairie phase settlements that are not in the analysis are rare in the American Bottom. At one such location, the Schlemmer site (11-S-382; Berres 1984; Szuter 1979), there were three Sand Prairie phase structures and a few exterior pits. One of the buildings was T-shaped. Another was small (9.7 m^2), contained very insubstantial foundations, and had a deep (70 cm) interior pit. Except for the T-shaped building, the architectural variety here is similar to that noted for the Sand Prairie phase in the analysis.

Bridges Site Contrasts

Sites beyond the limits of the American Bottom floodplain tend to show more differences from the analyzed sample than do unanalyzed floodplain sites. It seems that the farther away from the American Bottom floodplain they were, the more different they were. One good example of this is the Bridges site, which had considerable time depth and was far from the American Bottom. The Bridges site (Hargrave et al. 1983) is located in Marion County, Illinois, about 95 km from the Mississippi River. Its peculiar community plan is similar to American Bottom Emergent Mississippian hut compounds. A large central courtyard was marked by a central postpit that had been reused several times. The Bridges site chronology, however, is interpreted in such a way that it is not amenable to direct correlation with that of the American Bottom.

The Bridges site buildings were qualitatively and quantitatively different than those of the American Bottom in size, shape, floor plan, and basin remnants; they also frequently superimposed one another. Because interior features were so rare, buildings seldom compared to the types defined for the American Bottom. Possible exceptions were obscured by the confusion of superposition. Buildings tended to be larger and more square than their American Bottom counterparts. However, the Bridges site did have circular buildings very much like those of the Stirling phase. In this way, the Bridges site buildings are qualitatively different from the ones in the study but are valid points of contrast highlighting the regularity of the American Bottom patterns.

The Bridges site buildings tend to be larger than their American Bottom counterparts. Component C has seven very large buildings that range from 43 to 68 m², plus an outlier at 120 m². The smallest Bridges site Component C building (29.7 m²), in addition, is larger than the median area for any other component or phase (see Table 15).

Another distinguishing aspect of the Bridges site can be seen in the debris distribution. Only one building at the Bridges site (Structure 4) had basin remnants; although very shallow, they contained more limestone pieces than any of the structure basins in the study. Another building (Structure 6) had over four times as many rough rocks as any in the study; this unusual structure also would have ranked in the top ten for several other debris categories.

Most of the differences between the Bridges site and the American Bottom sites are related to the organization of the Bridges site itself and, thus, perhaps to its role in its own regional system. Special circumstances of the site, including its compound community plan and its distance from the American Bottom, demonstrate clearly that the well-defined sequences of events in the American Bottom were not present everywhere and show that if processes were similar elsewhere, they were expressed differently.

The Cahokia Trajectory

As previously mentioned, recent results of Cahokia site analyses and reporting have added a new dimension to the possibilities for American Bottom regional synthesis. These results include the works of Collins (1990), Dalan (1989), Fowler (1989, 1991), Holley (1989), Holley et al. (1990), Iseminger et al. (1990), Lopinot (1991), Pauketat (1991, 1993, 1994), Skele (1988), and Yerkes (1991). These works represent two thrusts: first, renewed enthusiasm on the part of Cahokia archaeologists to analyze thoroughly and to report the wealth of information available as the result of previous large-scale excavations; and second, analysis and reporting of results according to current standards in a timely manner by archaeologists taking advantage of new research opportunities. Two works are most relevant to the synthetic model (Mehrer 1988) put forth previously. These are Collins's (1990) report on recent (late 1980s) large-scale excavations at the ICT-II area and Pauketat's (1991, 1994) analysis of previous excavations (late 1960s and 1970s) at Tract 15A, the Dunham Tract, and Kunnemann Mound.

The ICT-II area was part of a prehistoric residential district just to the southeast and outside of Cahokia's central precinct (Collins 1990). It was occupied during the Lohmann, Stirling, and Moorehead phases. Excavations there opened an area of about 5,300 m^2 and recovered 88 structures and 368 other features from 18 households. Tract 15A and the Dunham Tract (or 15A-DT) are west of Cahokia's central precinct (Pauketat 1994). During the Edelhardt and Lohmann phases, 15A-DT was a residential district; during the Stirling phase the residences were cleared off and replaced by a series of woodhenges and a small set of special-purpose buildings; during the Moorehead phase they reverted to residential use. At 15A-DT, excavations opened an area of roughly 14,600 m^2, yielding 247 structures and 524 other features; individual households were not often definable. A small, insignificant Loyd phase occupation preceded the substantial Edelhardt occupation at 15A-DT. The Kunnemann Mound was built during the Stirling phase and so augments our understanding of the ceremonial use of the 15A-DT.

The following discussion helps put Cahokia in the context of the regional synthetic model by comparing and contrasting the recent findings at ICT-II, Tract 15A, and the Dunham Tract with those of this study. Even though the archaeological phases punctuate the continuum of evidence, an underlying assumption is that on a regional basis, and usually on a local basis also, the sequence of occupations represents a continuity of ever-changing community relations. This exercise shows how the trends at Cahokia were complimentary to those in the countryside, each setting comprising essential parts of the regional system and linked to one another by large-scale, long-term trends, but each setting was as distinct as its respective place on the landscape. At ICT-II, where households were discernible, detailed comparisons and contrasts are made between Cahokia and the rural households; at the larger 15A-DT, where households were not readily discernible, important regional trends of community planning and governance are most salient.

The results of both analyses of Cahokia tracts include subphase chronological units based on ceramic, lithic, and superposition data, among other data.

The subphase distinctions of the 15A-DT and ICT-II analyses do not match exactly, although they agree with one another in general trends. The analysis of large, complex, and long-term archaeological occupations, such as those at Cahokia, are difficult, and the complexity often obscures some detail. However, subtle distinctions in the trends of technology or art style can sometimes be expressed confidently as chronological markers if they are lent credibility by the circumstances of direct feature superimposition. Small isolated sites, such as the ones analyzed above, do not often present this opportunity, although they have their own virtues. These useful distinctions discovered at Cahokia will not be applied in detail here; rather, the important short-term trends that they reveal will be highlighted to amplify the details and coherence of the regional model.

Trends in the composition and arrangement of households and communities in Cahokia and in the countryside express how regional complexity was experienced at the lowest levels of social organization. Domestic architectural trends at Cahokia and in the hinterlands were similar throughout the Mississippian period. These include the growth of building size through time, the early adoption of wall-trench foundations, the appearance of interior storage pits during the Stirling phase, and the tendency toward equilateral floor plans during the Moorehead phase. Differences between households at Cahokia and those in the hinterland are apparent in the complexity of their spatial arrangements. Differences in complexity, profound during the Lohmann phase, became less noticeable in Stirling phase times; by Moorehead phase times, there was little distinction between them. The Sand Prairie phase is not represented at Cahokia's 15A-DT or ICT-II, as it is in the countryside.

Edelhardt Phase

Because ICT-II had no Edelhardt component, only Tract 15A can represent Cahokia at that time. The basic unit of Edelhardt community organization consisted of a courtyard group of small posthole structures placed around an open area marked with a central post (Pauketat 1991:218–221, 1994). These compounds resemble those of the Range site (Kelly 1990a; Kelly et al. 1989), as Pauketat points out (1991:221). Building size at Tract 15A, with floor areas averaging about 8.7 m², compares favorably with the ones at the nearby Edelhardt component of the BBB Motor site, where most of the buildings ranged between 5 m² and 12 m² (Figure 52). The BBB Motor site buildings, however, were not arranged in courtyard groups around central posts, even though they were placed in clusters of two, three, or more.

At this time, the Cahokia site is not unlike the Range site, with nuclear or extended families forming the basic coresidential group. Early in the Edelhardt phase, the buildings in Cahokia's courtyard groups were similar in size and shape to one another, but later during the phase, buildings were generally larger, with one markedly larger than the others (Pauketat 1991:248). The whole community at Cahokia was probably much larger in terms of area occupied and total population than the community at the Range site, but the similarities between the two sites serve to establish that this type of settlement was a regional phenomenon, and not peculiar to the Range site, which until recently was the sole well-studied example. The similarities between the two sites also establish a basis for contrast with the regional trends of the following Lohmann phase.

Lohmann Phase

The Lohmann phase is better represented at Cahokia than the Edelhardt phase, because both Tract 15A and ICT-II have components. At Tract 15A, the trends in building construction reinforce long-established regional trends. Posthole foundations are replaced by wall trenches, structures increase in size to average approximately 11 to 12 m². One possible early Lohmann courtyard at Tract 15A was similar in size, composition, arrangement, and placement to the preceding Edelhardt phase examples, which suggests continued occupation by individual corporate groups (Pauketat 1991:221–222, 1994:120–124). Other early Lohmann dwellings were not organized in courtyard groups. Late Lohmann buildings were bimodal in their size distribution, indicating a new level of complexity for household and/or community organization (Pauketat 1991:248). Circular buildings first make their appearance at Tract 15A late in Lohmann phase times. It is also important to remember that Cahokia was probably one of several towns that lured people away from the countryside, where they had lived in Edelhardt phase villages such as the one at the Range site. Therefore, one can conclude that all of Cahokia was not initially settled during Lohmann phase times but was probably one of the most rapidly growing population centers in the region.

For example, the initial settlement of ICT-II was a well-planned Lohmann phase residential neighborhood. The buildings at ICT-II were laid out on a grid similar to Fowler's (1969) Cahokia grid. The buildings were well-spaced and oriented with the cardinal directions. Three households were defined. A large T-shaped structure was the nodal point, or hub of several axes of symmetry, spatially integrating two households—one to the north and one to the south—each having a few domestic features placed in nearly mirror-image symmetry to others beyond the T-shaped structure. Two postpits near the T-shaped structure probably held standard-bearing poles (Collins 1990; Mehrer and Collins 1989). There were above-ground granaries and subsurface storage pits representing both communal and household storage practices. One relatively large storage pit was located inside a building. Such interior storage pits are rare prior to Stirling phase times, when they become familiar elements in household planning.

One of the ICT-II Lohmann phase households is interpreted to represent a mature single family or coresidential group (Collins 1990). It had five buildings around a small courtyard, where there were several hearths and firepits. A pit oven, granary, and sweatlodge were located nearby. This neatly arranged complex of domestic facilities includes more features and greater variety than its countryside counterparts (Mehrer and Collins 1989). Lohmann phase household organization at Cahokia appears to have been more rigidly planned than its Edelhardt phase precursors in the hinterlands and far more complex than its Lohmann phase contemporaries in the hinterlands.

The structured pattern of Lohmann phase households at ICT-II differs considerably from that of Tract 15A. No grid orientation was recognized at Tract 15A, as it was at ICT-II. This may reflect the fact that ICT-II was newly settled and the Tract 15A had already been established as a residential district by previous generations. Perhaps established members of the community who resided in the old part of town were allowed to maintain the neighborhood layout with which they were familiar, while newcomers were obliged to conform to a new plan designed to control community growth.

In contrast to Cahokia, hinterland households had fewer buildings and more pits. Although they were well organized, households in the hinterlands were not arranged in symmetrical patterns. Furthermore, they were isolated, and nodal points were rare or absent. Kelly (1990a:106–107) seems to prefer the interpretation of a nodal point community at the Range site during Lohmann phase times that included one or more circular structures. It is worth noting again that ceramics from Lohmann phase components have only recently been used to define the Lindhorst phase in the southern portion of our study area as an equivalent to the Lohmann phase, which remains useful in the northern portion (Kelly 1990a, 1990b).

Recent discussions of Cahokia (Conrad 1989; Fowler 1991; Yerkes 1991) emphasize the high level of social differentiation that was attained early at Cahokia. The elaborate Mound 72 complex includes the burials of high-status individuals and those of scores of sacrificial retainers who accompanied them to the grave. This dramatic show of social power, especially the control over the life and death of community members, is understood as a clear indication of social stratification. The Mound 72 burials show well that the transition from Edelhardt phase to Lohmann phase times was marked by a good deal of power becoming focused on high-ranking people. The mortuary evidence from Mound 72 and the community plan evidence from Tract 15A and ICT-II complement one another to support the notion of increasing social power being exercised in community planning and in ritual expenditure of valuable resources, including human life.

Stirling Phase

At Cahokia, the Stirling phase is represented strongly at ICT-II and Tract 15A, though in different ways. ICT-II had a well-planned residential neighborhood (Collins 1990), but Tract 15A had been converted from its previous use as a Lohmann phase residential district to a grand plaza that contained "post-circle" monuments, also called "woodhenges" (Pauketat 1991, 1994; Wittry 1964, 1969). Evidence for residential use at Tract 15A is limited to some debris from ceramics used domestically from an exceptionally large wall-trench building (about 12 x 18 m) that flanked the woodhenge plaza (Pauketat 1991:235). This dramatic shift in function of the Tract 15A space from residential to primarily monumental use is another strong indicator that the Cahokia community was being planned. The presence of strong community leaders, such as the individuals buried in Mound 72, suggests that the community plan could well have been directed by the hands of a few high-status figures.

Fundamental changes occurred during the transition from the Lohmann phase to the Stirling phase not only at Tract 15A but also at ICT-II. Both household organization and community plan at ICT-II changed during this time (Collins 1990). Stirling structures were built in the previously unoccupied periphery around the former Lohmann phase households. Houses were no longer arranged in a gridlike pattern; rather, their arrangement appears to have been focused on a small residential mound nearby and on a plaza where the Lohmann phase residences once stood. The center of the plaza was marked by a large postpit that probably held a standard-bearing pole. Flanking the plaza, six Stirling households were spaced at intervals in two rows that appear to radiate from the mound, which was located at one end of the plaza. On top of the mound was a large residential building.

Stirling phase ICT-II households typically had two large wall-trench structures with central hearths and large, deep interior storage pits. Often there were hearths and storage pits outside, too. Nearly all households had a postpit that may have supported a standard-bearing pole. There were also "additions" to structures and detached, three-sided buildings. Stirling phase buildings were built over and over on the original plots, indicating that families, lineages, or corporate groups must have had some long-term rights to individual lots. Household storage at ICT-II took a new form. Small, distinctive structures (<11 m²), often at the edge of a household, may have been family storehouses. Granaries such as those of the ICT-II Lohmann phase community were rare.

Stirling phase households may have had smaller families than their Lohmann phase predecessors because they had fewer buildings occupying less space. However, there were more Stirling phase households, and they apparently shared fewer communal domestic facilities (Collins 1990). Stirling phase families seem to have been organized according to a local neighborhood social hierarchy represented by the residence on the mound rather than by Cahokia-wide central authority represented by the gridlike community plan of Lohmann phase times. If so, the Stirling phase settlement represents a new level of neighborhood autonomy that arose about the time a massive stockade wall was built separating the neighborhood from Cahokia's Central Ceremonial Precinct, where Monks Mound and other large public buildings were located (Collins 1990; Mehrer and Collins 1989).

As the population reached its peak during the Stirling phase, households throughout the region were similarly organized, but communities were not. Locally dispersed communities in the hinterlands were composed of several isolated households without a formal community plan. In contrast, the ICT-II community had several households and a residential mound laid out around a small plaza. The households that made up these different settlements were analogous to one another even though their community plans were not (Mehrer and Collins 1989).

At ICT-II, the Stirling phase plaza and mound complex appears to have usurped the nodal functions of the T-shaped Lohmann phase community building. Nodal households in the hinterlands were the focus of rural community ties. The socially integrative functions of the local mound and plaza at Cahokia's ICT-II and those of the nodal households in the hinterland were correlates at the lower levels of a complex regional social hierarchy. These local communities, nucleated at Cahokia and dispersed in the countryside, represented a new stratum of social organization between the temple-town and family levels. This intermediate level of social power must have reduced the degree of polarization of social power at the highest and lowest levels (Mehrer and Collins 1989).

Moorehead Phase

Once again there was considerable change between phases at Cahokia. At this time at Tract 15A, the woodhenges had been dismantled and a few domestic structures occupied the area (Pauketat 1991:243, 1994:128–130, 138–140). The Moorehead buildings tended to be a bit larger and more equilateral than earlier ones, except for the enormous Stirling phase structure that accompanied the woodhenges. Moorehead buildings were more widely spaced than the clustered courtyard groups of the Lohmann phase. Pauketat (1991:247–248, 1994:140) recognizes in the Moorehead phase occupation evidence of declining complexity in community layout that seems to reflect reduced social complexity. Variations in structure size may be related to domestic function rather than to the different social standings of the families who occupied them; that is, household clusters were probably relatively similar to one another because the families who occupied them were probably of similar social status. There was similarly a break in the occupation of ICT-II between the Stirling and Moorehead phases. The Moorehead phase settlement was different from earlier ones there. The Moorehead phase household at ICT-II had a central group of three buildings placed around a small courtyard with a central hearth. To one side of this group was a fourth, lightly constructed building interpreted as a smokehouse or a hide-processing shelter. At the other side of the central group was an open area for storage, processing, and cooking (Collins 1990).

Placement of the household seems to have been based on local topography rather than on some Cahokia-wide community plan. Even though there were only about 70 cm of vertical topography in the tract, Moorehead phase buildings were found only on the highest spots (Collins 1991). Likewise, Moorehead phase inhabitants throughout the bottomland region preferred slightly higher elevations for their houses (Emerson and Milner 1981; Milner and Emerson 1981), perhaps because of environmental stresses. Several studies have demonstrated environmental stresses in the American Bottom during the Moorehead phase (Brown et al. 1988a, 1988b; Lopinot and Woods 1988). Overexploitation of trees on the floodplain and in the adjacent uplands may have caused increased water runoff that resulted in sediment-clogged floodplain waterways and more bottomland flooding, which may have threatened homes and crops (Mehrer and Collins 1989).

An important change in the Cahokia community plan during the Moorehead phase was that the Central Ceremonial Precinct reverted to residential use (Holley et al. 1988). This and other settlement changes at Cahokia appear to mark a decline in the importance of the centralized authority there as regional population waned. This decline may have been hastened by a redistribution of social power. The highest echelons of the regional social spectrum disappeared as populations dwindled, but local communities persisted in attenuated form. This is significant because it shows that the roles of households did not revert to pre-Mississippian patterns. The level of local-community integration that formed as part of a complex regional hierarchy did not completely dissolve after the regional system disintegrated (Mehrer and Collins 1989).

SYNOPSIS

Sites throughout the American Bottom had buildings and households that conformed to the types defined in this study. A few sites vary beyond the range noted for the analyzed sample, but most resemble the ones in this study and support the interpretations of the results presented here. Long-term trends of settlement change found among the analyzed sites were confirmed in comparisons with other rural households in and around the region as well as with those at nearby mound centers such as the Mitchell, Lunsford-Pulcher, and especially Cahokia sites. Some of the settlement patterns and trends exhibited at sites far away from the American Bottom were dissimilar to those derived from the analysis, indicating that regional patterns in the American Bottom probably reflect not only widespread cultural trends but also special conditions there.

Long-standing interpretations regarding the processes of population nucleation in the American Bottom based on the surface surveys of the 1960s and early 1970s were not confirmed. It has been shown here that as regional population nucleation was taking place at Cahokia and other mound centers, there was another process of population dispersal taking place in the backwater areas of the region. Furthermore, the neighborhoods and small communities that made up the large and small sites in the region were an important and robust element of the dynamic regional hierarchy, surviving the decline of the ceremonial centers without reverting to the pre-Mississippian mode of community organization.

Chapter 6

Conclusion
Changing Lifeways in a Rural Landscape

Seven centuries of Late Woodland and Emergent Mississippian cultural development spawned the American Bottom's regional expression of the Mississippian tradition. Some temporal trends of settlement organization are now clearly evident. Rural settlement was tied to the development of regional complexity in ways that stemmed from changes in the rural settlement hierarchy and division of labor. The process of population nucleation that began during the Late Woodland period continued through the Emergent Mississippian period, when hut compound communities developed into a two-tiered settlement hierarchy with large complex villages and small multifamily hamlets. This simple hierarchy was subsequently accentuated early in the Mississippian period, when the complex villages disintegrated as their constituent families either moved to the new, regionally important temple-towns or dispersed as isolated homesteads over the rural landscape, thereby leaving a gap in the hierarchy of social power at what was formerly the village level. The few mound centers were the regional foci of social integration, but there were apparently no smaller, nonmound nucleated villages such as those of the preceding Emergent Mississippian period to stand hierarchically between the temple-towns and the homesteads. This social and political void was filled in a few decades by the formation of dispersed communities made up of isolated rural families who were integrated by nodal families providing communal services and facilities to their neighbors. This type of dispersed community persisted through the Mississippian period and in an attenuated form even after the regional centers began to fall into disuse as complex regional systems disintegrated and population declined.

An archaeological focus on architecture, household organization, and community planning has proved useful for deriving long-term trends of social, economic, and political complexity. The linkage between built form and sociocultural patterns has been established in recent years on a firm foundation of studies in household archaeology, family life, vernacular architecture, and environmental planning.

Long-term trends of rural settlement emphasize the notion that the evolution of complex society was not simply a matter of growing power becoming concentrated at the highest social levels located in regional centers. There were important concomitant processes at low levels especially in the countryside. While *relative* social power necessarily declined at low levels, *absolute* power actually increased. This increase in absolute social power at low levels came in the form of family-level autonomy gained in rural domestic affairs, which were apparently unimportant to regional elites, and in private matters, such as wealth accumulation, that were kept secret. As a sociopolitical hierarchy increases in complexity, the details of affairs at low levels become increasingly obscure to members at high levels. Such details become unimportant to elites and they become more easily hidden, or kept private, by low-level members (Adams 1975, 1988). This increased degree of social power at the family-level originated initially with the loss of village-level authority, which had been usurped by leaders at the temple-towns, and with the growing isolation of rural families on the landscape. The dispersed communities, which emerged shortly, appear to have been well-integrated in social and political ways that focus on meeting houses and mortuary programs. But it seems unlikely, on the basis of the households' organizations and their positions on the landscape, that prominent local families controlled their neighbors' subsistence-related affairs to the degree that must have been true for their ancestors who had lived in the hut compound communities and complex villages of Emergent Mississippian times. This is also supported by the fact that private storage became widespread among ordinary families at the same time nodal families emerged to coordinate the affairs of the newly forming dispersed communities. Community concerns may have included the conservation of commonly held natural resources or participation in regional exchange networks but may not have included the accumulation of private domestic surplus production. Even so, the nodes were important within their communities and probably served as a means to maintain alliances among neighbors and between large and small communities.

It has become clear that there were widely shared norms regarding the organization of rural household facilities. There are several different repeating patterns of household layout and examples of common facilities that rose and fell in popularity throughout the region. It has also become clear that the level of planning that went into the rural households—for example, those of the Lohmann and Stirling phases—was not on par with that found at Cahokia in the ICT-II and to a lesser extent at Tract 15A. At the time that Cahokia's planning was carefully regulated, planning in the countryside was relatively casual, often somewhat idiosyncratic, and based on logistics rather than arbitrary axes of symmetry. There seems to have been a centralized planner overseeing the layout of Cahokia during these phases, but rural people who were often simultaneously owners, builders, and users of buildings in the countryside seem to have done their own planning to suit their family's needs and to fit society's general expectations of suitability in housing.

Rural families lived in relative isolation. Their homes were oriented primarily to the natural landscape and not to distant monuments or to cardinal directions. This concept supports the interpretation that country dwellers were more autonomous than their contemporaries who lived in the thoroughly structured temple-towns. It is likely that the elites who lived on the mounds had more social power over the people who lived in their shadows than they did over the farmers who lived out of their sight.

This structure of social power seems especially true for a society with a relatively new ethic regarding the attainment of status through wealth accumulation. Wealth items and exotic paraphernalia are a hallmark of Mississippian social distinctions, and this is reflected even in the relatively low-status nodal households in the study sample. The private accumulation of relatively mundane commodities such as food surpluses, tools, and raw materials can be inferred from the architecture and organization of the other, nonnodal households in the study. Enhanced privacy would have been necessary and desirable in a social climate that emphasized a new form of social hierarchy based in part on wealth accumulation, in a region where ancient traditional ideals must have been relatively egalitarian. After all, only about one hundred years separated the complex villages of the Lindeman phase from Cahokia at its most complex.

Trends of rural household organization and building design trace the development of regional cultural complexity. As regional systems became more complex, rural families organized their domestic space and their neighborhoods in new ways. They became increasingly isolated on the landscape and they began to incorporate useful new types of facilities into spatial schemes that were widely shared throughout the region. During the Stirling phase, when mound construction was most intense, rural households installed large, private interior storage facilities and organized themselves into dispersed communities. This seems appropriate for intensive agriculturalists who were expected to increase surplus production in support of public works—each farm family would have had to micromanage their holding with special emphasis on local environment, family labor pool, and the needs of their immediate neighbors. They probably would not have been able to manage increased production from limited resources in a political climate where daily affairs were influenced by regional policy makers. Undoubtedly a substantial surplus flowed from the countryside into the temple-towns, but that was probably not accomplished by routine interference by regional planners in intensely productive domestic labor.

Divisions of labor are apparent for this time in the form of households that specialized in hosting community activities. These nodal points appear to be the homes of locally prominent families who were part-time ceremonial specialists but who also produced their own food. There is no evidence for full-time handicraft or subsistence specialization in the countryside beyond the generally accepted notion that rural families functioned primarily to provide for their own subsistence and to produce a surplus for exchange or tribute. In the same sense, there is no evidence to suggest that these households existed merely to support the temple-towns with their surplus production.

During the final phases of the Mississippian tradition, the occupations of many households were not intense or prolonged. Family autonomy apparently waned along with regionally centralized power. During the decline of regional complexity, there was a change in the way that space was systematically allocated. The hierarchy of rural households persisted even as Monks Mound itself fell into common residential use, but private interior storage and well-ordered outdoor activity areas at rural households became limited to the nodal points. The Sand Prairie phase population, and hence the archaeological sample of the Sand Prairie phase, was so small that it is awkward to consider the social power of these times in the same way as that of earlier times. The continuity of the Sand Prairie phase with earlier phases is clear in the layouts of the household settlements, but most of the known examples come from adjacent sites: the Julien and Florence Street sites. With prehistoric populations at a low point and the regionally centralized hierarchy disintegrating, the regional trade and subsistence networks would have been changing and the number of social roles decreasing.

Adams's theory has been a useful heuristic device for studying the markers of social power. Adams's definition of social power as the control of energy provides the link between social processes and the material record. The analyses focused on facilities as the material evidence for the control of energy. In the rural household setting, an unambiguous indicator of one form of energy control is the bulk commodity storage facility, the storage pit. Private family storage made its first appearance when both mound centers were growing and the social hierarchy was developing most rapidly and when rural households were becoming integrated with one another to form dispersed communities on the landscape away from the temple-towns. The analysis has emphasized a broad assessment of the social power of rural households in a regional context rather than a study of energy capture or expenditure.

The use of Adams's theory facilitates the discussion of individual levels of social organization; with the theory, the study of households can proceed without a determination being made about whether they are parts of a state, a chiefdom, or some other specific form of government. Households and communities did exist as identifiable entities within the overarching regional system. Subsystems within Cahokia's sphere of influence have been analyzed according to their own characteristics regardless of how the overarching regional system would fit into an evolutionary taxonomy.

The methods of analysis and synthesis in this study, as well as its results, are relevant to research questions throughout the world because they focus on elements of settlement that are common to the basic units of many societies. Most important is the notion that changing lifeways in a rural landscape can be usefully studied as parts of a whole regional system. In this case, isolated farmsteads are identified as dynamic functional parts of a complex regional social system on the basis of patterns derived from an analysis of their features and debris. In other regions the same sorts of evidence might be used to study a population of large and small sites to reveal the unique character of their own times.

Notes

NOTES FOR CHAPTER 1

1. Radiocarbon assays used to assign dates to periods and phases employ no systematic calibration; the RCYBP values were simply subtracted from the present (A.D. 1950; see Bareis and Porter 1984: Appendix B).

2. For discussions of Cahokia as a major mound center, see, for example, Collins (1990), Fowler (1973c, 1974, 1975, 1978), Fowler and Hall (1975, 1978), Hall (1975a, 1975b), Kelly (1980), and Pauketat (1991); for the Mitchell site, see Porter (1973, 1974b).

3. Published reports of this work are numerous. The pertinent ones are cited in Chapter 3, which details my methods and the source of my materials.

4. Some useful ethnoarchaeological studies that examine living peoples with archaeological questions in mind include, for example, Binford (1987), Gould (1978), Hodder (1987), Horne (1982), Joyce and Johannessen (1993), Kent (1984, 1987), Kramer (1982a, 1982b), Oswald (1987), Robbins (1966).

5. For consideration of whether or not tribal organization is a necessary stage of cultural evolution, see Adams (1975:223-228), Fried (1975, 1978), and Sturtevant (1983). For recent applications of the tribal classification in studies of warfare and the interaction between states and nonstates, see Ferguson and Whitehead (1992a, 1992b).

6. For studies of settlement, see Binford (1983:144-192), Flannery (1976), Fletcher (1977), Hodder (1984), Pearson (1984), Peebles (1978, 1983), Smith (1978a), Wilk and Rathje (1982a), and Winter (1976). For studies of architecture, see Deetz (1977), Glassie (1968), Hunter-Anderson (1977), McGuire and Schiffer (1983), Rapoport (1969, 1980), Rudolph (1984), and South (1977a). For proxemics, the study of the cultural meanings of space, see the works of Hall (1966, 1968). For studies of spatial organization and ideology, society, economy, and political organization, see Bourdier and AlSayyad (1989a), Chisolm (1962), Eliade (1954:3-21), Levi-Strauss (1963:120-131), Netting (1989, 1993), Plog and Upham (1983), and Smith (1976).

NOTES FOR CHAPTER 2

1. The single-site analyses include those describing the sites in this study: Carbon Dioxide (Finney 1985), Range (Mehrer 1982a), Julien (Milner 1984a), Turner-DeMange (Milner 1983), BBB Motor (Emerson and Jackson 1984), Florence Street (Emerson et al. 1983), and Robert Schneider (Fortier 1985b). There are also many other works that form the foundation that I build on, mostly those by FAI-270 analysts and authors, including but not limited to Dale McElrath, Sissel Johannessen,

Paula Cross, Guy Prentice, Lucretia Kelly, John Kelly, William White, Linda Bonnell, Christine Szuter, Ann Stahl, James Porter, Charles Bareis, Duane Esarey, Joyce Williams, Steven Ozuk, Douglas Jackson, Jean Linder, Theresa Cartmell, and Ned Hanenberger. Other recent American Bottom authors include James Collins, Glen Freimuth, Timothy Pauketat, William Woods, Neal Lopinot, Terry Norris, and Thomas Berres.

2. Recent works on interrelated topics include Wilk and Ashmore (1988) and Wilk and Rathje (1982a) on household archaeology; Netting, Wilk, and Arnould (1984) and Wilk (1988) on households and family life; Bourdier and AlSayyad (1989a), Duly (1979), Guidoni (1975), Jain (1980), Oliver (1987), and Yagi (1980) on vernacular architecture; Netting (1989, 1993) on family-based intensive agriculture; and Conklin (1976), Duncan and Duncan (1976), and Rapoport (1976) on environmental planning.

3. The previous studies are the single-site descriptive reports mentioned above from which most of the present data were derived.

4. For a recent ethnohistorical ethnoarchaeological study of a sedentary group, see Brooks (1993). Basic theoretical constructs pertinent to the study of both sedentary life and nomadic life include the notion of an independent objective reality and the credible link between the static archaeological record and dynamic prehistoric behavior—both essential elements of middle-range theory. Activity area studies that deal with sedentary groups include works by Kramer (1982a) and Kent (1984), among many others. Activity area studies do not always offer an explicit scrutiny of middle-range theory but often use it inexplicitly.

NOTE FOR CHAPTER 4

1. Chapter 5 has an extended discussion of circular buildings.

NOTES FOR CHAPTER 5

1. See Binford (1983, 1987) for small sites. See Carrillo (1977), Deetz (1977), and South (1977a, 1977b) for examples of material culture residue and debris discard among European colonists in eastern North America.

2. The notion of dispersed communities has become an established part of Mississippian archaeology in the American Bottom. The notion goes back at least to Riordan's (1975) and Muller's (1978) recognition of "nodal point" settlements in the southern Illinois region. Nodal households were recognized among the sites in the American Bottom during the FAI-270 Project (Emerson and Milner 1981, 1982; Mehrer 1982a, 1982b; Milner and Emerson 1981). Dispersed communities continue to play an important part in discussions of Mississippian social, political, and economic dynamics throughout the Midwest (Emerson and Jackson 1984; Emerson and Lewis 1991; Milner 1990).

Works Cited

Adams, Richard Newbold
  1975   *Energy and Structure: A Theory of Social Power.* University of Texas Press, Austin.
  1977   Power in Human Societies: A Synthesis. In *The Anthropology of Power,* edited by Raymond D. Fogelson and Richard N. Adams, pp. 387–410. Academic Press, New York.
  1981   Natural Selection, Energetics, and "Cultural Materialism." *Current Anthropology* 22(6):603–604.
  1988   *The Eighth Day: Social Evolution as the Self-Organization of Energy.* University of Texas Press, Austin.
Adams, Robert McCormick
  1940   The Division of Cultural Materials from Archaeological Sites. *The Missouri Archaeologist* 6(2):15–17.
  1941   Archaeological Investigations in Jefferson County, Missouri. *Transactions of the Academy of Science of St. Louis* 30(5).
  1949   Archaeological Investigations in Jefferson County, Missouri. *The Missouri Archaeologist* 11(3 & 4).
Adams, Robert McCormick, and Frank Magre
  1939   Archaeological Surface Survey of Jefferson County, Missouri. *The Missouri Archaeologist* 5:11–23.
Adams, Robert McCormick, and Winslow M. Walker
  1942   Archaeological Surface Survey of New Madrid County, Missouri. *The Missouri Archaeologist* 8(2).
Ahler, Steven R., and Peter J. DePuydt
  1987   A Report on the 1931 Powell Mound Excavations, Madison County, Illinois. *Illinois State Museum Reports of Investigations* 43.
Aldenderfer, Mark S., and Roger K. Blashfield
  1984   *Cluster Analysis.* Sage University Papers, Quantitative Applications in the Social Sciences 07-004. Sage Publications, Beverly Hills.
Algaze, Guillermo
  1993   Expansionary Dynamics of Some Early Pristine States. *American Anthropologist* 95:302–333.
Anderson, Duane C.
  1987   Toward a Processual Understanding of the Initial Variant of the Middle Missouri Tradition: The Case of the Mill Creek Culture of Iowa. *American Antiquity* 52:522–537.
Ashmore, Wendy, and Richard R. Wilk
  1988   Household and Community in the Mesoamerican Past. In *Household*

and Community in the Mesoamerican Past, edited by Richard R. Wilk and Wendy Ashmore, pp. 1–27. University of New Mexico Press, Albuquerque.

Bareis, Charles J.

1975   Report of the 1972 University of Illinois-Urbana Excavations at the Cahokia Site. In *Cahokia Archaeology: Field Reports,* edited by Melvin Fowler, pp. 12–15. *Illinois State Museum, Research Series, Papers in Anthropology* 3. Springfield.

1976   *The Knoebel Site, St. Clair County, Illinois.* Illinois Archaeological Survey, Circular 1.

Bareis, Charles J., and James W. Porter (editors)

1984   *American Bottom Archaeology.* University of Illinois Press, Urbana.

Barker, Alex W., and Timothy R. Pauketat (editors)

1992   Lords of the Southeast: Social Inequality of Southeastern North America. *Archaeological Papers of the American Anthropological Association* 3.

Barrett, Samuel A.

1933   Ancient Aztalan. *Bulletin of the Public Museum of the City of Milwaukee* 13.

Bartram, William

1909   *Observations on the Creek and Cherokee Indians.* 1789. With prefatory and supplementary notes by E. G. Squier. Report. Complete. *Transactions of the American Ethnological Society* 3(1):1–81. (Facsimile reprint of 1853 edition)

1928   *Travels of William Bartram.* Mark Van Doren, editor. Dover Press, New York.

Benchley, Elizabeth D.

1974   *Mississippian Secondary Mound Loci: A Comparative Functional Analysis in a Time-Space Perspective.* Ph.D. dissertation, University of Wisconsin, Milwaukee. University Microfilms, Ann Arbor.

Bennett, John W.

1944   Archaeological Horizons in the Southern Illinois Region. *American Antiquity* 10:12–22.

Berres, Thomas Edward

1984   *A Formal Analysis of Ceramic Vessels from the Schlemmer Site (11-S-382): A Late Woodland/Mississippian Occupation in St. Clair County, Illinois.* Unpublished Master's thesis, Department of Anthropology, Western Michigan University, Kalamazoo.

Binford, Lewis R.

1964   A Consideration of Archaeological Research Design. *American Antiquity* 29:425–441.

1977   *For Theory Building in Archaeology.* Academic Press, New York.

1980   Willow Smoke and Dogs' Tails: Hunter-Gatherer Settlement Systems and Archaeological Site Formations. *American Antiquity* 45:4–20.

1983   *In Pursuit of the Past: Decoding the Archaeological Record.* Thames and Hudson, New York.

1987   Researching Ambiguity: Frames of Reference and Site Structure. In *Method and Theory for Activity Area Research: An Ethnoarchaeological*

Approach, edited by Susan Kent, pp. 449–512. Columbia University Press, New York.

Binford, Lewis R., Sally R. Binford, Robert Whallon, and Margret Ann Hardin
1970   Archaeology at Hatchery West. *Society for American Archaeology, Memoir* 24.

Black, Glenn A.
1967   *Angel site.* Indiana Historical Society, Indianapolis.

Blake, Leonard W.
1942   A Hopewell-Like Site near St. Louis. *The Missouri Archaeologist* 8(1):3–7.
1955   The Lambert-St. Louis Airport Site. *The Missouri Archaeologist* 17:24–42.

Bohannan, Paul
1954   Tiv Farm and Settlement. *Colonial Research Studies* 15.

Bourdier, Jean-Paul, and Nezar AlSayyad (editors)
1989a   *Dwellings, Settlements and Tradition: Cross-Cultural Perspectives.* University Press of America, New York.

Bourdier, Jean-Paul, and Nezar AlSayyad
1989b   Prologue. In *Dwellings, Settlements and Tradition: Cross-Cultural Perspectives,* edited by Jean-Paul Bourdier and Nezar AlSayyad, pp. 5–25. University Press of America, New York.

Brain, Jeffrey P.
1991   Cahokia from the Southern Periphery. In *New Perspectives on Cahokia: Views from the Periphery,* edited by James B. Stoltman, pp. 93–100. Prehistory Press. Madison, Wisconsin.

Brandt, Kieth A.
1972   American Bottom Settlements. Paper presented at the 37th annual meeting of the Society for American Archaeology, Bal Harbor, Florida.

Brooks, Robert L.
1993   Housheold Abandonment among Sedentary Plains Societies: Behavioral Sequences and Consequences in the Interpretation of the Archaeological Record. In *Abandonment of Settlements and Regions: Ethnoarchaeological and Archaeological Approaches,* edited by Catherine M. Cameron and Steve A. Tomka, pp. 178–187. Cambridge University Press, Cambridge.

Brown, James A.
1971   The Dimensions of Status in the Burials at Spiro. *American Antiquity* 36 (3, part 2):92–112.
1985   The Mississippian Period. In *Ancient Art of the American Woodland Indians,* pp. 93–145. Harry N. Abrams, Inc., New York.

Brown, James A. (editor)
1975   *Perspectives in Cahokia Archaeology.* Illinois Archaeological Survey, Bulletin 10. Urbana.

Bushnell, David I., Jr.
1904   The Cahokia and Surrounding Mound Groups. *Peabody Museum of American Archaeology and Ethnology, Papers* 3(1).
1907   Primitive Salt-Making in the Mississippi Valley. *Man: A Monthly Record of Anthropological Science* 7(13):16–21.
1908   Primitive Salt-Making in the Mississippi Valley. *Man: A Monthly Record of Anthropological Science* 8(35):64–70.
1919   *Native Villages and Village Sites East of the Mississippi.* Bureau of American Ethnology, Bulletin 69.

1922   Archaeological Reconnaissance of the Cahokia and Related Mound Groups. *Smithsonian Miscellaneous Collections* 72 (15):92-105.

Butzer, Karl W.
1982   *Archaeology as Human Ecology: Method and Theory for a Contextual Approach.* Cambridge University Press, Cambridge.

Cameron, Catherine M., and Steve A. Tomka (editors)
1993   *Abandonment of Settlements and Regions: Ethnoarchaeological and Archaeological Approaches.* Cambridge University Press, Cambridge.

Carrillo, Richard F.
1977   Archaeological Variability—Sociocultural Variability. In *Research Strategies in Historical Archeology,* edited by Stanley South, pp. 73–89. Academic Press, New York.

Chang, Kwang-Chih
1958   Study of the Neolithic Social Grouping: Examples from the New World. *American Anthropologist* 60:298–334.

Chisolm, Michael
1962   *Rural settlement and Land Use: An Essay in Location.* Hutchinson, London.

Chmurny, William Wayne
1973   *The Ecology of the Middle Mississippian Occupation of the American Bottom.* Ph.D. dissertation, University of Illinois, Urbana-Champaign. University Microfilms, Ann Arbor.

Claflin, John
1991   The Shire Site: Mississippian Outpost in the Central Illinois Prairie. In *New Perspectives on Cahokia: Views from the Periphery,* edited by James B. Stoltman, pp. 93–100. Prehistory Press. Madison, Wisconsin.

Clarke, David L.
1977   Spatial Information in Archaeology. In *Spatial Archaeology,* edited by David L. Clarke, pp. 1–32. Academic Press, New York.

Cole, Fay-Cooper et al.
1951   *Kincaid: A Prehistoric Illinois Metropolis.* University of Chicago Press.

Collins, James M.
1987   The ICT-II: An Evolutionary Model of Micro-Cahokia Residence. Paper presented at the 25th Annual Workshop on Illinois Archaeology, Collinsville, Illinois.

1988   *Cahokia Interpretive Center Tract—Location II Project Description and Feature Analysis.* Contract Archaeology Program, Southern Illinois University, Edwardsville. Draft report submitted to the Illinois Historic Preservation Agency, Springfield.

1990   The Archaeology of the Cahokia Mounds ICT-II: Site Structure. *Illinois Cultural Resources Study* 10. Illinois Historic Preservation Agency, Springfield.

Collins, James M., and Michael L. Chalfant
1993   A Second-Terrace Perspective on Monks Mound. *American Antiquity* 58:319–332.

Collins, James M., Michael L. Chalfant, and George R. Holley
1986   *Archaeological Testing of the Slump Area on the West Face of Monks Mound, Madison County, Illinois.* Contract Archaeology Program, Southern Illinois University, Edwardsville. Report submitted to John Mathes and Associates, Inc., Columbia, Illinois.

Conklin, Harold C.
1976   Ethnographic Semantic Analysis of Ifugao Landform Categories. In *Environmental Knowing: Theories, Research, and Methods*, edited by Gary T. Moore and Reginald B. Golledge, pp. 235–246. Dowden, Hutchinson & Ross, Inc., Stroudsburg, Pennsylvania.

Conrad, Lawrence A.
1989   The Southeastern Ceremonial Complex on the Northern Middle Mississippian Frontier: Late Prehistoric Politico-Religious Systems in the Central Illinois Valley. In *The Southeastern Ceremonial Complex: Artifacts and Analysis: The Cottonlandia Conference*, edited by Patricia Galloway, pp. 93–113. University of Nebraska Press, Lincoln.

Cottier, John W.
1977a   The 1972 Investigations at the Lilbourn Site. In *Investigation and Comparison of Two Fortified Mississippi Tradition Archaeological Sites in Southeastern Missouri: A Preliminary Compilation*, edited by Robert T. Bray, pp. 123–154. *The Missouri Archaeologist* 38.
1977b   Continued Investigations at the Lilbourn Site, 1973. In *Investigation and Comparison of Two Fortified Mississippi Tradition Archaeological Sites in Southeastern Missouri: A Preliminary Compilation*, edited by Robert T. Bray, pp. 155-185. *The Missouri Archaeologist* 38.

Cunningham, Clark E.
1973   Order in the Atoni House. In *Right and Left: Essays on Dual Symbolic Classification*, edited by Rodney Needham, pp. 204–238. University of Chicago Press, Chicago.

Dalan, Rinita A.
1989   Geophysical Investigations of the Prehistoric Cahokia Palisade Sequence. *Illinois Culture Resources Study* 8. Illinois Historic Preservation Agency, Springfield.

David, Nicholas
1971   The Fulani Compound and the Archaeologist. *World Archaeology* 3:111–131.

Deetz, James
1977   *In Small Things Forgotten: The Archeology of Early American Life.* Anchor Books, Garden City, New York.

Deuel, Thorne
1938   Lower Mississippi Traits in the Middle Phase in Illinois. *Transactions of the Illinois State Academy of Science* 31(2):68–70.

Dick, George C.
1955   Incised Pottery Decorations from Cahokia: A Middle Mississippi Site in Western Illinois. *The Missouri Archaeologist* 17(4):36–48.

Dixon, W. J. (editor)
1985   *BMDP Statistical Software Manual: 1985 printing.* University of California Press, Berkeley.

Duly, Colin
1979   *The Houses of Mankind.* Thames and Hudson, London.

Duncan, James S., and Nancy G. Duncan
1976   Housing as Presentation of Self and the Structure of Social Networks. In *Environmental Knowing: Theories, Research, and Methods*, edited by Gary

   T. Moore and Reginald B. Golledge, pp. 247–257. Dowden, Hutchinson
   & Ross, Inc., Stroudsburg, Pennsylvania.

Eliade, Mircea
   1954   *The Myth of the Eternal Return, or Cosmos and History.* Translated by
           Willard R. Trask. Princeton University Press, Princeton.

Emerson, Thomas E.
   1982   *Mississippian Stone Images in Illinois.* Illinois Archaeological Survey, Circu-
           lar 6. Urbana.
   1989   Water, Serpents, and the Underworld: An Exploration into Cahokian
           Symbolism. In *The Southeastern Ceremonial Complex: Artifacts and Analy-
           sis: The Cottonlankia Conference,* edited by Patricia Galloway, pp. 45–92.
           University of Nebraska Press, Lincoln.
   1992   The Mississippian Dispersed Village as a Social and Environmental Strat-
           egy. In *Late Prehistoric Agriculture: Observations from the Midwest,* edited
           by William I. Woods, pp. 198–216. Studies in Illinois Archaeology,
           Number 8. Illinois Historic Preservation Agency, Springfield.

Emerson, Thomas E., and Andrew C. Fortier
   1986   Early Woodland Cultural Variation, Subsistence, and Settlement in the
           Amican Bottom. In *Early Woodland Archeology,* edited by Kenneth B.
           Farnsworth and Thomas E. Emerson, pp. 475–522. Center for American
           Archeology, Kampsville Seminars in Archeology Vol. 2. Center for Amer-
           ican Archeology Press, Kampsville, Illinois.

Emerson, Thomas E., and Douglas K. Jackson
   1984   *The BBB Motor Site.* University of Illinois Press, Urbana.
   1987   Emergent Mississippian and Early Mississippian Homesteads at the
           Marcus Site. In *The Radic Site and the Marcus Site,* pp. 305–391. Univer-
           sity of Illinois Press, Urbana.

Emerson, Thomas E., and R. Barry Lewis
   1991   Cahokia and the Hinterlands: Middle Mississippian Cultures of the Mid-
           west. University of Illinois Press, Urbana.

Emerson, Thomas E., and George Milner R.
   1981   The Mississippian Occupation of the American Bottom: The Communi-
           ties. Paper presented at the Midwestern Archaeological Conference in
           Madison, Wisconsin.
   1982   Community Organization and Settlement Patterns of Peripheral Missis-
           sippian Sites in the American Bottom, Illinois. Paper presented at the
           47th annual meeting of the Society for American Archaeology, Min-
           neapolis.

Emerson, Thomas E., George R. Milner, and Douglas K. Jackson
   1983   *The Florence Street Site.* University of Illinois Press, Urbana.

Esarey, Duane, and Lawrence A. Conrad (compilers)
   1981   *The Orendorf Site Preliminary Working Papers, 1981.* Archaeological Re-
           search Laboratory, Western Illinois University, Macomb.

Esarey, Duane, with Timothy W. Good
   1981   Final report on FAI-270 and Illinois Route 460 related excavations at the
           Lohmann site, 11-S-49, St. Clair County, Illinois. Archaeological Research
           Laboratory, Western Illinois University. *FAI-270 Archaeological Mitigation
           Project Report 39.*

Esarey, Duane, and Timothy R. Pauketat
1992   *The Lohmann Site: An Early Mississippian Center in the American Bottom.* University of Illinois Press, Urbana.

Fairbanks, Charles H.
1946   The Macon Earth Lodge. *American Antiquity* 12:94–108.

Farnsworth, Kenneth B., Thomas E. Emerson, and Rebecca Miller Glenn
1991   Patterns of Late Woodland/Mississippian Interaction in the Lower Illinois Valley Drainage: A View from Starr Village. In *Cahokia and the Hinterlands: Middle Mississippian Cultures of the Midwest,* edited by Thomas E. Emerson and R. Barry Lewis, pp. 83–118. University of Illinois Press. Urbana, Illinois.

Faulkner, Charles H.
1977   The Winter House: An Early Southeast Tradition. *Midcontinental Journal of Archaeology* 2:141–159.

Ferguson, R. Brian, and Neil L. Whitehead (editors)
1992a   *War in the Tribal Zone: Expanding States and Indigenous Warfare.* School of American Research Press, Santa Fe.
1992b   The Violent Edge of Empire. In *War in the Tribal Zone: Expanding States and Indigenous Warfare,* edited by R. Brian Ferguson and Neil L. Whitehead, pp. 1–30. School of American Research Press, Santa Fe.

Finney, Fred A.
1985   The Carbon Dioxide Site (11-Mo-594). In *The Carbon Dioxide Site and The Robert Schneider Site,* pp. 1–167. University of Illinois Press, Urbana.

Finney, Fred A., and James B. Stoltman
1991   The Fred Edwards Site: A Case of Stirling Phase Culture Contact in Southwestern Wisconsin. In *New Perspectives on Cahokia: Views from the Periphery,* edited by James B. Stoltman, pp. 229–252. Prehistory Press, Madison, Wisconsin.

Flannery, Kent V.
1972   The Origins of the Village as a Settlement Type in Mesoamerica and the Near East: A Comparative Study. In *Man, Settlement, and Urbanism,* edited by Peter J. Ucko, Ruth Tringham, and G. W. Dimbleby, pp. 23–53. Duckworth, London.
1976   The Early Mesoamerican House. In *The Early Mesoamerican Village,* edited by Kent V. Flannery, pp. 16–24. Academic Press, New York.
1983   The Tierras Largas Phase and the Analytical Units of the Early Oaxacan Village. In *The Cloud People: Divergent Evolution of the Zapotec and Mixtec Civilizations,* edited by Kent V. Flannery and Joyce Marcus, pp. 43–45. Academic Press, New York.

Flannery, Kent V., and Marcus C. Winter
1976   Analyzing Household Activities. In *The Early Mesoamerican Village,* edited by Kent V. Flannery, pp. 34–47. Academic Press, New York.

Fletcher, Alice C., and Francis LaFlesche
1972   *The Omaha Tribe.* Reprinted. University of Nebraska Press, Lincoln. Originally published 1911, in the 27th *Annual Report of the Bureau of American Ethnology to the Secretary of the Smithsonian Institution, 1905–1906,* Government Printing Office, Washington, D.C.

Fletcher, Roland
  1977   Settlement Studies (Micro and Semi-Micro). In *Spatial Archaeology,* edited by David L. Clarke, pp. 47–162. Academic Press, London.
Fortier, Andrew C.
  1983   Settlement and Subsistence at the Go-Kart Site: A Late Archaic Tittering-ton Occupation in the American Bottom, Illinois. In *Archaic Hunters and Gatherers in the American Midwest,* edited by James L. Phillips and James A. Brown, pp. 243–260. Academic Press, New York.
  1985a   *Selected Sites in the Hill Lake Locality.* University of Illinois Press, Urbana.
  1985b   The Robert Schneider Site. In *The Carbon Dioxide Site and The Robert Schneider Site,* pp. 169–313. University of Illinois Press, Urbana.
  1993   American Bottom House Types of the Archaic and Woodland Periods: An Overview. *Illinois Archaeology* 5:260–275.
Fortier, Andrew C., Fred A. Finney, and Richard B. Lacampagne
  1983   *The Mund Site (11-S-435).* University of Illinois Press, Urbana.
Fortier, Andrew C., Thomas E. Emerson, and Fred A. Finney
  1984a   Early Woodland and Middle Woodland Periods. In *American Bottom Archaeology,* edited by Charles J. Bareis and James W. Porter, pp. 59–103. University of Illinois Press, Urbana.
Fortier, Andrew C., Richard B. Lacampagne, and Fred A. Finney
  1984b   *The Fish Lake Site.* University of Illinois Press, Urbana.
Fowler, Melvin L.
  1973a   The Cahokia Site. In *Explorations into Cahokia Archaeology,* edited by Melvin L. Fowler, pp. 1–30. Illinois Archaeological Survey, Bulletin 7. Urbana.
  1974   Cahokia: Ancient Capital of the Midwest. *Addison-Wesley Module in Anthropology* 48:3–38.
  1975   A Pre-Columbian Urban Center on the Mississippi. *Scientific American* 233(2):92–101.
  1978   Cahokia and the American Bottom: Settlement Archaeology. In *Mississippian Settlement Patterns,* edited by Bruce D. Smith, pp. 455–478. Academic Press, New York.
  1989   The Cahokia Atlas: A Historical Atlas of Cahokia Archaeology. *Studies in Illinois Archaeology* 6. Illinois Historic Preservation Agency, Springfield.
  1991   Mound 72 and Early Mississippian at Cahokia. In *New Perspectives on Cahokia: Views from the Periphery. Monographs in World Archaeology* 2, edited by James B. Stoltman, pp. 1–28. Prehistory Press, Madison, Wisconsin.
Fowler, Melvin L. (editor)
  1962   *First Annual Report: American Bottoms Archaeology, July 1, 1961–June 30, 1962.* Illinois Archaeological Survey, University of Illinois, Urbana.
  1963   *Second Annual Report: American Bottoms Archaeology, July 1, 1962–June 30, 1963.* Illinois Archaeological Survey, University of Illinois, Urbana.
  1964   *Third Annual Report: American Bottoms Archaeology, July 1, 1963–June 30, 1964.* Illinois Archaeological Survey, University of Illinois, Urbana.
  1973b   *Cahokia Archaeology: Field Reports.* Illinois State Museum, Research Series, Papers in Anthropology 3, Springfield.

1973c   *Explorations into Cahokia Archaeology.* Illinois Archaeological Survey, Bulletin 7, Urbana.

Fowler, Melvin L., and Robert L. Hall
1972   *Archaeological Phases at Cahokia.* Illinois State Museum, Papers in Anthropology 1. Springfield.
1975   Archaeological phases at Cahokia. In *Perspectives in Cahokia Archaeology,* edited by James A. Brown, pp. 1–14. Illinois Archaeological Survey, Bulletin 10. Urbana.
1978   Late Prehistory of the Illinois Area. In *Northeast,* edited by Bruce G. Trigger, pp. 560-568. *Handbook of North American Indians* Vol. 15, William C. Sturtevant, general editor. Smithsonian Institution, Washington, D.C.

Fowler, P. J.
1983   *The Farming of Prehistoric Britain.* Cambridge University Press, Cambridge.

Freimuth, Glen A.
1974   The Lunsford-Pulcher Site: An Examination of Selected Traits and Their Social Implications in American Bottom Prehistory. Pre-dissertation paper, Department of Anthropology, University of Illinois, Urbana-Champaign.

Fried, Morton H.
1960   On the Evolution of Social Stratification and the State. In *Culture in History: Essays in Honor of Paul Radin,* edited by Stanley Diamond, pp. 713–731. Columbia University Press, New York.
1967   *The Evolution of Political Society: An Essay in Political Anthropology.* Random House, New York.
1975   *The Notion of Tribe.* Cummings Publishing, Menlo Park.
1978   Tribe to State or State to Tribe in Ancient China? In *The Origins of Chinese Civilization,* edited by David N. Keightley, pp. 467–493. University of California, Berkeley.

Fuchs, A. R., and M. Meyer-Brodnitz
1989   The Emergence of the Central Hall House-Type in the Context of Nineteenth Century Palestine. In *Dwellings, Settlements and Tradition: Cross-Cultural Perspectives,* edited by Jean-Paul Bourdier and Nezar AlSayyad, pp. 403–424. University Press of America, New York.

Gibbon, Guy E.
1974   A Model of Mississippian Development and Its Implications for the Red Wing Area. In *Aspects of Upper Great Lakes Anthropology: Papers in Honor of Lloyd A. Wilford,* edited by Elden Johnson, pp. 129–137. Minnesota Prehistoric Archaeology Series 11. Minnesota Historical Society, St. Paul.
1979   *The Mississippian Occupation of the Red Wing Area.* Minnesota Prehistoric Archaeology Series 13. Minnesota Historical Society, St. Paul.
1984   *Anthropological Archaeology.* Columbia University Press, New York.

Gibbon, Guy E., and Clark A. Dobbs
1991   The Mississippian Presence in the Red Wing Area, Minnesota. In *New Perspectives on Cahokia: Views from the Periphery,* edited by James B. Stoltman, pp. 281–305. Prehistory Press. Madison, Wisconsin.

Glassie, Henry
1968   *Pattern in the Material Folk Culture of the Eastern United States.* University of Pennsylvania Press, Philadelphia.

Goldstein, Lynne
   1991   The Implications of Aztalan's Location. In *New Perspectives on Cahokia: Views from the Periphery,* edited by James B. Stoltman, pp. 209–227. Prehistory Press. Madison, Wisconsin.
Gould, Richard (editor)
   1978   *Explorations in Ethnoarchaeology.* University of New Mexico Press, Albuquerque.
Gregg, Michael L.
   1975a   A Population Estimate for Cahokia. In *Perspectives in Cahokia Archaeology,* edited by James A. Brown, pp. 126–136. Illinois Archaeological Survey, Bulletin 10, Urbana.
   1975b   *Settlement Morphology and Production Specialization: The Horseshoe Lake Site, A Case Study.* Ph.D. dissertation, University of Wisconsin, Milwaukee. University Microfilms, Ann Arbor.
Griffin, James B.
   1941   Report on Pottery from the St. Louis Area. *The Missouri Archaeologist* 7(2):1–17.
   1949   The Cahokia Ceramic Complexes. In *Proceedings of the Fifth Plains Conference for Archaeology,* edited by John L. Champe, pp. 44–58. University of Nebraska Laboratory of Anthropology, Notebook 1.
   1977   The University of Michigan Excavations at the Pulcher Site in 1950. *American Antiquity* 42:462–488.
   1984   Historical Perspective. In *American Bottom Archaeology,* edited by Charles J. Bareis and James W. Porter, pp. xv–xviii. University of Illinois Press, Urbana.
Griffin, James B., and Albert C. Spaulding
   1951   The Central Mississippi Valley Archaeological Survey, Season 1950—A Preliminary Report. *Journal of the Illinois State Archaeological Society* n.s., 1:74–80, 84.
Griffith, Roberta Jean
   1962   *Ramey Incised Pottery.* Master's thesis, Department of Art, Southern Illinois University, Carbondale.
   1981   *Ramey Incised Pottery.* Illinois Archaeological Survey, Circular 5. Urbana.
Grimm, R. E. (editor)
   1950   Cahokia Brought to Life. *The Greater St. Louis Archaeological Society* n.d. [1950]
Guidoni, Enrico
   1975   *Primitive Architecture.* Translated by Robert Erich Wolf. Rizzoli International Publications, Inc., New York.
Haas, Jonathan
   1982   *The Evolution of the Prehistoric State.* Columbia University Press, New York.
Hall, Edward T.
   1966   *The Hidden Dimension.* Doubleday and Company, Garden City.
   1968   Proxemics. *Current Anthropology* 9:83–108.
Hall, Robert L.
   1975a   Chronology and Phases at Cahokia. In *Perspectives in Cahokia Archaeology,* edited by James A. Brown, pp. 15–31. Illinois Archaeological Survey, Bulletin 10. Urbana.
   1975b   Some Problems of Identity and Process in Cahokia Archaeology. Revision

of a paper prepared for discussion November 10-15, 1974, at an advanced seminar on Mississippian cultural development organized by Stephen Williams, Harvard University and sponsored by the School of American Research, Santa Fe, New Mexico.

1991   Cahokia Identity and Interaction Models of Cahokia Mississippian. In *Cahokia and the Hinterlands: Middle Mississippian Cultures of the Midwest,* edited by Thomas E. Emerson and R. Barry Lewis, pp. 3–34. University of Illinois Press, Urbana, Illinois.

Hanenberger, Ned
1986   Late Archaic and Mississippian Occupations at the Olszewski Borrow Pit Site (11-S-465). Department of Anthropology, University of Illinois at Urbana-Champaign, *FAI-270 Archaeological Mitigation Project Report* 73.

Hanenberger, Ned, and Mark W. Mehrer
in prep   *The Range Site 3: Mississippian and Oneota Occupations (11-S-47).* University of Illinois Press, Urbana.

Hargrave, Michael L.
1982   Archaeological Investigations at the Bluff Shadow Site, Monroe County, Illinois. Southern Illinois University at Carbondale, *Center for Archaeological Investigations, Research Paper* 31.

1991   *A Selectionist Perspective on Change in Late Prehistoric (A.D. 600–1400) Domestic Architecture in the American Bottom Region of Southern Illinois.* Ph.D. Dissertation. Department of Anthropology, Southern Illinois University at Carbondale. University Microfilms International. Ann Arbor.

Hargrave, Michael L., Gerald A. Oetelaar, Neal H. Lopinot, Brian B. Butler, and Deborah A. Billings
1983   The Bridges Site (11-Mr-11): A Late Prehistoric Settlement in the Central Kaskaskia Valley. *Research Paper* 39. Center for Archaeological Investigations, Southern Illinois University Press, Carbondale.

Harn, Alan D.
1971   An Archaeological Survey of the American Bottoms in Madison and St. Clair Counties, Illinois. *Illinois State Museum, Reports of Investigations* 21:19–39.

1978   Mississippian Settlement Patterns in the Central Illinois River Valley. In *Mississippian Settlement Patterns,* edited by Bruce D. Smith, pp. 233–268. Academic Press, New York.

1991   The Eveland Site: Inroad to Spoon River Mississippian Society. In *New Perspectives on Cahokia: Views from the Periphery,* edited by James B. Stoltman, pp. 129–153. Prehistory Press, Madison, Wisconsin.

Hartwig, Frederick, with Brian E. Dearing
1979   *Exploratory Data Analysis.* Sage University Papers, Quantitative Applications in the Social Sciences 07-016. Sage Publications, Beverly Hills.

Hayden, Brian, and Aubrey Cannon
1982   The Corporate Group as an Archaeological Unit. *Journal of Anthroplogical Archaeology* 1:132–158.

1983   Where the Garbage Goes: Refuse Disposal in the Maya Highlands. *Journal of Anthropological Archaeology* 2:117–163.

Heider, Karl G.
1966   Archaeological Assumptions and Ethnographical Facts: A Cautionary Tale

from New Guinea. *Southwestern Journal of Anthropology* 23:52–64.

1979   *Grand Valley Dani: Peaceful Warriors.* Holt, Rinehart and Winston, New York.

Hines, Philip

1977   On Social Organization in the Middle Mississippian: States or Chiefdoms? *Current Anthropology* 18:337–338.

Hirth, Kenneth G.

1993   The Household as an Analytical Unit: Problems in Method and Theory. In *Prehispanic Domestic Units in Western Mesoamerica: Studies of the Household, Compound, and Residence,* edited by Robert S. Santley and Kenneth G. Hirth, pp. 21–36. CRC Press, Boca Raton.

Hodder, Ian

1984   Burials, Houses, Women and Men in the European Neolithic. In *Ideology, Power and Prehistory,* edited by Daniel Miller and Christopher Tilley, pp. 51–68. Cambridge University Press, Cambridge.

1987   The Meaning of Discard: Ash and Domestic Space in Baringo. In *Method and Theory for Activity Area Research: An Ethnoarchaeological Approach,* edited by Susan Kent, pp. 424–447. Columbia University Press, New York.

Hodson, F. R.

1969   Searching for Structure within Multivariate Archaeological Data. *World Archaeology* 1(1):90–105.

1970   Cluster Analysis and Archaeology: Some New Developments and Applications. *World Archaeology* 1(3):299–320.

Holley, George R.

1989   The Archaeology of the Cahokia Mounds ICT-II: Ceramics. *Illinois Cultural Resources Study* 11. Illinois Historic Preservation Agency, Springfield.

Holley, George R. Rinita A. Dalan, and Philip A. Smith

1993   Investigations in the Cahokia Site Grand Plaza. *American Antiquity* 58:306–318.

Holley, George R., Neal H. Lopinot, Rinita A. Dalan, and William I. Woods

1990   South Palisade Investigations. *Illinois Cultural Resources Study* 14. Illinois Historic Preservation Agency, Springfield.

Horne, Lee

1982   The Household in Space: Dispersed Holdings in an Iranian Village. *American Behavioral Scientist* 25:677–685.

Hunter-Anderson, Rosalind L.

1977   A Theoretical Approach to the Study of House Form. In *For Theory Building in Archaeology: Essays on Faunal Remains, Aquatic Resources, Spatial Analysis, and Systemic Modeling,* edited by Lewis R. Binford, pp. 287–315. Academic Press, New York.

Hus, Henri

1908   An Ecological Cross-Section of the Mississippi River in the Region of St. Louis, Missouri. *Missouri Botanical Garden, Annual Report* 19:127–258.

Iseminger, William R., Timothy R. Pauketat, Brad Koldehoff, Lucretia S. Kelly, and Leonard Blake

1990   East Palisade Investigations. *Illinois Cultural Resources Study* 14.

Illinois Historic Preservation Agency, Springfield.

Jackson, Douglas K.

1980a   Final Report on Archaeological Investigations at the Sandy Ridge Farm Site (11-S-660). Department of Anthropology, University of Illinois at Urbana-Champaign, *FAI-270 Archaeological Mitigation Project Report* 20.

1980b   *Final Report on Mitigation at the Bryon Site (11-S-432).* FAI-270 Archaeological Mitigation Project Report 1. Department of Anthropology, University of Illinois, Urbana-Champaign.

Jain, Kulbshan

1980   Form—A Consequence of Context. *Process: Architecture* 15:17–34.

Johannessen, Sissel

1984   Paleoethnobotany. In *American Bottom Archaeology,* edited by Charles J. Bareis and James W. Porter, pp. 197–214. University of Illinois Press, Urbana.

1993a   Farmers of the Late Woodland. In *Foraging and Farming in the Eastern Woodlands,* edited by C. Margaret Scarry, pp. 57–77. University of Florida Press, Gainesville.

1993b   Food, Dishes, and Society in the Mississippi Valley. In *Foraging and Farming in the Eastern Woodlands,* edited by C. Margaret Scarry, pp. 182–205. University of Florida Press, Gainesville.

Johnson, Allen W., and Timothy Earle

1987   *The Evolution of Human Societies: From Foraging Group to Agrarian State.* Stanford University Press, Stanford, California.

Johnson, Elden

1991   Cambria and Cahokia's Northwestern Periphery. In *New Perspectives on Cahokia: Views from the Periphery,* edited by James B. Stoltman, pp. 307–317. Prehistory Press, Madison, Wisconsin.

Joyce, Arthur A., and Sissel Johannessen

1993   Abandonment and the Production of Archaeological Variability at Domestic Sites. In *Abandonment of Settlements and Regions: Ethnoarchaeological and Archaeological Approaches,* edited by Catherine M. Cameron and Steve A. Tomka, pp. 138–153. Cambridge University Press, Cambridge.

Kelley, A. R.

1933   Some Problems of Recent Cahokia Archaeology. *Transactions of the Illinois State Academy of Science* 25(4):101–103.

Kelly, John E.

1980   *Formative Developments at Cahokia and the Adjacent American Bottom: A Merrell Tract Perspective.* Ph.D. dissertation, University of Wisconsin, Madison. Archaeological Research Laboratory, Western Illinois University, Macomb, Illinois.

1990a   Range Site Community Patterns and the Mississippian Emergence. In *The Mississippian Emergence,* edited by Bruce D. Smith, pp. 67–112. Smithsonian Institution Press, Washington, D.C.

1990b   The Emergence of Mississippian Culture in the American Bottom Region. In *The Mississippian Emergence,* edited by Bruce D. Smith, pp. 112–152. Smithsonian Institution Press, Washington, D.C.

1991   The Evidence for Prehistoric Exchange and Its Implications for the Development of Cahokia. In *New Perspectives on Cahokia: Views from the Periphery,* edited by James B. Stoltman, pp. 65–92. Prehistory Press, Madison, Wisconsin.

1992   The Impact of Maize on the Development of Nucleated Settlements: An American Bottom Example. In *Late Prehistoric Agriculture: Observations from the Midwest,* edited by William I. Woods, pp. 167–197. Studies in Illinois Archaeology No. 8. Illinois Historic Preservation Agency, Springfield.

1993   The Pulcher Site: An Archaeological and Historical Overview. *Illinois Archaeology* 5:434–451.

Kelly, John E., Jean R. Linder, and Theresa J. Cartmell
1979   The Archaeological Intensive Survey of the Proposed FAI-270 Alignment in the American Bottom Region of Southern Illinois. *Illinois Transportation Archaeology, Scientific Reports* 1. Springfield.

Kelly, John E., Fred A. Finney, Dale L. McElrath, and Steven J. Ozuk
1984a   Late Woodland Period. In *American Bottom Archaeology,* edited by Charles J. Bareis and James W. Porter, pp. 104–127. University of Illinois Press, Urbana.

Kelly, John E., Steven J. Ozuk, Douglas K. Jackson, Dale L. McElrath, Fred A. Finney, and Duane Esarey
1984b   Emergent Mississippian Period. In *American Bottom Archaeology,* edited by Charles J. Bareis and James W. Porter, pp. 128–157. University of Illinois Press, Urbana.

Kelly, John E., Steven J. Ozuk, and Joyce A. Williams
1990   *The Range Site 2: The Emergent Mississippian Dohack and Range Phase Occupations (11-S-47).* University of Illinois Press, Urbana.

Kelly, John E., Andrew C. Fortier, Steven J. Ozuk, and Joyce A. Williams
1987   *The Range Site: Archaic through Late Woodland Occupations.* University of Illinois Press, Urbana.

Kelly, Lucretia S., and Paula G. Cross
1984   Zooarchaeology. In *American Bottom Archaeology,* edited by Charles J. Bareis and James W. Porter, pp. 215–232. University of Illinois Press, Urbana.

Kent, Susan
1984   *Analyzing Activity Areas: An Ethnoarchaeological Study of the Use of Space.* University of New Mexico Press, Albuquerque.

Kent, Susan (editor)
1987   *Method and Theory for Activity Area Research: An Ethnoarchaeological Approach.* Columbia University Press, New York.

Kramer, Carol
1982a   *Village Ethnoarchaeology: Rural Iran in Archaeological Perspective.* Academic Press, New York.

1982b   Ethnographic Households and Archaeological Interpretations: A Case from Iranian Kurdistan. *American Behavioral Scientist* 25:663–675.

Larson, Lewis H.
1972   Functional Considerations of Warfare in the Southeast during the

Mississippi Period. *American Antiquity* 37:383–392.

Larsson, Anita

1989   Traditional Versus Modern Housing in Botswana—An Analysis from the User's Perspective. In *Dwellings, Settlements and Tradition: Cross-Cultural Perspectives,* edited by Jean-Paul Bourdier and Nezar AlSayyad, pp. 503–525. University Press of America, New York.

Levi-Strauss, Claude

1963   *Structural Anthropology.* Translated by Claire Jacobson. Basic Books, New York.

Lewis, R. Barry

1982   *Excavations at Two Mississippian Hamlets in the Cairo Lowland of Southeast Missouri.* Illinois Archaeological Survey, Special Publication 2. Urbana.

Lewis, Thomas M. N., and Madeline Kneberg

1946   *Hiwassee Island: An Archaeological Account of Four Tennessee Indian Peoples.* The University of Tennessee Press, Knoxville.

Linder, Jean R., John E. Kelly, George R. Milner, and James W. Porter

1975   An Archaeological Survey of the Mississippi Valley in St. Clair, Monroe, and Randolph Counties. In *Preliminary Report of the 1974 Historic Sites Survey: Archaeological Reconnaissance of Selected Areas in the State of Illinois, Part 1, Summary Section A,* pp. 28–41. Illinois Archaeological Survey, Department of Anthropology, University of Illinois, Urbana.

Lopinot, Neal H.

1991   The Archaeology of the Cahokia Mounds ICT-II: Biological Remains. *Illinois Cultural Resources Study* 13. Illinois Historic Preservation Agency, Springfield.

Macnie, John

1895   *Elements of Geometry: Plain and Solid.* American Book Company.

Markman, Charles W.

1991   Above the American Bottom: The Late Woodland-Mississippian Transition in Northeast Illinois. In *New Perspectives on Cahokia: Views from the Periphery,* edited by James B. Stoltman, pp. 177–208. Prehistory Press. Madison, Wisconsin.

McConaughy, Mark A.

1991   The Rench Site Late Late Woodland/Mississippian Farming Hamlet from the Central Illinois River Valley: Food for Thought. In *New Perspectives on Cahokia: Views from the Periphery,* edited by James B. Stoltman, pp. 101–128. Prehistory Press. Madison, Wisconsin.

McElrath, Dale L., Thomas E. Emerson, Andrew C. Fortier, and James L. Phillips

1984   Late Archaic Period. In *American Bottom Archaeology,* edited by Charles J. Bareis and James W. Porter, pp. 34–58. University of Illinois Press, Urbana.

McElrath, Dale L., and Andrew C. Fortier

1983   *The Missouri Pacific #2 Site.* University of Illinois Press, Urbana.

McElrath, Dale L., Joyce A. Williams, Thomas O. Maher, and Michael C. Meinkoth

1987   Emergent Mississippian and Mississippian Communities at the Radic Site (11-Ms-584). *Department of Anthropology, University of Illinois at*

Urbana-Champaign, FAI-270 Archaeological Mitigation Project, Report 74.

McElrath, Dale L., and Fred A. Finney
1987   *The George Reeves Site.* University of Illinois Press, Urbana.

McGuire, Randall H., and Michael B. Schiffer
1983   A Theory of Architectural Design. *Journal of Anthropological Archaeology* 2:277–303.

McKern, William C.
1939   The Midwestern Taxonomic Method as an Aid to Archaeological Study. *American Antiquity* 4:301–313.

Mehrer, Mark W.
1982a   *A Mississippian Community at the Range Site (11-S-47), St. Clair County, Illinois.* Master's thesis, Department of Anthropology, University of Illinois, Urbana-Champaign.
1982b   A Mississippian Homestead at the Range Site in St. Clair County, Illinois. Paper presented at the Midwest Archaeological Conference, Cleveland, Ohio.
1983   Middle Mississippian Architecture in the American Bottom Area. Paper presented at the 48th annual meeting of the Society for American Archaeology, Pittsburgh.
1986a   The Built Environment and Emerging Social Complexity: A View from the Bottom Up. Paper presented at the 2d Built Form and Culture Research Conference, Lawrence, Kansas.
1986b   The Mississippian Households of Cahokia's Hinterlands. Paper presented at the 51st annual meeting of the Society for American Archaeology, New Orleans.
1988   The Settlement Patterns and Social Power of Cahokia's Hinterland Households. Unpublished Ph.D. dissertation, Department of Anthropology, University of Illinois, Urbana-Champaign.

Mehrer, Mark W., and James M. Collins
1989   *Household Archaeology at Cahokia and in Its Hinterlands.* Paper delivered at the 54th annual meeting of the Society for American Archaeology, Atlanta, April.

Milner, George R.
1982   *Measuring Prehistoric Levels of Health: A Study of Mississippian Period Skeletal Remains from the American Bottom, Illinois.* Ph.D. dissertation, Northwestern University, Evanston. University Microfilms, Ann Arbor.
1983   *The Turner and DeMange Sites.* University of Illinois Press, Urbana.
1984a   *The Julien Site.* University of Illinois Press, Urbana.
1984b   *The Robinson's Lake Site.* University of Illinois Press, Urbana.
1984c   Social and Temporal Implications of Variation among American Bottom Mississippian Cemeteries. *American Antiquity* 49:468–488.
1986   Mississippian Period Population Density in a Segment of the Central Mississippi River Valley. *American Antiquity* 51:227–238.
1990   The Late Prehistoric Cahokia Cultural System of the Mississippi River Valley: Foundations, Florescence, and Fragmentation. *Journal of World Prehistory* 4:1–43.
1991   American Bottom Mississippian Cultures: Internal Developments and

External Relations. In *New Perspectives on Cahokia: Views from the Periphery*, edited by James B. Stoltman, pp. 29–47. Prehistory Press, Madison, Wisconsin.

Milner, George R., and Thomas E. Emerson
1981   The Mississippian Occupation of the American Bottom: The Farmsteads. Paper presented at the Midwest Archaeological Conference, Madison, Wisconsin.

Milner, George R., Thomas E. Emerson, Mark W. Mehrer, Joyce A. Williams, and Duane Esarey
1984   Mississippian and Oneota Period. In *American Bottom Archaeology*, edited by Charles J. Bareis and James W. Porter, pp. 158–186. University of Illinois Press, Urbana.

Moorehead, Warren K.
1922   *The Cahokia Mounds: With 16 Plates: A Preliminary Paper.* University of Illinois, Urbana.
1923   *The Cahokia Mounds.* Contributions from the Museum of Natural History No. 28. Urbana, Illinois.
1929   Explorations of 1922, 1924, and 1927. In *The Cahokia Mounds, Part I.* University of Illinois, Bulletin 26 (4). Urbana.

Morrison, Donald G.
1969   On the Interpretation of Discriminant Analysis. *Journal of Marketing Research* 6:156–163.

Morse, Dan F., and Phylis A. Morse
1983   *Archaeology of the Central Mississippi Valley.* Academic Press, New York

Muller, Jon
1978   The Kincaid System: Mississippian Settlement in the Environs of a Large Site. In *Mississippian Settlement Patterns,* edited by Bruce D. Smith, pp. 269–292. Academic Press, New York.

Munger, Paul and Robert McCormick Adams
1941   Fabric Impressions of Pottery from the Elizabeth Harrell Site, Missouri. *American Antiquity* 7:166–171.

Munson, Patrick J.
1971   An Archaeological Survey of the Wood River Terrace and Adjacent Bottoms and Bluffs in Madison County, Illinois. *Illinois State Museum, Reports of Investigations* 21:3–17.
1974   Terraces, Meander Loops, and Archaeology in the American Bottoms, Illinois. *Transactions of the Illinois State Academy of Science* 67:384–392.

Netting, Robert McC.
1989   Smallholders, Householders, Freeholders: Why the Family Farm Works Well Worldwide. In *The Household Economy,* edited by Richard Wilk, pp. 221–244. Westview Press, Boulder, Colorado.
1993   *Smallholders, Householders: Farm Families and the Ecology of Intensive, Sustainable Agriculture.* Stanford University Press, Stanford, California.

Netting, Robert McC., Richard R. Wilk, and Eric J. Arnould
1984   Introduction. In *Households: Comparative and Historical Studies of the Domestic Group,* edited by Robert McC. Netting, Richard R. Wilk, and Eric J. Arnould, pp. xiii–xxxviii. University of California Press, Berkeley.

Nie, Norman H. C. Hadlai Hull, Jean G. Jenkins, Karin Steinbrenner, and Dale H.
Bent
1975   *SPSS: Statistical Package for the Social Sciences.* McGraw-Hill, New York.

Norris, Terry
1978   *Excavations at the Lily Lake Site: 1975 Season.* Contract Series, Reports in
Contract Archaeology 4. Southern Illinois University, Edwardsville.

O'Brien, Patricia J.
1972a   *A Formal Analysis of Cahokia Ceramics from the Powell Tract.* Illinois
Archaeological Survey, Monograph 3. Urbana.
1972b   Urbanism, Cahokia and Middle Mississippian. *Archaeology* 25:189–197.
1978a   A Western Mississippian Settlement System. In *Mississippian Settlement
Patterns,* edited by Bruce D. Smith, pp. 1–19. Academic Press, New York.
1978b   Steed-Kisker and Mississippian Influences on the Central Plains. In *The
Central Plains Tradition: Internal Development and External Relationships,*
edited by Donald J. Blakeslee, pp. 67–80. Office of the State Archaeologist, Report 11. Iowa City.

Oliver, Paul
1987   *Dwellings: The House across the World.* University of Texas Press, Austin.

Oswald, Dana Beth
1987   The Organization of Space in Residential Buildings: A Cross-cultural Perspective. In *Method and Theory for Activity Area Research: An Ethnoarchaeological Approach,* edited by Susan Kent, pp. 295–344. Columbia University Press, New York.

Parmalee, Paul W.
1957   Vertebrate Remains from the Cahokia Site, Illinois. *Transactions of the
Illinois State Academy of Science* 50:235–242.

Pauketat, Timothy R.
1987   Mississippian Domestic Economy and Formation Processes: A Response
to Prentice. *Midcontinental Journal of Archaeology* 12:77–88.
1991   *The Dynamics of Pre-State Political Centralization in the North American
Midcontinent.* Unpublished Ph.D. dissertation, University of Michigan.
1993   Temples for Cahokia Lords: Preston Holder's 1955–1956 Excavations of
Kunnemann Mound. *Museum of Anthropology, University of Michigan,
Memoir* 28.
1994   *The Ascent of Chiefs: Cahokia and Mississippian Politics in Native North
America.* The University of Alabama Press, Tuscaloosa.

Pauketat, Timothy R., and William I. Woods
1986   Middle Mississippian Structure Analysis: The Lawrence Primas Site
(11-Ms-895) in the American Bottom. *Wisconsin Archaeologist*
67:104–127.

Pearson, Michael Parker
1984   Economic and Ideological Change: Cyclical Growth in the Pre-State Societies of Jutland. In *Ideology, Power and Prehistory,* edited by Daniel Miller
and Christopher Tilley, pp. 69–92. Cambridge University Press, Cambridge.

Peebles, Christopher S.
1971   Moundville and Surrounding Sites: Some Structural Considerations of

Mortuary Practices II. In *Approaches to the Social Dimensions of Mortuary Practices,* edited by James A. Brown, pp. 68–91. Society for American Archaeology, Memoir 25.

1978   Determinants of Settlement Size and Location in the Moundville Phase. In *Mississippian Settlement Patterns,* edited by Bruce D. Smith, pp. 369–416. Academic Press, New York.

1983   Moundville: Late Prehistoric Sociopolitical Organization in the Southeastern United States. In *The Development of Political Organization in Native North America,* edited by Elizabeth Tooker, pp. 183–198. 1979 Proceedings of the American Ethnological Society. Washington, D.C.

Peebles, Christopher S., and Susan M. Kus

1977   Some Archaeological Correlates of Ranked Societies. *American Antiquity* 42:421–448.

Perino, Gregory

1947a   Cultural Problems at Cahokia. *Illinois State Archaeological Society, Journal* 4(3):14–17.

1947b   Cahokia Notes. *Illinois State Archaeological Society, Journal* 5(2):57–60.

1959   Recent Information from Cahokia and Its Satellites. *Central States Archaeological Journal* 6(4):130–138.

Perino [Pernio (sic)], Gregory

1967   The Cherry Valley Mounds, Cross County, Arkansas and Banks Mound 3, Crittenden County, Arkansas. *The Central States Archaeological Societies, Inc., Memoir* 1.

Phillips, James, L., Robert L. Hall, and Richard W. Yerkes

1980   *Investigations at the Labras Lake Site, Volume 1, Archaeology.* Department of Anthropology, University of Illinois, Chicago.

Phillips, James L., and Bruce G. Gladfelter

1983   The Labras Lake Site and the Paleogeographic Setting of the Late Archaic in the American Bottom. In *Archaic Hunters and Gatherers in the American Midwest,* edited by James L. Phillips and James A. Brown, pp. 197–218. Academic Press, New York.

Phillips, James L., and James A. Brown (editors)

1983   *Archaic Hunters and Gatherers in the American Midwest.* Academic Press, New York.

Phillips, Philip

1940   Middle American Influences on the Archaeology of the Southeastern United States. In *The Maya and Their Neighbors: Essays on Middle American Anthropology and Archaeology,* edited by Clarence L. Hay, Ralph L. Linton, Samuel K. Lothrop, Harry L. Shapiro, and George C. Vaillant, pp. 349–367. Dover Press, New York.

1970   Archaeological Survey in the Lower Yazoo Basin, Mississippi, 1949–1955. *Peabody Museum of Archaeology and Ethnology, Papers* 60.

Phillips, Philip, James A. Ford, and James B. Griffin

1951   Archaeological Survey in the Lower Mississippi Alluvial Valley, 1940–1947. *Peabody Museum of Archaeology and Ethnology, Papers* 25.

Piesinger, Constance

1972   The Mansker Site: A Late Prehistoric Village in Southern Illinois. Master's thesis, Department of Anthropology, University of Wisconsin, Madison.

Plog, Fred, and Steadman Upham
1983   The Analysis of Prehistoric Political Organization. In *The Development of Political Organization in Native North America,* edited by Elizabeth Tooker, pp. 199–213. 1979 Proceedings of the American Ethnological Society. Washington, D.C.

Porter, James W.
1971   An Archaeological Survey of the Mississippi Valley in St. Clair, Monroe, and Randolph Counties. In *Preliminary Report of the 1971 Historic Sites Survey Archaeological Reconnaissance of Selected Areas in the State of Illinois, Part 1, Summary Section 4.* Illinois Archaeological Survey, Department of Anthropology, University of Illinois, Urbana.

1972   An Archaeological Survey of the Mississippi Valley in St. Clair, Monroe, and Randolph Counties. In *Preliminary Report of the 1972 Historic Sites Survey Archaeological Reconnaissance of Selected Areas in the State of Illinois, Part 1, Summary Section A,* pp. 25–33. Illinois Archaeological Survey, Department of Anthropology, University of Illinois, Urbana.

1973   The Mitchell Site and Prehistoric Exchange Systems at Cahokia: A.D. 1000–300. In *Explorations into Cahokia Archaeology,* edited by Melvin L. Fowler, pp. 137–164. Illinois Archaeological Survey, Bulletin 7. Urbana.

1974a   An Archaeological Survey of the Mississippi Valley in St. Clair, Monroe, and Randolph Counties. In *Preliminary Report of the 1973 Historic Sites Survey Archaeological Reconnaissance of Selected Areas in the State of Illinois, Part 1, Summary Section A.* Illinois Archaeological Survey, Department of Anthropology, University of Illinois, Urbana.

1974b   *Cahokia Archaeology as Viewed from the Mitchell Site: A Satellite Community at A.D. 1150-1200.* Ph.D. dissertation, University of Wisconsin, Madison. University Microfilms, Ann Arbor.

Prentice, Guy
1983   Cottage Industries: Concepts and Implications. *Midcontinental Journal of Archaeology* 8:17–48.

1985   Economic Differentiation among Mississippian Farmsteads. *Midcontinental Journal of Archaeology* 10:77–122.

1986   An Analysis of the Symbolism Expressed by the Birger Figurine. *American Antiquity* 51:239–266.

Prentice, Guy, and Mark W. Mehrer
1981   The Lab Woofie Site (11-S-346): An Unplowed Mississippian Site in the American Bottom Region of Illinois. *Midcontinental Journal of Archaeology* 6:35–53.

Price, James E., and James B. Griffin
1979   *The Snodgrass Site of the Powers Phase of Southeast Missouri.* Museum of Anthropology, Anthropological Papers, No. 66. University of Michigan, Ann Arbor.

Rapoport, Amos
1969   *House Form and Culture.* Prentice-Hall, Englewood Cliffs.

1976   Environmental Cognition in Cross-Cultural Perspective. In *Environmental Knowing: Theories, Research, and Methods,* edited by Gary T. Moore and Reginald B. Golledge, pp. 220–234. Dowden, Hutchinson & Ross, Inc., Stroudsburg, Pennsylvania.

1980 Vernacular Architecure and the Cultural Determinants of Form. In *Buildings and Society: Essays on the Social Development of the Built Environment,* edited by Anthony D. King, pp. 283–305. Routledge & Kegan Paul, London.

Reed, Nelson A., John W. Bennett, and James Warren Porter
1968 Solid Core Drilling of Monks Mound: Technique and Findings. *American Antiquity* 33:137–148.

Reynolds, Peter J.
1974 Experimental Iron Age Storage Pits: An Interim Report. *Proceedings of the Prehistoric Society* 40:118–131.

Rindos, David, and Sissel Johannessen
1991 Human-Plant Interactions and Cultural Change in the American Bottom. In *Cahokia and the Hinterlands: Middle Mississippian Cultures of the Midwest,* edited by Thomas E. Emerson and R. Barry Lewis, pp. 35–45. University of Illinois Press, Urbana, Illinois.

Riordan, Robert
1975 *Ceramics and Chronology: Mississippian Settlement in the Black Bottom, Southern Illinois.* Ph.D. dissertation, Southern Illinois University, Carbondale. University Microfilms, Ann Arbor.

Robbins, Michael C.
1966 House Types and Settlement Patterns: An Application of Ethnology to Archaeological Interpretation. *Minnesota Archaeologist* 28(1):3–26.

Rodell, Roland L.
1991 The Diamond Bluff Site Complex and Cahokia Influence in the Red Wing Locality. In *New Perspectives on Cahokia: Views from the Periphery,* edited by James B. Stoltman, pp. 253–280. Prehistory Press. Madison, Wisconsin.

Root, Delores
1984 *Material Dimensions of Social Inequality in Non-Stratified Societies: An Archaeological Perspective.* Ph.D. dissertation, University of Massachusetts. University Microfilms, Ann Arbor.

Rudolph, James L.
1984 Earthlodges and Platform Mounds: Changing Public Architecture in the Southeastern United States. *Southeastern Archaeology* 3(1):33–45.

Schiffer, Michael B.
1976 *Behavioral Archaeology.* Academic Press, New York.

Service, Elman R.
1962 *Primitive Social Organization: An Evolutionary Perspective.* Random House, New York.
1975 *Origins of the State and Civilization: The Process of Cultural Evolution.* W. W. Norton and Company, New York.

Shami, Seteney
1989 Settlement and Resettlement in Umm Qeis: Spatial Organization of a Jordanian Village. In *Dwellings, Settlements and Tradition: Cross-Cultural Perspectives,* edited by Jean-Paul Bourdier and Nezar AlSayyad, pp. 451–476. University Press of America, New York.

Skele, Mikels
1987 Monks Mound: A Genetic Topography. Master's thesis, Department

of Geography and Earth Science, Southern Illinois University, Edwardsville.

1988 The Great Knob: Interpretations of Monks Mound. *Studies in Illinois Archaeology* 4. Illinois Historic Preservation Agency, Springfield.

Smail, William

1951 Some Early Projectile Points from the St. Louis Area. *Journal of the Illinois State Archaeological Society* 2(1):11–16.

Smith, Bruce D. (editor)

1978a *Mississippian Settlement Patterns.* Academic Press, New York.

Smith, Bruce D.

1978b *Prehistoric Patterns of Human Behavior: A Case Study in the Mississippi Valley.* Academic Press, New York.

1978c Variation in Mississippian Settlement Patterns. In *Mississippian Settlement Patterns,* edited by Bruce D. Smith, pp. 479–503. Academic Press, New York.

1984 Mississippian Expansion: Tracing the Historical Development of an Explanatory Model. *Southeastern Archaeology* 3:13–32.

1992 Prehistoric Plant Husbandry in Eastern North America. In *The Origins of Agriculture: An International Perspective,* edited by C. Wesley Cowan and Patty Jo Watson, pp. 101–119. Smithsonian Institution Press, Washington, D.C.

1992 *Rivers of Change: Essays on Early Agriculture in Eastern North America.* Smithsonian Institution Press, Washington and London.

Smith, Carol A.

1976 Exchange Systems and the Spatial Distribution of Elites: The Organization of Stratification in Agrarian Societies. In *Regional Analysis: Volume 2, Social Systems,* edited by Carol A. Smith, pp. 309–374. Academic Press, New York.

Smith, Harriet M.

1973 The Murdock Mound, Cahokia Site. In *Explorations into Cahokia Archaeology,* edited by Melvin L. Fowler, pp. 49–88. Illinois Archaeological Survey, Bulletin 7. Urbana.

Sneath, Peter H. A., and Robert R. Sokal

1973 *Numerical Taxonomy: The Principles and Practice of Numerical Classification.* W. H. Freeman and Company, San Francisco.

South, Stanley

1977a *Method and Theory in Historical Archeology.* Academic Press, New York.

1977b Research Strategies in Historical Archeology: The Scientific Paradigm. In *Research Strategies in Historical Archeology,* edited by Stanley South, pp. 1–12. Academic Press, New York.

Stahl, Ann Brower

1985 *The Dohack Site.* University of Illinois Press, Urbana.

Steensberg, Axel

1980 *New Guinea Gardens: A Study of Husbandry with Parallels in Prehistoric Europe.* Academic Press, New York.

Stephens, Jeanette E.

1993 Settlement Plans and Community Social Interaction: An Example for the Knoebel Site in Southwestern Illinois. *Illinois Archaeology* 5:344–354.

Stoltman, James B.
1991a   New Perspectives on Cahokia: Views from the Periphery. *Monographs in World Archaeology* 2. Prehistory Press, Madison, Wisconsin.
1991b   Cahokia as Seen from the Peripheries. In *New Perspectives on Cahokia: Views from the Periphery,* edited by James B. Stoltman, pp. 349–354. Prehistory Press, Madison, Wisconsin.

Strong, William Duncan
1935   *An Introduction to Nebraska Archaeology.* Smithsonian Miscellaneous Collections 93(10).

Sturtevant, William C.
1983   Tribe and State in the Sixteenth and Twentieth Centuries. In *The Development of Political Organization in Native North America,* edited by Elizabeth Tooker, pp. 3–16. 1979 Proceedings of the American Ethnological Society. Washington, D.C.

Swanton, John R.
1946   *The Indians of the Southeastern United States.* Bureau of American Ethnology, Bulletin 137. Washington, D.C.

Szuter, Christine R.
1979   The Schlemmer Site: A Late Woodland-Mississippian Site in the American Bottom. Master's thesis, Department of Anthropology, Loyola University, Chicago.

Taylor, Walter W.
1964   *A Study of Archeology.* Reprint of American Anthropological Association Memoir 69, originally published in 1948. Southern Illinois University Press, Carbondale, Illinois.

Temple, Wayne C.
1957   The Piasa Bird: Fact or Fancy? *Illinois State Historical Society, Journal* 49(3):3–22.

Thomas, C. Joe
1938   Lower Mississippi Traits in the Middle Phase in Illinois. *Illinois State Academy of Science, Transactions* 31(2):68–70.

Thomas, Cyrus
1894   Report on the Mound Explorations of the Bureau of Ethnology. Accompanying paper in *12th Annual Report to the Bureau of American Ethnology, 1890–1891.* Government Printing Office, Washington, D.C.

Thompson, J. E.
1934   *Geometry for the Practical Man.* D. Van Nostrand Company, New York.

Tiffany, Joseph A.
1991   Modeling Mill Creek-Mississippian Interaction. In *New Perspectives on Cahokia: Views from the Periphery,* edited by James B. Stoltman, pp. 319–347. Prehistory Press. Madison, Wisconsin.

Titterington, Paul F.
1935   Certain Bluff Mounds of Western Jersey County, Illinois. *American Antiquity* 1:6–46.
1938   *The Cahokia Mound Group and Its Village Site Materials.* Privately printed, St. Louis.
1943   The Jersey County, Illinois, Bluff Focus. *American Antiquity* 9:240–245.
1947   Shell Gorget-Jersey County Bluff Focus. *Journal of the Illinois State Archaeological Society* 5:55.

1950 Some Non-Pottery Sites in the St. Louis Area. *Journal of the Illinois State Archaeological Society* 1:18–31.

Trigger, Bruce G.
1990 Monumental Architecture: A Thermodynamic Explanation of Symbolic Behaviour. *World Archaeology* 22:119–132.

United States Department of the Interior (USDI)
1970 *Classes of Land-Surface Form.* Map, Sheet 62. United States Department of the Interior, Geological Survey, Washington, D.C.

Vogel, Joseph O.
1975 Trends in Cahokia Ceramics: Preliminary Study of the Collections from Tracts 15A and 15B. In *Perspectives in Cahokia Archaeology,* edited by James A. Brown, pp. 32–125. Illinois Archaeological Survey, Bulletin 10. Urbana.

Wagner, Mark J.
1986 The Jamestown Site (21C4-14). Ms. of file, American Resources Group, Carbondale, Illinois.

Wagner, Philip
1960 *The Human Use of the Earth.* The Free Press, New York.

Wagner, Robert W.
1959 An Analysis of the Material Culture of the James Ramey Mound. Master's thesis, Department of Anthropology, University of Illinois, Urbana-Champaign.

Walker, Winslow M., and Robert McCormick Adams
1946 Excavations in the Matthews Site, New Madrid County, Missouri. *Transactions of the Academy of Science of Saint Louis* 31(4).

Walthall, John A., and Elizabeth D. Benchley
1987 *The River L'Abbe Mission: A French Colonial Church for the Cahokia Illini on Monks Mound.* Studies in Illinois Archaeology, No. 2. Illinois Historic Preservation Agency, Springfield.

Waterson, Roxana
1989 Migration, Traditon and Change in Some Vernacular Architectures of Indonesia. In *Dwellings, Settlements and Tradition: Cross-Cultural Perspectives,* edited by Jean-Paul Bourdier and Nezar AlSayyad, pp. 477–501. University Press of America, New York.

Webb, William S.
1952 *The Jonathan Creek Village, Site 4, Marshall County, Kentucky.* Reports on Anthropology Vol. 8, No. 1. University of Kentucky.

Wedel, Waldo R.
1945 On the Illinois Confederacy and Middle Mississippi Culture in Illinois. *American Antiquity* 10:383–386.

Weltfish, Gene
1977 *The Lost Universe: Pawnee Life and Culture.* University of Nebraska Press, Lincoln.

White, William P., and Linda M. Bonnell
1981 *Geomorphic Investigations at the Range Site (11-S-47).* FAI-270 Archaeological Mitigation Project Geomorphological Report 6. Department of Anthropology, University of Illinois, Urbana-Champaign.

White, William P., Sissel Johannessen, Paula G. Cross, and Lucretia S. Kelly
1984 Environmental Setting. In *American Bottom Archaeology,* edited by Charles

J. Bareis and James W. Porter, pp. 15–33. University of Illinois Press, Urbana.

Wilk, Richard R.
1983   Little House in the Jungle: The Causes of Variation in House Size among Modern Kekchi Maya. *Journal of Anthropological Archaeology* 2:99–116.
1988   Maya Household Organization: Evidence and Analogies. In *Household and Community in the Mesoamerican Past,* edited by Richard R. Wilk and Wendy Ashmore, pp. 135–151. University of New Mexico Press, Albuquerque.

Wilk, Richard R., and Wendy Ashmore (editors)
1988   *Household and Community in the Mesoamerican Past.* University of New Mexico Press, Albuquerque.

Wilk, Richard R., and William L. Rathje
1982a   Household Archaeology. *American Behavioral Scientist* 25:617–639.

Wilk, Richard R., and William L. Rathje (editors)
1982b   *Archaeology of the Household: Building a Prehistory of Domestic Life.* American Behavioral Scientist Vol. 25. Sage Publications, Beverly Hills.

Willey, Gordon R.
1966   *An Introduction to American Archaeology: Volume 1: North and Middle America.* Prentice-Hall, Englewood Cliffs, New Jersey.

Williams, Joyce, and Richard B. Lacampagne
1982   *Final Report on Archaeological Investigations at the Adler Site (11-S-64).* FAI-270 Archaeological Mitigation Project Report 43. Department of Anthropology, University of Illinois, Urbana-Champaign.

Williams, Samuel Cole (editor)
1930   *Adair's History of the American Indians.* Promontory Press, New York.

Williams, Stephen
1954   *An Archeological Study of the Mississippian Culture in Southeast Missouri.* Ph.D. dissertation, Yale University, New Haven. University Microfilms, Ann Arbor.

Williams, Stephen, and Jeffrey P. Brain
1983   Excavations at the Lake George Site: Yazoo County, Mississippi, 1958–1960. *Peabody Museum of Archaeology and Ethnology, Papers* 74.

Williams, Stephen, and John M. Goggin
1956   The Long-Nosed God Mask in the Eastern United States. *The Missouri Archaeologist* 18(3):1–72.

Winter, Marcus C.
1976   The Archeological Household Cluster in the Valley of Oaxaca. In *The Early Mesoamerican Village,* edited by Kent V. Flannery, pp. 25–31. Academic Press, New York.

Wittry, Warren L.
1961   Notes and News: Northern Mississippi Valley. *American Antiquity* 26:586–590.
1969   The American Woodhenge. In *Explorations into Cahokia Archaeology,* edited by Melvin L. Fowler, pp. 43–48. Illinois Archaeological Survey, Bulletin 7.

Wittry, Warren L., and Joseph O. Vogel
1962   Illinois State Museum Projects: October 1961 to June 1962. In *First*

Annual Report: American Bottoms Archaeology, July 1, 1961-June 30, 1962, edited by Melvin L. Fowler, pp. 14–30. Illinois Archaeological Survey, Urbana.

Wolforth, Thomas Robert
1989   Small Settlements and Population Movement in the Mississippian Settlement Pattern. Unpublished Master's thesis, Department of Anthropology, University of Wisconsin, Milwaukee.

Woods, William Irving
1986   *Prehistoric Settlement and Subsistence in the Upland Cahokia Creek Drainage.* Ph.D. dissertation, Department of Geography, University of Wisconsin, Milwaukee.

Woods, William I. and George R. Holley
1991   Upland Mississippian Settlement in the American Bottom Region. In *Cahokia and the Hinterlands: Middle Mississippian Cultures of the Midwest,* edited by Thomas E. Emerson and R. Barry Lewis, pp. 46–60. University of Illinois Press, Urbana, Illinois.

Wray, Donald E., and Hale Smith
1944   An Hypothesis for the Identification of the Illinois Confederacy with the Middle Mississippi Culture in Illinois. *American Antiquity* 10:23–27.

Yagi, Koji
1980   Human Environment. *Process: Architecture* 15:13–16.

Yellen, John E.
1977   *Archaeological Approaches to the Present: Models for Reconstructing the Past.* Academic Press, New York.

Yerkes, Richard W.
1987   *Prehistoric Life on the Mississippi Floodplain: Stone Tool Use, Settlement Organization, and Subsistence Practices at the Labras Lake Site, Illinois.* University of Chicago Press, Chicago.

1991   Specialization in Shell Artifact Production at Cahokia. In *New Perspectives on Cahokia: Views from the Periphery. Monographs in World Archaeology* 2, edited by James B. Stoltman, pp. 49–64. Prehistory Press, Madison, Wisconsin.

Index

Adams, Richard Newbold, 29–30, 166–67

agriculture: development summarized, 9; during Emergent Mississippian period, 138, 139; households and, 122; during Patrick phase, 137. *See also* maize agriculture; storage facilities, for agricultural products

AlSayyad, Nezar, 26–27

American Bottom: archaeological resources summarized, 4–5; chronology, 10, 11, 12–14, 55; cultural evolution in, 15–19; geographical location, 4, 5; history of investigations in, 9–12; natural setting, 9, 135; study area defined, 4, 6

Anderson, Duane C., 8

Anderson, James, xvi

Angel site, 149

Archaeological Survey of the Cahokia Region, 10

architecture, 129–31; building typology and, 95; of circular structures, 12, 129–30, 147–50; domestic architecture, 4, 12, 14, 134, 140, 156; Emergent Mississippian through Mississippian trends in, 99–101; Historic period, 129, 131–32; household configurations and, 116; Late Woodland, 12, 14, 129; in methodology for analysis, 61; number of buildings and diversity in, 99–100; occupational history and, 102; vernacular, 25–26; worldview and, 130–31. *See also* buildings, analysis of

Atoni households, 135

Aztalan, 8

Bareis, Charles J., xvii

Bartram, William, 131–32

BBB Motor site: building analysis, 95–97, 98, 101–3; community plan, 140, 141; compared to Cahokia site, 156; data available for, 56; Edelhardt phase, 49, 50, 53, 95–97, 102–3, 106–7, 140–41, 143; environmental setting, 48; exotic items from, 117; exterior pits at, 107; feature analysis, 77, 84, 95; hearths at, 117; household analysis, 109, 117; interior pits at, 95–96, 99, 107; mortuary/temple nodes at, 117; phases summarized, 34; plan maps, 48–49, 106; postholes at, 96; posthole structures at, 50; proximity to other sites, 48; social organization at, 140, 141; Stirling phase at, 49, 53, 101–3, 109, 117

benches: in circular structures, 97, 99, 103, 129, 148–49, 150; in civic-ceremonial nodes, 119, 152; at Julien site, 119; postholes for, 90, 92, 97, 149; in rectangular structures, 103, 119

Big Men, 133, 140

Birger figurine, 117

Bishop site, 48

Bluff Shadow site, 146

Bold Counselor complex, 13

bone tools, 54, 63

bottles, 120

Bourdier, Jean-Paul, 26–27

Bridges site, 153–54